After Tragedy Strikes

After Tragedy Strikes

WHY CLAIMS OF TRAUMA AND LOSS
PROMOTE PUBLIC OUTRAGE AND
ENCOURAGE POLITICAL POLARIZATION

Thomas D. Beamish

UNIVERSITY OF CALIFORNIA PRESS

University of California Press
Oakland, California

© 2024 by Thomas D. Beamish

Library of Congress Cataloging-in-Publication Data

Names: Beamish, Thomas D., author.
Title: After tragedy strikes : why claims of trauma and loss promote
    public outrage and encourage political polarization / Thomas D.
    Beamish.
Description: Oakland, California : University of California Press,
    [2024] | Includes bibliographical references and index.
Identifiers: LCCN 2023037641 (print) | LCCN 2023037642 (ebook) |
    ISBN 9780520401068 (cloth) | ISBN 9780520401075 (paperback) |
    ISBN 9780520401082 (ebook)
Subjects: LCSH: Psychic trauma—Political aspects—United States—
    21st century. | Psychic trauma—Social aspects—United States—
    21st century. | Secondary traumatic stress—Political aspects—United
    States—21st century. | Secondary traumatic stress—Social aspects—
    United States—21st century. | Psychic trauma and mass media—
    United States—21st century.
Classification: LCC BF175.5.P75 B44 2024 (print) | LCC BF175.5.P75
    (ebook) | DDC 306.2—dc23/eng/20231205
LC record available at https://lccn.loc.gov/2023037641
LC ebook record available at https://lccn.loc.gov/2023037642

33 32 31 30 29 28 27 26 25 24
10 9 8 7 6 5 4 3 2 1

Contents

Illustrations

Acknowledgments

The ideas explored in this book simmered for a good time before my active investigation of them. My interest began in the decade following the 9/11 terrorist attacks as I sensed a change. There seemed to be a significant increase in media-curated and hyperpoliticized crisis events. Framed as tragedies, they involved highly publicized outpourings of grief, anger, and accusation; spontaneous tributes and memorials; and protest demonstrations, among other sorts of public spectacle highlighted in news coverage in their aftermath. The media coverage of such "public tragedies" also focused on those victimized or those who claimed to be victims and their stories of pain, suffering, and trauma. Coverage emphasized what could (or should) have been done but wasn't and frequently included social blame for the factors and forces judged responsible. While individual perpetrators were often at the center of these tragedies, their actions were typically cast as representing something larger, something deeper, something societal. Explanations of these events and those harmed by them were not attributed to individual, accidental, or fated causes. In these hyperpoliticized and tragic cases, the publics' response also seemed to take shape through increasingly stylized means: well-publicized victims' funds, memorials and commemorations, art and iconography, targeted policies, and with these, associated outpourings of remembrance, grief, anger, and social protest. While no single case on its own might have caught my attention, the sheer volume of coverage devoted to case after case of tragedy cast in this way and the increasingly choreographed public political responses struck me as emergent.

My initial curiosity and research efforts focused on British Petroleum's Deepwater Horizon oil spill in 2010. Once oil spillage from the seafloor was capped and blame was placed on BP's safety record, the oil industry in general, and federal and state regulatory responses, those affected in the Gulf region demanded compensation for their losses. Given the billions of dollars involved, Kenneth Feinberg, an attorney made famous by mediation and dispute resolution in other tragic events, was given responsibility for dispensing victims' remuneration after that spill. Feinberg had previously overseen calculating the damages and determining who gets compensation for Vietnam veterans exposed to Agent Orange (1985) and then, in 2001, the 9/11 fund. After presiding over the 9/11 fund, Fienberg would then supervise the dispensation of funds for the students and faculty killed in the Virginia Tech mass shooting (2007), then for the Deepwater Horizon spill (2010), and then for the "One Fund," victims' assistance established in the wake of the Boston Marathon bombings (2013). Most recently, Feinberg oversaw the distribution of support funds for the 737 MAX crash victim families (2019).

Having recently completed another book project in which I had focused on the role that political narratives play in civic and community-based risk disputes, I was sensitive to how competing political discourses can shape how issues and events are understood, remembered, and consequently responded to in the public domain. I was interested in the shape claims took and in how those making such claims were sorted into "deserving" and "undeserving" of compensation and, therefore, recognition as victims. Put another way, I wanted to understand better how recognition and denial were justified. Indeed, I had found in my just completed research on risk disputes that control over claims making—what was locally recognized as true, right, and acceptable—went a long way toward controlling how the events under debate were understood and remembered and therefore how they influenced future issues and events.

Regrettably, I could not pursue this research because access to the data on victims' claims was off limits; acquiring funds required that claim makers sign nondisclosure agreements to receive a payout. Although in the Deepwater Horizon case Feinberg was government appointed, he ultimately distributed money on behalf of those seeking to resolve the issue(s) quickly—in the case of this spill, British Petroleum. Consequently, the process was largely closed to outside eyes and therefore my research interest. Stymied, I began thinking in broader terms about tragic circumstances, the trauma and loss associated with them, and what made one and not another victim eligible for recognition and remuneration. This was not simply an issue of victim claims but also, just as important, when and why the public recognizes trauma, loss, and victimization and expresses sympathy for it. Without widespread sympathy and recognition, support is unlikely.

Serendipitously, I was contacted by Chip Clarke, who as a member of the sociology board for the Russell Sage Foundation Series was soliciting and vetting potential book projects. Chip was the impetus and early motivation to write up my ideas as a prospectus and pursue a book on "the victims of tragedy." While that manuscript was never submitted to Russell Sage, Chip's comments on an early book prospectus began the book effort. Chip also provided, years later, a thoughtful review of the manuscript in its final stages, for which I am also grateful.

After this, I began researching cases that exemplified my growing impressions of highly publicized and politicized trauma and loss. While finishing a prior project, several cases gained my attention. I began to track and compare their media coverage to similar cases that had not achieved the same national notoriety. In 2015, Flint, Michigan's toxic water story struck me as an exemplary case, given the role of government and the partisan political rhetoric that enveloped it. Soon after, Hurricane Maria hit Puerto Rico (circa 2017), leaving the island devastated. The political rhetoric surrounding the federal emergency response was also markedly polarized and surprising. This engendered great sympathy for the island's residents and sewed conflict with the sitting Trump administration. Then in 2018, the mass shooting at Marjory Stoneman Douglas High School in Parkland, Florida, represented a new level of politicized tragedy that played out not in the internet's dark corners but in mainstream media outlets. Students, some of whom had been at the shooting, had been injured, or had lost loved ones to it, mobilized in the name of gun control, blaming political elites and legislators. And in response to victim mobilization in the aftermath of that shooting, so too did those who supported gun rights and conservative causes, publicly ridiculing the students and victims of the shooting for their efforts in a way that I had not experienced in the past. Claims making was hyperbolic, to say the least.

My initial impressions were confirmed as I dug deeper into these highly publicized and politicized tragedies and compared them to less notorious cases with virtually the same tragic characteristics. They were also clarified. The political aspect of these sad events was not secondary or peripheral but largely defined them. There was more to the story of "publicly tragic" events than I had first recognized. Having done some pilot research in 2019, I began a sabbatical to get deeply into drafting this book. I could never have known that the COVID pandemic would hit three months into my leave. Over the next year and a half, in the crucible of the COVID pandemic and then the tumultuous 2020 summer of protest following George Floyd's murder, the discourses and processes I had been researching accelerated, showing public tragedies and the narrative trope that underlay them—what I term the *trauma script* in this book—to be the galvanizing political story of our time.

As for those who helped me along as this book project unfolded, Nicole Biggart was essential to germinating and framing my early ideas. Nicole volunteered comments on my initial writing and, more than that, engaged in conversations about what I was claiming and what it might mean, which helped structure the ideas that are now argued in the book. Also instrumental at this time was Deb Neiemier, whom I had been working with for years on climate-related research. She listened to my ideas in the margins of that work as I worked through them and frequently disagreed, arguing counterpoints. Both agreement and disagreement can improve one's thoughts; Deb's certainly did. Also important were office and dinner chats with Stephanie Mudge and Ryken Grattet, who shared their understanding and opinions on the ideas I sought to develop. My dad, Thom Beamish, provided insights, arguments, and grist on ideas and issues that orbit the center of this book. Talking to him, an intellectual who does not subscribe to my professional orientation as a sociologist (and the biases contained therein), significantly improved my thinking on the issues and ideas herein. I would also like to thank David Smilde, who read and assessed the manuscript in its later stages and shared insightful comments and critiques that improved the manuscript and my argument immensely.

David also opened his political sociology seminar at Tulane University, where an author-meets-critics' discussion of the yet-to-be-published manuscript further enhanced my sense of the project and the conclusions I was drawing from it. All provided me with constructive feedback and welcome encouragement that I required to finish this book.

Special gratitude goes to Vicki Smith for her unwavering support and editorial efforts on my behalf, which cannot be sufficiently expressed in a sentence or paragraph. Vicki has been a friend and intellectual confidante for over twenty years at UC Davis. Whether it was classroom issues or my latest manuscript, she has provided a nonjudgmental point of reference and perspective that I treasure. Early on, when my ideas regarding the book were still in their infancy, Vicki commented on pieces of writing as I developed different aspects of the book. As department chair, Vicki supported my efforts by reading grant proposals and a book prospectus. Her continued insightful and constructive comments on chapter drafts and the book's overall argument(s) were instrumental to its completion. As the book matured, she read the draft several times and provided the kind of edits and comments no author could rightly ask of a colleague. She knows this manuscript awfully well. I am endlessly grateful.

Finally, I want to thank all my friends, colleagues, and students who are unnamed but have spoken with me about this project over the years, both directly and indirectly, and helped develop the ideas and arguments advanced herein. I would also like to thank the anonymous reviewers who shared their views as I worked on bettering the manuscript; they, too, however critical in their opinions of it, were integral to the book's improvement and completion. Last, at the University of California Press, thanks to Sociology Editor Naomi Schneider for shepherding the project to its completion and Assistant Editor Aline Dolinh, who helped finalize the manuscript. Of course, none of those I have mentioned bear responsibility for the ideas or shortcomings of the manuscript. Those are entirely mine.

Introduction

THE POLITICS OF PUBLIC TRAGEDY

Crisis, misfortune, and suffering—in a word, *tragedy*—are a universal part of the human experience. They always have been and likely always will be. While trauma and loss of seemingly limitless variety can occur anywhere, affecting individuals, communities, and even nations, most suffering is experienced as personal tragedy. Some tragedies, however, rise above the sad but inevitable traumas that populate everyday life and become hyper-politicized and notorious public events: they become *public tragedies* in which suffering is made publicly visible and lamentable. Such tragedies trigger and are defined by a comparable set of public political reactions, including accusations and social blame, denial and denunciation, out-pourings of grief and anger, spontaneous memorialization and collective action, and a struggle to define the collective meaning and memory of the event (cf. Doka 2003b). Natural disasters, school shootings, terrorist attacks, and economic crises can become public tragedies. Sexual assaults, primarily of women, by abusive executives recently emerged as a public tragedy, as has African Americans being brutalized by police, which has sown widespread political unrest, protest, and rioting across the United States. The COVID-19 pandemic, seemingly a natural disaster, quickly transitioned into a public tragedy as deaths mounted and a pervasive sense of mismanagement, distrust, and blame directed at federal and state governments for inaction, on the one hand, and rights violations, on the other, led to political controversy that engulfed the nation and the world.

Traumatic events that spur public shock, outrage, and accusation, and from them denial and denunciation, can rapidly develop into national political events, even international social and political controversies, further elevating the spectacle and the social conflicts associated with them. Indeed, public tragedies do more than simply shock the public; they now help to define public issues, political platforms, policy fiats, and more. Yet countless traumas with causes and outcomes that are essentially the same do not become widely recognized and socially inflamed and therefore are not politically consequential. They do not become publicly tragic.

What transforms an event that has typically been understood in the past as an "individual misfortune" or "fateful disaster" into a public tragedy that today can seize the public's attention and galvanize the emotions of millions? Why have public reactions to distinctive types of individual and collective crises increasingly taken shape through very similar types of claims and accusations? Why do present-day Americans regularly sympathize with those harmed in ways that can transform a localized trauma into a widely reviled public tragedy, triggering protest and controversy and perhaps even political transformation? I strive to answer these questions in *After Tragedy Strikes*. They are significant for several reasons. First, prior research and theory suggest this was not the case in the past (Bovens and 't Hart 2016; Giddens 1999; Quarantelli 1998; Rubin 2012; Steinberg 2006). Well into the twentieth century, trauma and loss were typically attributed to God's plan, fate, bad luck, and blameless accident or, in line with the U.S. liberal political tradition, attributed to individual responsibility (Butler 2012a; Fukuyama 2022; Kuipers and 't Hart 2014; Levy 2012; Rubin 2012). This was often the case even when losses were known to have been caused or worsened by human actions or omissions (Godbey 2006; Levy 2012; Platt 1999).

While very public, hyperpoliticized, and tragic events involving outpourings of grief and anger, claims of victimization, spontaneous memorialization, social blame, and collective action are not new, they were considerably rarer in the past. Their surge in frequency, indeed their present commonness, shows their qualitatively greater significance in the early twenty-first century. Their regularity has also exposed a shift in how trauma and loss are perceived, sympathized with, and collectively responded to. For reasons I outline in the following pages, suffering is now afforded much more attention than it gained in the past. Indeed, I argue that sympathy for claims of societal victimization and the valorization of "victimhood" as a type of claim and political identity are distinctive sociopolitical features of the contemporary. These sentiments stand behind and animate public tragedies. I further argue that reflecting transformations in public beliefs and sentiment, public tragedies have become our time's definitive social and political events. Public tragedies are, in this sense, epochal. From the September 11 terror attacks to Hurricane Katrina, Harvey Weinstein's sexual assault cases, George Floyd's murder by police, and the COVID-19 pandemic, these events and others that co-occurred, are occurring, and have yet to occur represent a change in what qualifies as a "tragic circumstance" and therefore in how they are increasingly cast and responded to in the United States and elsewhere. Events and sentiments like these are also increasingly associated with partisan political polarization, even sectarian claims, as those harmed blame society or a societal proxy and the institutions, organizations, and/or groups associated with them, who respond by denying blame and denouncing their detractors. The question, then, becomes: *What has changed?*

PUBLIC TRAGEDIES ARE POLITICAL EVENTS

Natural and human-made disasters and social crises are often understood as "disastrous" because of the objective extent of the damage(s) they have wrought or the horrific crime(s) they exemplify (Alexander 2004:8). In this essentializing perspective, the intensity of a tornado, the cost associated with a hurricane, the number of persons harmed in a mass shooting, the importance of the person harmed, or the heinousness of the harm inflicted on victims defines the trauma and therefore its notoriety. In *After Tragedy Strikes*, by contrast, I approach public tragedies as social and political events. I argue that their increased frequency and association with public spectacle involve a transformation in the politics of our time. They do not simply happen but are politically made. They are, at heart, issues and events that, through their political and cultural framing, come to represent an existential threat to the social and moral order. As public tragedies, they ultimately reflect a kind of moral critique and "panic" regarding societal issues and relations (Cohen 2011). These critiques of society and social relations, founded in the crucible of trauma and loss, then become a source for political action. This makes public tragedies notorious and potentially transformative political events. I therefore distinguish public tragedies from those "disasters," "calamities," and other sorts of trauma and loss that may cause significant personal and collective damage and human suffering but do not challenge the social and moral order. Put another way, while the material qualities of a disaster certainly matter, they are not on their own enough to generate a public tragedy.

Focusing explicitly on "public tragedies," Lattanzi-Licht and Doka (2003) seek to determine what sets them apart from other disasters and, importantly for this book, how the public experiences them. In his opening remarks, Doka (2003b) expresses surprise that while there is a great deal of literature on "specific public tragedies . . . there is little written about public tragedy *sui generis*" (4). In fact, there is a dearth of research on public tragedies as a class of societal-wide trauma distinct from simple disasters, crises, and loss, even though, as I argue, the transformative power of public tragedy reigns supreme in the twenty-first century. Lattanzi-Licht and Doka (2003) describe public tragedies as traumatic events that, while involving any number of causes and outcomes, evoke a similar public response: outpourings of anger and grief, spontaneous memorialization, collective action, and attempts at finding meaning in the loss. Several factors, in combination, work to heighten public notoriety, including cause, scope, severity, and duration; the public's affinity with those harmed; the level of suffering involved; and the "social value" of the victims. Also significant is whether the trauma was intended, expected, or preventable (8–10). While these factors represent a catalog of the necessary conditions for an event to become publicly tragic, *necessary* does not mean *sufficient*.

I focus less on quantified, actual, and material trauma and loss and more on why specific crisis events are politicized through social and cultural framings—how they are, in turn, taken up in the public domain such that they become public tragedies. By "public domain," I refer to communications that scale beyond the individual, group, or even local level to those levels where heterogeneous individuals, groups, political interests and parties, social movements, and the news media virtually congregate. Here they converse and debate, seeking to shape and control the discussion of events and the outcomes associated with them (Calhoun 1998; Fraser 1990; Habermas 1979, 1991; Lichterman 1996). Therefore, I am concerned with how a given case of trauma and loss is publicly explained and remembered such that it benefits a political interest, comes to existentially threaten the public or some significant subset of it, and through that interest or threat becomes "publicly tragic."

Public tragedy is typically accompanied by outrage and moral accusations, claims of victimization, and social blame for the trauma and loss. Social blame is a core aspect of public tragedy; it attributes harm to social and relational forces rather than blaming individuals or superordinate forces like fate or bad luck (Oorschot and Halman 2000). As Erikson points out, injuries of the former kind are especially distressing and prone to moralization and conflict because they reflect basic interactional issues such as distrust, deception, dishonesty, and betrayal (1994:231). As I show, public reaction is often further stoked and shaped by political elites, the media, and/or victims' advocates; therapeutic professionals; and social movement entrepreneurs, all historically novel and organized interest groups native to the late twentieth and early twenty-first centuries. Beyond the actual suffering, then, public tragedies are inherently political constructs as much as they are deeply traumatic cultural experiences.

While not addressing public tragedies as discrete political events, some have studied trauma and developed exemplary accounts of how horrific circumstances shape cultural views, not only of immediate victims but also of associated collectivities and even subsequent generations (Alexander 2004; Eyerman 2001). These scholars have advanced an understanding of "cultural trauma" based on what collective memories of prolonged suffering can do to individuals, social groups, and even whole societies. Through case studies of slavery, genocide, massacres, civil wars, colonialism, and terrorism, they have found that "cultural trauma occurs when members of a collective feel they have been subjected to a horrendous event that leaves indelible marks upon their group consciousness" (Alexander 2004:4; see also Eyerman, Alexander, and Breese 2015; Kleinman,

Das, and Lock 1997). These documented traumas have social causes that injure the psyche, leaving in their wake feelings of distrust and vulnerability from which recovery is difficult or impossible.

Focusing on exceptional cases of suffering and deeply traumatized groups, the cultural trauma view provides a template for understanding pervasive damage caused by a wide range of conditions (Alexander 2004; Sztompka 2000). And yet the cultural trauma view ultimately adheres to a psychological definition that treats "the trauma" as the driver behind social change. It depicts cultural trauma as a process at the collective level that runs parallel to the development of actual psychological trauma at the individual level. It is during culture work on the part of the afflicted—the active engagement and shaping of collective memories around a shared story of suffering—that cultural group identities emerge, trauma is "felt," and the conditions for a culture of trauma are established.

Rather than centering on a specific group's cultural experience and identity construction, I focus on the standardized language of suffering—in discourse and claims making—that has emerged in arguments made about trauma and loss in the context and aftermath of crisis. In my theorization of public tragedies, the collective memories that anchor cultural trauma do not "cause" an event to become publicly tragic, even if they play a role in its construction. As I show, the emergence of public tragedies as powerful political events reveals a highly conventionalized language of victimhood and a response that transcends specific events and associated cultural memories and identities. Following on Boltanski and Thévenot's (2006) work on repertoires of evaluation and "orders of worth," I argue that people rely on a relatively fixed number of justifications in assessing whether an act benefits or conflicts with the common good (see also Dodier 1995; Lamont and Thévenot 2000; Moody and Thévenot 2000).[1] Similarly, I have found that victims of trauma and loss, those who support them, and those who would deny them recognition also rely on a relatively narrow language to foment outrage and elicit support from the wider public or to deny them such support.

1. Such conventionalized justifications include the *market sphere* (performance), *industrial sphere* (efficiency), *civic sphere* (equality and solidarity), *domestic sphere* (parochial and traditional trustworthiness), *inspirational sphere* (expressed in creativity, emotion, or religious grace), and *renown sphere* (public opinion and fame) (Boltanski and Thévenot 2006).

Therefore, while claims of victimhood can be based on authentic cases and genuinely "felt" cultural trauma, such claims and the conventionalized language they invoke need not be genuine for people to use them as a political rhetoric to promote a position, whether their own or that of others. Indeed, I argue that an expanded appreciation for and definition of "the traumatic" (by therapeutic professionals, victims' advocates, and activists; see Fassin and Rechtman 2009), along with the emergence of trauma as a conventionalized narrative (Sehgal 2021; Self 2021), have significantly widened the standardized language's applicability, legitimacy, and power (Bennett 2022; Pandell 2022). Because of its newfound power to define experience, the discourse of trauma has become a leading political "script," applied to almost any type of personal or collective suffering. While used to articulate authentic trauma and loss, what I call the "trauma script" also aims to cultivate sympathy and support, whether those who use it or respond to it are themselves victims of trauma or not.

A CONVENTIONALIZED SCRIPT OF TRAUMA AND LOSS

Why term it the trauma script? According to Goffman (1959), social scripts are frameworks that guide human interpretation and behavior. They signal to people that distinct situations and scenarios require specific performances, in much the same way as a script functions in a play or film. Implicit scripts specify not only how one is to act but also when and whether the context for performance is "front" (public) or "backstage" (private). Therefore, the script concept suggests that specific scenarios can "trigger" the use of specific narratives. Similarly, scripts communicate that narratives can cue other social scripts that guide participants toward socially "appropriate" responses. The trauma script is just such a conventionalized narrative, triggering relatively predictable responses when used to frame and explain trauma and loss. Events that associate harm with the trauma script have the power to command attention and gain the kind of notoriety required to become publicly tragic in the twenty-first century (cf. Davis 2005b; Ewick and Sibley 1995; Loseke 2001). The trauma script is a contemporary cultural framing and explanation of trauma and loss that centers on blameless victims who have suffered unnecessarily at the hands of others and therefore pivots on social blame. Social blame suggests unfair treatment and suffering caused by a group or collective (Oorschot and Halman 2000). The ultimate "perpetrator," according to the trauma script, is therefore society or some aspect of it.

After Tragedy Strikes situates public tragedies as explicitly political events in contemporary twenty-first-century social and political discourse and relations. Public tragedies appropriate now-routine, standardized narratives of harm—the trauma script—to communicate and politicize trauma and loss to gain public attention and political recognition. This mechanism reflects qualitative changes in the role that trauma—as an idea, a condition, a claim type, and increasingly a political stratagem—plays in politics, political conflict, and social change more generally.

To support this assertion, I track a range of traumatic events as they took shape in public discourse, to gain a clearer sense of how and why some crises emerge as politically consequential public tragedies while other, objectively similar events do not. I focus less on the details of crisis, trauma, and loss or on cultural traumas (especially as they affect groups) and more on the emergence of contemporary public tragedies as volatile political crises made relevant by epochal conditions and animated by a highly conventionalized discourse. Events that I consider to be public tragedies currently propel the news cycle, anchoring mainstream politics and political campaigns. They also generate the rhetoric deployed by victims' advocates and many social movement entrepreneurs on the left and right. I draw on insights from a range of works on public tragedy (Hayes, Waddell, and Smudde 2017; Jorgensen-Earp and Lanzilotti 1998; Lattanzi-Licht and Doka 2003; Ott and Aoki 2002), culture and trauma (Alexander 2004; Campbell and Manning 2018; Eyerman, Alexander, and Breese 2015; Fassin and Rechtman 2009; Lukianoff and Haidt 2018), victims and victimology (Best 1997; Christie 1986; Davis 2005a; Fattah 2000; Lamb 1999a, 1999b), risk and risk management (Beamish 2015; Freudenburg 2001; Gephart 1993; Kuipers and 't Hart 2014; 't Hart 1993), and risk society theory (Bauman 2007; Beck 1992; Giddens 1990) to address the core issues that lie at the center of this effort. Ultimately, by situating public tragedies in contemporary social and institutional relations I analyze why they, and the narratives that comprise them, have emerged as the twenty-first century's quintessential political events.

THE CONDITIONS FOR PUBLIC TRAGEDIES

In this book I show how and why some events involving trauma and loss "take off," gaining tremendous social influence by becoming publicly tragic, while objectively similar traumas do not. Theoretically, I address a contemporary "structure of feeling" (Williams 1961) in the United States—and, I suggest, across Western postindustrial states—that has cultivated broad identification with and sympathy for those who are viewed as having been victimized by conditions and actions attributed to society. This structure of feeling has its origins in several intersecting forces and trends I take up in detail in chapter 1, "A World at Risk." To document and exemplify the process of public tragedy construction in the United States, I conduct a comparative analysis of the role social institutions (such as government, mass media, and victims' advocates) play and how they actively shape public experience and understanding of events through competitive political construction and framing. As such, my analytic focus is on tragedies as public, political, and discursive contests. They are sui generis: an emergent and currently ascendant type of politics founded in the crucible of crisis, reflecting a specific, relatively conventionalized political claims making that actors deploy to gain the upper hand in political dialogue and dispute (cf. Boltanski 1999; Lamont and Thévenot 2000; Thévenot, Moody, and Lafaye 2000). Currently, political contests of this kind involve stylized claims of persecution, innocence, trauma, loss, victimization, and ultimately social blame. Those who deploy such claims seek to foment moral panic to prevail in public disputes. Public tragedies are therefore events of active political framing, leading to public struggle over what will (and will not) be recognized as traumatic and, with that designation, who will (and will not) gain power over explanations of the event and attributions of blame and deservingness.

I show that, as the twenty-first century unfolds, claims and conflicts of this kind are no longer peripheral or confined to groups that have developed identities around horrific histories of abuse (cf. Alexander 2002; Eyerman 2001). Rather, the media regularly and strategically mobilizes the discourse of trauma as a trope to shock audiences and promote viewer attention. The trope is also exploited by a range of professional mediators and pundits, including therapeutic professionals, political elites, academics, experts, victims' advocates, and social movement organizations, to gain recognition, adherents, and resources for their causes (cf. Best 1997).

The contemporary resonance of the trauma script and the emergence of public tragedies in the United States reveal the intersection of current trends in thinking and feeling underlying the transformation from "modern society" to "risk society." As a kind of event, public tragedies are epochal. Williams (1961) contended that every era has a zeitgeist, a structure of feeling: a collective worldview through which people experience that period's social, political, and material dynamics. He developed the concept "structure of feeling" to capture the different ways of thinking that compete for expression. They emerge from and in competition with the dominant forms of thinking and doing. The structure of feeling emerges out of the fissures and lapses that always exist amid the official, the authoritative, and the conventional understandings of the day. Williams stressed "feeling" rather than "thought" to signal that what is at stake may not be fully articulated but can remain inferred in public reactions to official actions, omissions, and interpretations. Such is the case for the sentiments that animate public tragedies, where public responses to official proclamations and actions reveal a range of feelings characteristic of our time. Such feelings include distrust of and cynicism toward authority as well as more general feelings of precarity, vulnerability, and victimization by social forces that "feel" out of control. These feelings further manifest as a penchant to blame society—that is, engage in social blaming—for personal and collective instances of trauma, loss, and suffering.

Contemporary partisan politics in the United States, which has with time become increasingly sectarian (Finkel et al. 2020), has further weaponized these feelings of vulnerability. Political elites increasingly rely on rhetoric that no longer promises shared prosperity and security but instead targets subpublics, emphasizing what will benefit their constituents (often also elites) and implicitly themselves (Brenner 2003, 2020). Elites also use the trauma script to mobilize their constituents and strengthen their claims making. Within this context of heightened partisanship and a sense of precarity and imperilment, claims to victimization have also achieved greater institutional legitimacy and political leverage because of the professional efforts of what Best (1997) labeled the "victim industry."

Psychologists, sociologists, the humanities (indeed much of the academy), those in the legal profession, social workers, and medical and therapeutic professionals who specialize in topics as diverse as trauma care, hospice and grieving, crisis response, inequality, victims advocacy, and victimology, among many others, have staked out agendas in their fields to both advocate for and assist those who have been harmed by society (Butler 2012a; Hawdon and Ryan 2011; Hayes et. al. 2017; Kropf and Jones 2014; Neal 1998; Platt 1999). One might even say trauma's conventionalization as a concept and script exemplifies Giddens's (1984) notion of the "double hermeneutic"—a situation in which theories and ideas of human behavior, like the technical and forensic term *trauma*, become everyday lay concepts used in political rhetoric to explain personal and collective issues and justify responses to them. This then feeds back into technical and forensic uses. As such, "victim of trauma," for example, has become an idiom and rhetorical device as much as it is a technical phrase that explains harm of some kind (cf. Fassin and Rechtman 2009).

SOCIAL BLAME AND PERSONAL BLAMELESSNESS

Due to the contemporary structure of feeling, the trauma script and the politics associated with risk society have given credibility and political power to social blaming. They provide victims and those who work on their behalf a potent justification for political advocacy (Best 1999; Kuipers and 't Hart 2014). Social blame expresses a view of trauma and loss that attributes cause to human-derived social and relational forces rather than blaming victims, individuals (perpetrators), or superordinate forces like fate or bad luck (Oorschot and Halman 2000). Human-centric social blaming reflects collective forms of blame in which an individual's actions are held to represent a group, an organization, and/or society. These forces and factors make them collective experiences and thus "public" rather than private. Based on social movement claims, educational curriculums, and news and entertainment media information, the public has become more aware of suffering while also connecting their personal experiences to the actions and omissions of governance institutions. People now routinely blame culture and society for their trauma, loss, and hardship. Importantly, when trauma, loss, and victimization are believed to be socially caused, this can tear the "fabric of community life," forcing open "fault lines that once ran silently through the structure of the larger community, dividing it into divisive fragments" (Erikson 1994:236). Social blame is ultimately a moral criticism, suggesting that those (unjustifiably) harmed have been victimized by the community or society of which they are members (Malle, Guglielmo, and Monroe 2014). This is the stuff of public tragedy.

Why, then, have claims of victimhood become ascendant, and why do they currently resonate so profoundly with the American public across the social and political spectrum? Most contemporary accounts presume that such claims are normatively "true" or "false." Indeed, some advocate a social science founded squarely on "true" claims of social suffering and an attempt to ameliorate it (Wilkinson and Kleinman 2016). In *After Tragedy Strikes*, I do not assume the truth or falsity of such claims. Rather, I investigate how and why they have found their coherence and political power in an emergent, conventionalized understanding of trauma and loss: the trauma script.[2] The trauma script has become a political explanation that through repetition acts as a "social heuristic," which is now used time and again to make sense of trauma and loss. Social heuristics are shared commonsense methods that aid in interpretation and personal decision-making. They align one's individual thinking and therefore decisions with collectively recognized and conventionalized understandings of everyday problems and issues (Beamish and Biggart 2009, 2011, 2015; Biggart and Beamish 2003; Marsh 2002).

In this script, blameless victims are suggested to have suffered from unforeseeable and unnecessary harm, and that harm is socially blamed on the actions or omissions of society or a societal proxy. Societal proxies include the state, industry, civil society, and "culture." They take institutional form through government (and governance), the police, science and technology, the professions, education, politics, and the rule of law. Blame is also placed on societal factors and social forces—structural qualities, such as race, class, and gender, and cultural identities, such as LGBTQ,

2. On the role of "conventions" in social and economic life, see Biggart and Beamish (2003); Boltanski (1999); Boltanski and Thévenot (2006); Dodier (1993); and Sibler (1993).

disability, or religious affiliation—which are viewed as either the reason for victimization or the "privilege" through which victimization is avoided. People frequently invoke the trauma script even when the apparent cause of harm could alternately be personal responsibility, an individual, chance, a simple accident, or fate, as it likely would have been in a different historical period. This is important because it mirrors a transition away from such personal explanations and toward a greater acceptance of the public discourse of victimhood and suffering. In the new framework, troubles formerly believed to be private (such as sexual abuse, addiction, domestic violence, sexism, and racism) become seen as societally centered problems that require political resolution (Beckett 1996; Rice 1995; Rothenberg 2003).

As a conventionalized cultural narrative, the trauma script is important because it can engender sympathy among and involvement by the public when used as a lens through which to view trauma and loss. As a way of interpreting loss, the script overlaps but is distinct from the "ideal victim" (Christie 1986), which has been widely used in the study of victims and the sympathy they do (and do not) receive (Dunn 2004; Rothenberg 2002, 2003). According to Christie (1986), the ideal victim framework features a vulnerable person engaged in respectable behavior who is harmed by an evil perpetrator who is a stranger to them. While focused on the individual level of victim and perpetrator, Christie's conceptualization introduces cultural nuance to the category of victim, highlighting the role that cultural and moral worthiness play in the degree of public sympathy and support. Sympathy for a victim, in his account, typically reflects how closely that victim's story coheres with the cultural ideal. The more they correspond, the more moral legitimacy the victim and their claims are likely to command.

Unlike Christie's ideal victim concept and its focus on an individual victim and perpetrator of crime, the trauma script concept identifies victims who have been mistreated by societal conditions. It culturally resonates with Americans, I argue, because the public currently identifies with the vulnerability and blamelessness conveyed by this explanation of victimization. That is, when deployed to explain trauma and loss, the framework of the trauma script can elicit widespread sympathy for the harmed, channeling social blame and moral outrage at those persons, groups, organizations, or institutions held responsible, thus vaulting public trage-dies into the political domain.

By *cultural framework*, I refer to an accessible and coherent cluster of ideas, beliefs, and values that people rely on to interpret incoming infor-mation and events. Such beliefs and values give rise to our emotional and moral judgments and to political arguments about fundamental group re-sponsibilities and limitations (Alexander 2004; Kavolis 1977). I use the term *trauma* to connect my effort to prior research regarding the rela-tively recent emergence of psychic trauma as a recognized and socially pri-oritized form of victimhood (Fassin and Rechtman 2009). I also connect it to research on cultural trauma as a "remembered" loss that plays a role in (re)defining responsibility and group identity (Alexander et al. 2004).

WHAT DOES *TRAGIC* MEAN TODAY?

Both Greek and Western literary traditions suggest that tragedy reflects a protagonist's internal, personal struggle with decisions and actions that beget great suffering (Nussbaum 2001). The meaning of tragedy has changed over time. In the Greek tradition, tragedy conveys a scenario in which bad things happen to good people, and personal redemption is im-possible. In the Greek trope, the protagonist must choose between two irreconcilable but uniformly tragic outcomes (Nussbaum 2001). Later, as a Shakespearean literary term and Christian cultural aesthetic, in a trag-edy morally good people (through well-intentioned acts) are brought low by character flaws. The best efforts of a character are corrupted by moral weakness, leading to profound, regretful, and tragic suffering (Burke 1984).

Over most of its history, the liberal cultural tradition in the United States depicted social ills as caused by individuals, reflecting their moral character and behavior (Fukuyama 2022). As a literary form, tragedy fit well with the liberal tradition. Yet over the course of the twentieth cen-tury, an increasing proportion of the American public began to reject this tradition, at least as it related to assigning blame for the social issues and personal vulnerabilities they have felt and experienced. This emergent view of tragedy goes against neoliberalism (the focus of much recent social and political theory as a top-down agenda pushed by social, political, and economic elites; see Bourdieu 1999; Fukuyama 2022; Mudge 2008) and an emphasis on individual responsibility. In the twenty-first century, the American public increasingly blames not themselves or their immediate peers but society (writ large) for the social issues and problems they confront. For instance, polling of American attitudes shows that the public has shifted away from accounts of success founded on work ethic, effort, and skill and toward social conditions to explain why some are rich and others are poor. Fully two-thirds of U.S. adults polled believe that some people are rich because they have more advantages than most people. And a larger majority—three-quarters—believe that people are poor because they have faced more obstacles in life. Far fewer, about a third of those polled, suggest that people become rich because they have worked harder than others (Pew Research Center 2020).

Mirroring the public's penchant to situate personal success and failure socially, people are also more apt to blame their own ills on society. Public tragedies, animated by the trauma script, convey a struggle in which good people are brought low by societal conditions over which they have little or no control. This sort of tragic struggle is not internal and personal but external and socially focused. It involves a scenario in which bad things happen to good people who have no choice; the heartrending outcome occurs no matter what the good person does.

In virtually all such cases, the claim (an accusation) is that had societal trustees fulfilled their charge, no harm would have befallen the victims, or at least the harm would have been significantly diminished. Therefore, the traumatic event is society's fault. Because victims are blameless, the injuries they experience are unjust. Even when an individual perpetrator is responsible, their actions can be framed via the trauma script to reflect higher-level forces and factors representative of societal problems and issues that are ultimately cast as political in character. One such example is the horrific spate of school shootings perpetrated by individuals but attributed by a majority of the American public to permissive gun laws and corrupt politicians (Shepard 2018). Polls by the Pew Research Center show that in 1993, 57% of Americans ranked controlling gun ownership as a priority over protecting gun rights. By 2018, in the aftermath of several mass shootings, support for stricter gun laws among registered voters had risen to 68%, compared with just 25% who opposed stricter gun laws and supported gun rights (Shepard 2018). Increasingly, the government and with it "society" are viewed as responsible for such shootings, if not for certain actions then for certain omissions—namely not doing enough to identify potential perpetrators, not regulating access to guns, or not preventing the conditions that make gun violence more likely. Horrific acts like this are therefore "caused" by groups, organizations, and trustee institutions that either act negligently or fail to take the right action when faced with dangerous trends or actual shooting scenarios. They become proxies that ultimately explain the harms they have indirectly produced. And when the causes of traumatic events and the damage they create are widely viewed as reflecting the extant social order or as a threat to it, they are more likely to become publicly tragic.

At heart, then, the emergence and ascendance of public tragedies reflects the resonance of the trauma script, which further reveals changing views of society and the individual's current relationship to it. Core issues of human dignity, equity, authority, liberty, and autonomy, and whether or not the "modern" nation-state and society protect or endanger them, have increasingly become flashpoints for social blame and political conflict (Nussbaum 2001:xiii–xxxix).

What brought about this contemporary concern with personal and collective security and the escalation in social blame? Blame, as reflected in the trauma script, resonates because it taps the public's current sense of vulnerability and the incongruous expectations of the state and its surrogates and social institutions generally (briefly sketched here, and further developed in chapter 1). Risks ranging from hurricanes to crime waves have cultivated dependence on societal trustees while simultaneously encouraging distrust of them. I argue that on the one hand, the public expects trustee authorities to secure their well-being, but on the other hand, we have a fair degree of cynicism regarding whether authorities will do so (Meek 2016). How the general public now views the state and its surrogates exposes a paradoxical relationship that lies at the very core of contemporary risk societies such as ours. Indeed, failure to alleviate risk—or at least the *perceived failure* to do so—has become a recurring allegation against the state and the status quo, leading to recurrent "risk disputes" and, as a result, political protests and collective actions (Beamish 2001, 2015; Boin and 't Hart 2007; Freudenburg 2001; Mazur 2010; Wildavsky 1988). Public tragedies are thus instances in which the government or societal structures or factors are perceived to be "at fault" for harming the public and, therefore, undermining the moral order. Events and issues of this kind are quintessentially "public" insofar as the public dimension distinguishes their collective nature and therefore signifies them as shared experiences. This sets public events apart from issues and events understood to be private concerns representing personal involvements.

GOING PUBLIC

To understand what distinguishes public tragedies from private harms requires that one acknowledge that most risks and the harms associated with them are not considered public in character. Indeed, most harms are still considered private affairs, even when experienced by many. This varies greatly, of course, with time and place, but a wide range of issues in the United States, from unemployment to the common cold, are considered neither "disastrous" nor "publicly tragic" but personal in nature. In truth, they are public problems insofar as the public at large experiences them en masse. Still, they are typically understood as personal problems governed by individual qualities like health, merit, effort, luck, or even fate. Only when formerly private troubles disrupt the social order, such that private issues are reinterpreted as collective problems, can they emerge as public experiences. Yet even when an event becomes a public and collective experience—such as in the case of natural disasters—it may not become publicly tragic.

As suggested earlier, the *tragic* aspect highlights a contemporary cultural outlook that emphasizes personal and collective vulnerability to human-manufactured risks (Giddens 1999). Public tragedies reflect and involve a view of society's actions (or omissions) as refracted through social factors and structural qualities that are deemed harmful to blameless victims. Clearly, this understanding pivots on the individual's perceived relationship to society, one in which a loss of control is central. Trauma and loss viewed as tragic resonate and provoke sympathy precisely because they highlight undeserved victimization by risks that few Americans have any control over but that threaten us all. As such, public tragedies reflect and align with a now pervasive unease with risks in life generated by societal relations and the trauma and loss associated with them (Best 1997; Erikson 1994; Fassin and Rechtman 2009; Jeffery and Candea 2006).

The amount of sustained public attention and notoriety that tragedies must gain to achieve widespread recognition also helps explain why they become public tragedies. It distinguishes them from similarly devastating events that do not gain such recognition but can be just as horrific to those who suffer them. I argue that this primarily reflects contemporary media logics and a new communication ecology that have obvious consequences for contemporary public views and the political discourses that emerge in the aftermath of any given crisis (which I address in chapter 3). Public tragedies gain notoriety through sustained broadcast and internet news reports, blogs, electronic bulletin boards, YouTube clips, TikTok memes, Twitter (now X) feeds, and Facebook and Instagram posts, among other communication channels. These diverse platforms portray alarming scenes that can be watched, shared, and commented on repeatedly, sometimes by millions. The interaction of these discursive streams sets off a dynamic broadcast-internet media feedback loop that in turn can supercharge an event. What was initially a private crisis can suddenly gain enough exposure to enter the public domain, becoming a clarion call for those who sympathize with, moralize about, or are outraged by it. Once trending, the issue can simultaneously explode across multiple media formats, feeding yet another wave of coverage, political controversy, and even collective action (Chadwick and Howard 2009; Margetts et al. 2015). In this way, a public tragedy is born.

Once the public is galvanized, the tragedy reflects more than the distress and trauma suffered by its immediate victims. Through association, an event framed as a public tragedy therefore comes to represent—to signify—widely recognized conditions, worries, and risks. As a genre of trauma and loss, those harmed become symbols of the "harms that could happen to any of us." As such, a public tragedy can trigger new fears that a group, community, or all of society is in jeopardy. Victims' advocates and their adversaries face off about who or what is to blame while calling on "the public" to join them in political campaigns, collective actions, and moral reckonings. At this point, public tragedies and the groups that claim to experience cultural trauma begin to play off one another (Alexander et al. 2004). As suggested, the trauma script is not partisan. People across the political spectrum engage in claims making of this kind. People on the political left frequently appropriate the script to suggest persecution based on race, class, and gender, as well as government and corporate indifference. On the right, virtually the same script is used to suggest that government overreach limits individual autonomy and that reverse discrimination victimizes hard-working "Americans" (by which is often meant "whites"; see Hochschild 2018).

Traumatic events and subsequent claims resonate within different subpublics that can quickly turn into antagonistic social and political enclaves. Concern and attention can continue for days, weeks, months, and even years, as the initial shocking and tragic event is followed by similar events and the same issues are subsequently raised by new victims, pundits, politicians, intellectuals and academics, activists, and movements. They can be amplified through legal action in the courts. Indeed, when stoked by extensive news coverage, the events can promote political polarization and sectarianism, the moralized identification with one political group or movement against others (Finkel et al. 2020).

In response, the general public's reaction can come to resemble that of the immediate victims, involving disbelief, grief, fear, and outrage that can further promote feelings of vulnerability, insecurity, and endangerment and a deep sense of having been collectively wronged (Alexander 2004; Boltanski 1999; Doka 2003a; Eyerman et al. 2015; Fassin and Rechtman 2009). This is even more likely when a given segment of the public strongly identifies with those who have been traumatized, seeing them as part of their "moral" or "cultural" community (Morris 1996; see also Erikson 1976, 1994). These conditions are also ripe for political manipulation because the story of victims coping with unprovoked, societally inspired, and crippling harms—the trauma script—currently resonates across a wide swath of the American public on both the political left and right. This is something not lost on political elites, pundits, and social movement entrepreneurs.

AT RISK

Human fault and its moral companion, blame, imbue trauma and loss not only with human cause but with human *intention* as reflected in animus, betrayal, and negligence. Blame polarizes explanation, forcing the causes of harm into good/bad and right/wrong oppositional categories (Baum, Fleming, and Singer 1983; Erikson 1976, 1990). What is more, blame is easily politicized: socially blaming an extant institution, group, or person for trauma and loss can serve a political function, exposing weakness in the existing order that requires redress for the wrongs committed (Kuipers and 't Hart 2014). Finally, trauma and loss believed to have been directly caused by humans or institutions or indirectly aggravated by human or institutional indiscretion tend to undermine the ties that bind and animate community life. This in turn creates a context in which suspicion and distrust can flourish and social and political conflict become likely.

Reflecting the hyperpartisanship of our time, the trauma script shadows public dialogue and political rhetoric regarding human suffering partly because it offers such a socially and politically powerful moral explanation (cf. Luker 1984). Because events culturally framed by the trauma script are much more likely to gain sympathy and support from those who identify with the victimized (Best 1997) but are met with denial and denunciation from those blamed, the events in question are also much more likely to become controversial and heavily politicized. This fuels further issue polarization, galvanizing subpublics to engage in political conflict, including debate, denunciation, collective action, and resistance.

At root, the suspicion and social blame that animate public tragedies reflect historic levels of social and institutional distrust. Trust in the church, the presidency, public schools, the Congress, the police, and the criminal justice system, among more than a dozen such major institutions, has, according to polling, decreased over time (Gallup 2022). At the same time, distrust of such institutions has grown, in some cases, precipitously. Indeed, according to Gallup the average level of confidence expressed by U.S. adults across the fourteen major trustee institutions Gallup annually tracks is at its lowest since its polling of them began in the 1970s (Jones 2022).[3] The trends, with few exceptions, are clear. Many Americans have lost faith in many of the institutions that are entrusted with their lives.

3. The fourteen major institutions that Gallup has used since the 1970s to track U.S. confidence are the church/organized religion, the military, the Supreme Court, the presidency, Congress, public schools, newspapers, television news, organized labor, the medical system, the police, the criminal justice system, big business, and banks. Small business, big technology, internet news, and health maintenance organizations were added in the 1990s.

This state of affairs reflects and involves metaconditions detailed by several noteworthy social theorists of modernity, late capitalism, and "risk society" (Bauman 2007; Beck 1992; Erikson 1994; Freudenburg 1993; Giddens 1990; Habermas 1975; Short 1984). Changes in belief and ideology at the societal level involve several entwined issues, which I explore in subsequent chapters. Briefly, we live at a time of transition from modern social relations to those of a risk society (Bauman 2013b; Beck 2009; Beck, Giddens, and Lash 1994; Giddens 1990, 1999; Lash 2000; Lash, Szerszynski, and Wynne 1996). The certainty that faith in progress gave modernity, and the sacrifice it justified, no longer securely tie citizens to the state or citizens to one another. Freed from modernity, the future is now radically uncertain. It is inflected with cynicism regarding the capacity and will of societal trustees like the state, industry, and allied societal institutions— those individuals, organizations, and institutions responsible for maintaining social order—to reliably secure the common good (Beamish 2015; Bude 2017; Freudenburg and Pastor 1992; Habermas 1975).[4] In short, the legitimizing beliefs that underlaid modern society focused on expanding opportunities, distributing goods, and promising progress. In the current risk society, growing public cynicism is reflected in social and economic retrenchment, risk allocation, and a belief that life and politics are governed by zero-sum trade-offs. These latter conditions have stimulated a politics of risk in which grievance and risk avoidance have become the day's leading social and political causes (to be explored in chapter 2).

THE STRUCTURE OF THIS BOOK

After Tragedy Strikes asks how trauma and loss have come to be seen in this way and why they have emerged in the twenty-first century as the predominant crucible for social and political conflict and change. Chapter 1 outlines in detail the societal and historical conditions from which public tragedies have emerged as epochal political events. I document how public tragedies emerged from modern social relations in contemporary risk

---

4. Government, industry, and other societal institutions like science, technology, education, politics, and rule of law represent types of *trustee authority*.

society and show how this exposed a sea change in cultural understandings regarding human trauma, suffering, and loss. The chapter delineates how the simultaneous emergence of risk society, in conjunction with new beliefs about persecution, victimization, and victimhood, lend themselves to the heightened politicization of crises from which hyperpoliticized and notorious public tragedies are more likely to arise.

Chapter 2 focuses on government and governance responses to social crises. In principle, when managing risks on behalf of the public, the government should seek to ameliorate harm and assist in saving lives, reassure the afflicted, and moderate the trauma and loss these victims experience. Governments also respond to limit the damage crisis events can inflict on broader concerns, such as the national economy and local, regional, and national well-being. Yet government response can also embody less principled interests, such as political expediency, political capital, and trying to maintain the appearance of success. Governmental officials may strive to avoid blame for actions or inactions that result in victims or full-blown humanitarian crises. When the government's actions or omissions are regarded as having failed the public, highly publicized and politicized cases of public tragedy can result. Consequently, avoiding blame has become an increasingly conspicuous feature of contemporary crisis management and disaster response. In seeking to ameliorate harm and assist victims of contemporary crises, public officials and their surrogates often simply try to avoid being blamed for the suffering they are expected to alleviate. As I show, blame avoidance and the politics that plays out around it are significant elements of all public tragedies. They act as fuel to the fire.

I analyze contemporary news media logics and a new communication ecology in chapter 3. They also indelibly contribute to the rise of notorious and publicly tragic events. The chapter explores the media's role in framing crisis events to expose what sets the publicly tragic apart from everyday unfortunate but seemingly routine traumas. Through an account of today's reigning media logics and a brief empirical comparison of the news media's framing of six cases of crisis, I explore how contemporary news frames do (and do not) align with the trauma script. I examine how in some cases news framing cultivates public understandings and the emotions associated with public tragedy, while in other, similar cases they do not. I also show how the contemporary news media and social media's communication ecology represent a hybrid system of communication that accelerates the news media cycle and opens the public to new levels of spectacle and hyperbole. In so doing, this hybrid system amplifies the impact and emotion associated with stories of trauma, loss, and victimization. In short, the media plays a defining role in the making of public tragedies.

Chapter 4 focuses on political mobilization of victims and victims' advocates in the aftermath of crises. At the center of publicly tragic events are those subjected to trauma and loss: the victims. The perceived damage they experience supplies public tragedies with their center points: public sympathy, moral outrage, social blame, and political victimhood. The accusatory power behind political victimhood reflects the use of the trauma script to explain suffering and cultivate the public's sympathy, outrage, and blame for their situation. The power of the trauma script to inspire sympathy and attention is further expressed in a new type of social acclaim I term *tragic celebrity*. Once achieved, tragic celebrity can propel victims and the issues associated with them into the political domain. Through content analysis of news covering George Floyd's murder, I demonstrate the role of these elements in fomenting public tragedy. This chapter also explores the use of public tragedy in victim advocacy and political campaigns. Collective actions, social movements, and even formal political campaigns currently rely on the trauma script to motivate public sympathy, outrage, and support for their causes and platforms.

The book's conclusion reasserts the need for a deeper understanding of the origins and manifestations of public tragedy. As I have noted, surprisingly, little has been written about public tragedy sui generis. There are several reasons for exploring the emergence and influence of public tragedies on the feelings and affairs of the United States and the world. First, public tragedies expose the structure of feeling in the current era, exposing sociological facets of society. They provide clues to the future direction of our political culture, particularly considering the ample evidence that contemporary public response to trauma and loss differs from past reactions. We see this difference in the outpourings of grief, memorialization, and collective action that follow events that achieve the status of public tragedy. We see it also in the prevalent claim that society is to blame for tragic suffering and the trauma and loss that result. This was unusual until the late twentieth century; it is not even uncommon in the twenty-first century. Second, public tragedies also matter because of what they represent politically, as they exert considerable influence over the "body politic." They currently fuel public outrage and encourage political polarization in the United States. Therefore, it is crucial to understand why some events become publicly tragic and how they can reshape an already shaken moral order. Put another way, unpacking how some events come to signify an existential threat to a sizable segment of the public is of the utmost sociological importance in the twenty-first century.

1 A World at Risk

MODERNITY, VULNERABILITY,
AND PUBLIC TRAGEDY

Public tragedies, as political events, emerge from a contemporary framing of trauma and loss that claims that blameless victims have suffered unnecessarily at the hands of others. This framing reflects the trauma script, a now conventionalized cultural explanation of harm that centers on claims of victimization and the assignment of social blame. Social blame suggests unfair treatment and suffering at the hands of a group or collective (cf. Kleinman, Das, and Lock 1997). The ultimate "perpetrator" in public tragedies is, therefore, society or some aspect of it. When invoking the script, even if people do not directly blame society, they still implicitly link it to trauma and loss based on the failings of its "proxies": institutions, structures, and culture. Crisis, when framed via the trauma script, also tends to galvanize the public because it highlights victims' accusations (Jeffery and Candea 2006; Kleinman et al. 1997); links prior tragedies and cultural traumas to current ones (Alexander 2002; Eyerman 2015; Platt 1999); and involves public expressions such as outpourings of anger, grief, spontaneous memorialization, and social protest (Doka 2003a; Veil, Sellnow, and Heald 2011). The victims have not just been harmed but "wronged"—whether deliberately, negligently, or accidentally—leading to moral outrage, blame, and political controversy.

Until the late twentieth century, responses to trauma and loss rarely took the shape of today's increasingly frequent public tragedies (Bovens and 't Hart 2016; Giddens 1999; Quarantelli 1998; Rubin 2012; Steinberg 2006). The trauma script and its actualization as public tragedy clearly embody a historically uncommon understanding and response to suffering. An important question is, therefore: "What has changed?" In this chapter I focus on social conditions and historical transformations that preconfigure the contemporary structure of feeling. A historical examination helps explain how and why the trauma script has come to resonate so powerfully with the American public. It also explains how and why public tragedies have become transformational in the twenty-first century. Again, I argue that the proliferation of public tragedies is epochal; they represent a sea change in societal mentalité and cultural understandings of human trauma, loss, and suffering and, hence, the response to them.

To explore the changes and conditions that explain public tragedies, I employ a genealogical account (Foucault 1984), detailing a transition that has taken place from "modern society" to our current "risk society." I recount material, ideological, and perceptual trends that have culminated in conditions and beliefs that markedly differ from those that prevailed at the close of World War II. They signal a move from one kind of society to another. I analyze how this transition was reflected in and partly driven by the rise of the modern welfare state. This paralleled the state's increasingly interventionist governance policies, culminating in what I term the "U.S. federalization of risk." By federalization of risk, I mean that in the U.S. context, the national government, as distinguished from the states that constitute it as a federation, has progressively adopted and expanded a proactive approach to risk interdiction and management.

The penchant for intervening and managing has, in turn, spurred countervailing opinions among the public. On the one hand, U.S. federal interventionism (and equivalent policies on the part of state and local governments) led the public to now expect these entities to reduce risk and enhance security. On the other hand, interventionism has spurred resistance and fear among the public as the state and its surrogates generated new risks, leading to accusations of "government overreach." I conclude the chapter by examining the concomitant emergence of a victim mentalité: its role in generating public sympathy and its political efficacy for strengthening claims of trauma and suffering. The conditions of risk society and the concurrent rise of "political victimhood" have cultivated a social and political context that explains why public tragedies have become pivotal political events in the opening decades of the twenty-first century.

AN EPOCHAL SHIFT

According to Foucault (1984), a genealogical analysis is a method for investigating the elements and categories of a recognized "thing" that is treated as if it were "without history." Such a thing is taken for granted; it becomes a reified object. Foucault used genealogical analysis to investigate crime and punishment, mental illness, sexuality, and governmentality, among other topics, in order to get at how these "things" had come to be viewed as normal. Similarly, I construct a genealogical account of public tragedy. Why, as a type of political event, has public tragedy become an increasingly "normal" response to trauma and loss?

As discussed in the introduction, crises involving life and death were previously often presumed to be the outcome of God's hand, bad luck (i.e., chance), accident, or personal responsibility. In some cases trauma and loss, even death, were rationalized as the "price of progress," a sad but necessary sacrifice for America's future. For example, in the context of industrialization, death and injury were commonplace for those who worked in the nation's factories and built its roads, bridges, dams, and cityscapes (Freeman 2018; Levy 2012; Sinclair 2003). Injury and death as a function of "modern nation-building" and the general lack of concern shown for worker welfare highlight a societal context and structure of feeling much different from today.

Part of this also surely reflects the opacity of the day, when the public (as a public) rarely ever saw or heard about industrial accidents or government wrongdoing, let alone the injuries and deaths that resulted. Moreover, the ability of the public to readily communicate their suffering outside of a very limited network of persons was also severely limited until recently. Clearly the current and ubiquitous attention to fear and suffering and public reactions to them were nearly impossible before the emergence of the contemporary communication ecology, with its round-the-clock news and social media communications, as I argue in chapter 4. But the subdued public response was also reflected in an American political-cultural view and commitment to "progress," which at least publicly had quasi-religious significance for much of the country; the sacrifice was necessary for all to move forward. And if fate, chance, or personal responsibility explained those harms and who or what was to be held to account, then what use was outrage and social protest? Public response to trauma and loss of this kind was accordingly relatively muted compared with many of today's public displays of sympathy and indignation. Indeed, one might even say the general response was callous by today's standards. For instance, postcrisis "tourism" was common in the nineteenth century. In the aftermath of catastrophe, spectators would often flock to horrific scenes of carnage where they would tour the devastation, entertained by dreadful scenes of death and destruction (Godbey 2006; McCullough 1968).

As I argue, it was not until the late twentieth century that human cause and social blame infused all matters of consequence. In what has been labeled the "Anthropocene"—a human-dominated epoch that supplanted the Holocene (Crutzen 2006; Crutzen and Schwägerl 2011; Steffen et al. 2011)—a now conventionalized political and cultural framework has, with increased frequency, been used to explain all kinds of trauma and loss. Indeed, as laid out in the introduction, trauma and its use in this way have become a rhetorical trope widely used in movements and politics but also in news making and entertainment (Bennett 2022; Pandell 2022; Sehgal 2021). A question that requires redress, then, is from where this transformation in sentiment and the discourse representing it derives.

RISK SOCIETY, THE RISK-MANAGEMENT STATE, AND A RISK PARADOX

My answer begins with the role of risk in governance. The government's role in risk interdiction and crisis response has transformed over time. Currently, most of the federal budget is devoted to risk management, ostensibly to protect the American public from harm. Indeed, roughly 75% of the U.S. federal budget reflects direct risk-mitigation provisions through health care, national security, and social security spending. The remaining quarter addresses a range of what are also ostensibly risk-mitigation-focused policies and programs such as law enforcement, natural disaster response, unemployment insurance, environmental protections, and food assistance (Friedman 2019).[1]

Taking one obvious risk-related expense—domestic disaster relief—and comparing federal government expenditures across time illustrates the point that the role of the U.S. federal government in reacting to and mitigating risk has become the primary axis for governance. It is increasingly viewed as an entitlement among much of the American public (Platt 1999; Rubin 2012). Between 1970 and 2019, disaster relief funding (DRF) appropriations increased tenfold, from roughly $13 million appropriated between 1970 and 1979 to $138 million between 2010 and 2019 (calculated in 2018 dollars; Painter 2019). While individual catastrophes in any given year can distort year-to-year comparisons, the trend line for DRF appropriations, like other risk-related expenditures, has gone steadily up as disaster relief and risk-alleviation measures have generally become a governance priority and an expectation among the American public (Rubin 2012).[2]

In fact, the U.S. public has progressively demanded this intervention. Paradoxically, social distrust of government efforts to manage risk of all kinds has also become more pronounced with time (Pew Research Center 2019). The incongruous beliefs and expectations that currently animate the public's understanding of risk and governance expose a mentalité that takes shape in what I have termed elsewhere "the politics of risk" in risk societies (Beamish 2015). Why have public expectations concerning risk and its management changed over time? And how are these changes

1. Roughly 30% of federal spending goes toward health care, 24% to national security, and 23% to social security; the remaining 23% goes to a range of programs, including law enforcement, natural disaster prevention and mitigation, unemployment insurance, environmental protection, and food assistance. Even the interest payments are largely a function of debt accrued on prior risk-reduction expenditures (see Friedman 2019).

2. Annual funding of the Disaster Relief Fund was not fully established in its current form until 1966. While funding of this kind became more common after the civil war (circa 1870s), it was not conceived of as a U.S. federal obligation until well after WWII. Up until this time, disaster relief and recovery was still considered primarily a matter for private individuals, private nongovernmental organizations, local government, and in extreme cases state government (Painter 2019; Platt 1999; Rubin 2012).

linked to the emergence of both the trauma script as an explanation of harm and public tragedies as a manifestation of this explanation?

In preindustrial society, crises and the trauma and loss they produced were typically understood as "fated." However, the intensification of "modern" industrialism brought with it human-wrought systems of productivity from which flowed the promise of benefits—capital, taxes, wages—and a broad sense of control over natural processes. So-called modern societies pursued technological innovation, economic expansion, and social change to achieve ever-higher levels of liberty, rationality, organization, and prosperity, and with these, "civilization." Parsons (1985), among others, referred to this as the "modernization process" (see also Weber 1978). Anthony Giddens describes modernity as a shorthand term for industrial civilization in which the world is viewed as open to human transformation through economic institutions such as industrial production and a market economy and in which a range of social and political institutions like the nation-state, technoscience, and democracy are central (Giddens 1998:94; see also Giddens 1990).

Modernity, as an ideal, is further founded on teleological ideas concerning "human progress" and the progress of society that emerged during the enlightenment. Many enlightenment philosophers presented social improvements as inexorable: they saw the modern age as a time of advancement, improvement, and progress (Harvey 1989; Marcuse 1964). Social theorists like Parsons (1985; following Weber 1978) suggested that Western civilization was inevitably moving toward ever-more-rationalized social relations. These ideas converged, in the mid-twentieth century, in "modernization theory" and a singular model of rationally developed civilization called modernity (Coleman 1965; Levy 1967; Parsons 1951, 1985). This model informed prescriptive and pragmatic development policy primarily funded by so-called modern societies. The model tasked global institutions, such as the World Bank and International Monetary Fund, with supporting the modernization of other societies, pushing them to develop in their image: the "modern state" (Apter 1965; Organski 1965; Rostow 1990).

As technological innovation, economic expansion, and social change were pursued in the name of progress, such transformations generated new forms of risk (Bauman 1992). This is modernity's *risk paradox*: modern societies were forced to reflexively respond to their prior actions to adjust to the challenges. In other words, actions and steps taken by the state to achieve progress created new risks for people, hence requiring new rounds of decisions and actions. According to theorists of risk society, the transformation from modern society to risk society reflects the unintended outcome of modernity's successes, not its failures. The control that technoscience and systems rationalization seemed to exert over natural processes ushered in an age of risk that paradoxically undermined that very control. Put another way, modernizing processes that were supposed to protect society from age-old threats—famine, pestilence, the elements, natural hazards—in turn introduced new "manufactured risks" that were by-products of advanced technoscientific systems: chemical toxicity, biological corruption, environmental decline, nuclear apocalypse, and more recently the newfound specter of AI-driven human extinction risk (Knight 2023; Roose 2023). The promise of control at the heart of modernity has thus been exposed as an illusion (Giddens 1999).

But the transformations were not simply "technological" in the typical sense of the term. They were also social, cultural, and ontological (Giddens 1990; Kinnvall and Mitzen 2020). Successive rounds of "progress" produced previously unforeseen threats to the social order, undermining the sureness and security ostensibly promised by modernity. Rapid technological innovation accelerated rates of social change and, with them, cultural dislocation. Rapidly rising expectations regarding progress have also often outpaced actual life gains. These conditions, as some suggest, have led to high rates of "relative deprivation" and with it, at the very least, social unhappiness and at worst, social unrest (Davies 1974; Gurr 1970; Smith and Pettigrew 2015). They may also lead to "deaths of despair" in which people kill themselves by suicide, alcoholism, and drug overdoses, which have increased in recent years (Case and Deaton 2021). Indeed, far-ranging beliefs and structural changes to society—the hallmarks of modernity—have eroded social institutions, in turn leading to social conflict. Dependence on wage work was accompanied by a rise in life-making precarity. The increases in personal liberty and the emergence of the nuclear family led to an equivalent decline of tradition. The invention of instantaneous communication fueled the escalation of disinformation, and the emergence of democratic political hierarchies led to populism, sectarianism, and policy paralysis.

Modern and modernizing institutions such as democracy, egalitarianism, scientism, techno-utopianism, industrialism, bureaucracy, merit systems, secularism, and individualism have both created benefits and generated new risks. They were and remain paradoxical in their effects: they ushered in an age of increased control and simultaneously, radical uncertainty. In short, the institutional forces associated with progress undermined many of the assumptions and beliefs that motivated the modern project, subverting and in turn fomenting a transition toward a risk society (Beck 1992, 2009).

In risk societies, social and political concerns no longer revolve around modernity's advantages, such as wealth acquisition and benefit allocation, but rather around an accelerating contest over modernity's dark side: *risk and its distribution*. When we perceive human life, property, or cherished values to be threatened and their future status uncertain, we say they are "at risk." We worry there is a chance they may be harmed or lost altogether (Beamish 2015:8). This sense of threat manifests in the contemporary effort to predict and manage all perceived threats to personal and collective well-being (Berstein 1996). As modern industrial society matured, creating both benefits and manufactured risk, these conditions simultaneously stimulated a deep reservoir of foreboding, a fear of victimization due to seemingly out-of-control conditions.

Yet risk as a concept has also moved outside technoscience and has mainstreamed; it is now routinely used in social and political struggles and disputes as a means of contestation and as a forensic device (Beamish 2015; Douglas 1990). In this regard, risk can be characterized as both a technology—an ability to forecast the chance of success or failure—and a perception—that something of value is uncertain and therefore under threat. Risk is both. The "politics of risk," therefore, represents a fundamental shift away from "modernist politics," with its focus on consensus through growth (of human resources, physical capital, natural resources, technoscience) and the distribution of benefits (investments, wages, taxes). We have moved, instead, toward a politics of risk in which concerns over the distribution of societal risks—deflation, defunding, regression—have become paramount.

Taking a more granular perspective, how then does risk society fundamentally differ from modern society? Risk society is distinguishable in several ways; its unique elements also help us understand why the trauma script resonates so profoundly with the public and why crises have consistently become publicly tragic. Per its nom de guerre, foremost among them is a contemporary obsession with risk. Beck (1992) suggests that three current conditions fueled the rise of risk societal relations. First, to achieve increased prosperity, power, and control, both the state and industry in modernizing societies pursued scientific expertise, technological innovation, and techno-organizational systems that created significant risks to humanity's future (Beck 1992:21; 1999:34–37). These include complex fields of production and consumption such as "systems" for resource extraction, energy, chemicals, agriculture, manufacturing, medicine, military, finance, transportation, information, and communication. Yet even as modern societies became preoccupied with preventing and managing risks through forecasting and probability models, the global threats that have been manufactured through technoscientific organization can no longer be adequately predicted. Consequently, discussions of society's past, present, and future increasingly center on risk as leaders and citizens obsess over exposure to it, its prevention, and its management (Beck and Levy 2013).

Second, modern risks are menacing but also inescapable irrespective of one's social standing (i.e., class, race, and gender). Modernity's risks threaten everybody, even if unequally. While the more vulnerable in society suffer from greater exposure to such threats, modern risks ultimately threaten everyone, everywhere, all the time, making risk a universal concern (Beck 1992:23). Finally, once those risks manifest, the organizational and administrative systems that created them are the only bodies through which they can be managed. A layperson cannot intuitively or via native senses—sight, smell, hearing, touch—know how to measure a chemical or radioactive dose. Nor can they detect biological markers and modifications or produce vaccinations without access to training, the proper equipment, and capital. Paradoxically, the risky technoscientific systems that generate such epic risks require further investment in technoscience. Only by continued investment can they invent and deploy technical strategies to manage the risks created in prior rounds of innovation, production, and consumption. This has become a continuous recursive loop that Bauman (1992, 2007) refers to as a "solution-problem dynamic"; it never resolves. Rather, it produces more unresolvable societal disquiet and angst with each iteration as risky "solutions" pile up.

Risk and Vulnerability

A deep sense of personal and collective imperilment has emerged out of modernity's risk paradox. Reflecting this, any proposed development or innovation involves risk and, therefore, a likely dispute over who will benefit and who will bear the costs. Importantly—and paradoxically— understanding and living with such risks often requires reliance on the same public officials, technical experts, and technological systems that produced or managed the risks and benefits in question. The public is left with further uncertainty about what is and is not threatening.

Yet the uncertainty characteristic of risk society does not end there. The experts who manage such risky technoscientific systems often disagree on the trade-offs of risks or benefits, their probability of success or failure, or the likely consequences of catastrophic accidents. Disputes regarding risks and benefits are now endemic. Risk disputes over such things frequently spill over into the public, where they can quickly become hyperpoliticized moral schisms. Disparate actors debate what is right and good or wrong and immoral rather than what is technically and factually correct or the best pragmatic course of action (Beck 1992:155–56). This impasse promotes pervasive skepticism and social distrust among and between actors: in the state, industry, civil society, and within and between institutions such as technoscience, education, law, the courts, and among and between citizens (Gallup 2022; Pew Research Center 2019). For example, a review of its annual surveys of public trust by the Pew Research Center (2022) shows that two-thirds of U.S. adults report believing that other Americans have little or no confidence in the federal government or in other citizens. Majorities think the public's confidence is likewise decreasing over time. Most respondents also expressed that the shortage of trust in the government and other citizens makes solving the nation's problems less likely. And they are correct, as long-running surveys of the American public show: public confidence in the government and other major social institutions has fallen since the 1970s and is currently near historic lows (Gallup 2022; Nadeem 2022; Pew Research Center 2022; Rainie and Perrin 2019; Rainie, Keeter, and Perrin 2018).

These forms of distrust and dispute also reflect the fact that many technical systems, and the experts and institutions that manage them, were initiated in modern contexts and based on modern conceptualizations. They are ill-equipped to resolve the political conflicts characteristic of a risk society or manage the risks endemic to it. Modern ideas such as objectivity, neutrality, and fact in science illustrate the point. When modern state building commenced (circa the seventeenth through nineteenth centuries), advocates for science styled it as a neutral arbiter of "the facts." Positivistic science relied on the trained professionalism of scientists who developed research methods they believed promised objectivity. Indeed, as an institution and practice, the legitimacy of scientific research largely rests on its perceived impartiality (Kuhn 1970; Latour 1987, 2012) and contrasts with the role that magic, religion, and tradition have played in supplying understandings of the world. Science functioned outside of religion and ideology, in the modern perspective. Yet in risk society, the politicization of the very term *objectivity* and with it, *science*, as well as the rampant use of disinformation to weaken factual claims, has for many undermined the credibility of science and the expertise on which it is based (Aronowitz 1996; Brysse et al. 2013; Latour 2004; Oreskes and Conway 2011; Sokal and Bricmont 1999).

Political theorist Jürgen Habermas (1975) suggested that the modern state has also confronted a legitimacy crisis that resulted from its contradictory role adjudicating modern market-capitalist economies. The modern state has actively promoted its role as a neutral arbiter in legal, political, and social disputes to gain the fealty of its citizenry. Yet over time it became clear to much of the American public that this was not the case. At the close of World War II in the United States, industrial elites, the U.S. government, and unionized labor entered into a relatively stable accord that endured for a generation of workers (Bowles, Gordon, and Weisskopf 1984; Rubin 1995). While the social charter that emerged during this industrial era was "nowhere written," it came to represent a tacit set of rights and expectations among American workers (Fantasia 1988; Fantasia and Voss 2004; Reinarman 1987). Indeed, it can be argued that it was fundamental to the legitimacy of the U.S. political-economic order in the post–World War II era (Fantasia 1988, 1995).

Yet over time the state emerged as primarily a defender of capital, not labor. It showed its hand as a partisan interest that promoted societal development by stimulating the "modernizing process" through capital accumulation. For instance, modern states have repeatedly intervened on behalf of capital interests rather than labor or small business interests to avert the periodic economic crises associated with market cycles (Harvey 1982). Over time it has become clear that state neutrality had never existed. In Habermas's (1975) rendering, the state progressively undermined its standing as a believable arbiter of social order. This has in turn also eroded public belief in the "modern project" and with it progress itself.

These social dynamics accelerated in the late twentieth century. Deindustrialization and the sustained movement of manufacturing jobs overseas, the rise of temporary work and a gig economy, and precarious employment across the board helped foster a relatively radical partisan political climate (Bluestone and Harrison 1982; Kalleberg 2000; Kalleberg, Reskin, and Hudson 2000; cf. Smith 1998, 2001). In contemporary political discourse, political elites increasingly rely on rhetoric that is no longer committed to shared prosperity and security for all Americans. Rather, they woo and entice, targeting subgroups (including other elites) who support their candidacies using particularistic promises. Donor politics and zero-sum rhetoric have fueled a growing sense among the American public that both personal futures and fortunes and those of the nation are declining. This sense that American democracy is threatened has also sowed a great deal of cynicism and distrust among the American public (Parker, Morin, and Horowitz 2019).

From this sociological crucible, public tragedies have emerged as galvanizing political events. They provoke the public because they resonate with a pervasive sense of vulnerability to societally induced risks. Indeed, social expectations regarding the responsibility of the state and its surrogates to secure the public well-being can even transform "natural" and "unpredictable" crises—from terrorism to natural disasters to pandemics—into highly politicized national political controversies that then become referenda on governance (Boin and Kuipers 2018; Habermas 1975; Meek 2016). Failure to effectively alleviate the risks of modernity—or at least the *perceived failure* to do so—has become a recurring claim against the state, society, and the status quo. Ultimately, it forms a basis for both collective action and political resistance (Beamish 2001, 2015; Freudenburg 2001; Mazur 2010; Wildavsky 1988).

The risk concept reflects a preoccupation with alleviating uncertainty and securing the future. Calculation of risk, as a concept, is aspirational. Risk is also a technology that conceptually controls uncertainty by turning it into a measurable quantity: the probability of cost and loss or benefit and gain. In risk society, modernity's promise of benefit now competes with the risk of harm in the future. All societal plans are now infused with a fundamental struggle over how risk and benefit will be distributed (i.e., who will benefit and who will suffer). But because of prior decisions, projects, and the risks associated with them, skepticism and social distrust now typify relations between the state, industry, and the citizenry and among citizens themselves (Beamish et al. 1998; Brenan 2019b; Hardin 2002, 2004; Montinola 2004). One can observe these dynamics in the now-frequent claim that the government and its surrogates (i.e., trustees) have failed to fulfill their obligations to the public trust. Accusations of "official recreancy"—a failure to follow through on an obligation—are now commonplace (Freudenburg 1993, 2000, 2001). Such accusations both explain and are reflected in declining levels of trust among Americans in the nation's major institutions (Jones 2022). They also reflect the application of the trauma script to understand trauma and loss, which generates the moral outrage that animates publicly tragic events. Such accusations define virtually all public tragedies.

Risk Society and a Victim's Mentalité

Reflecting the risk-society dynamic, fear of becoming a victim (i.e., being victimized) has become the leading political cause of our time. A deepening sense of vulnerability has likewise encouraged an abiding sympathy for victims and cases of "victimization" (Best 1997; Campbell and Manning 2018; Lukianoff and Haidt 2015). I argue that the simultaneous fear of becoming a victim and sympathy for those who have been victimized lies at the emotional heart of risk society and with it public tragedies. It is no coincidence, then, that the disasters and traumatic events that receive the most public attention, sympathy, and politicization are those in which someone is viewed as having been unfairly harmed by societal forces that feel out of control to many Americans. Even where responsibility is in doubt, accusation and social blame bolster the view that if the victims had been treated differently—had a law existed or been enforced, had society acknowledged their suffering, or had they been assisted sooner—their harms and suffering would have been greatly diminished, if not avoided altogether. In this context, the state and other trustee institutions are frequent targets for blame, in both their actions and omissions.

Again, the modern risk paradox suggests that risks beget solutions and that solutions beget more risks. This puts the government and its surrogates in an unenviable position. On the one hand, the public often assumes that most risks should be preventable, or at least that societal trustees should significantly diminish them (Boin and 't Hart 2007; Slovic 1994, 2000). The sense that the government and its surrogates are responsible becomes acute when the harms appear to be exceptionally unfair. These are also the events that are most likely to become publicly tragic.

On the other hand, deep-seated distrust of the government and its surrogates commonly ensues from the modern risk paradox: people view many risks and the harms as society's fault. Of course there are plenty of mistakes and instances of misconduct and wrongdoing associated with today's crises. In the context of these incongruous and even contradictory assumptions and expectations, the public routinely blames the government and its surrogates—rightly and wrongly—for failing to protect people from risk. Because the dynamics of risk society have cultivated a deep sense of vulnerability, tragic circumstances have acquired greater meaning and significance, too. Events of this kind are often both framed by the media as "threats to us" and experienced as "if it were us." Indeed, when the mass and social media frame crisis events as "warnings," "lessons," and "things to be feared," they amplify people's feelings of vulnerability (Altheide 2013). Widespread fear and vulnerability provide a pretext for nonlocal crises to be emotionally experienced as proximate tragedies. This reflects the sympathy virtual viewers now feel for the victims of trauma and loss in conjunction with media framings of crisis that frequently seek to take advantage of and promote these feelings of insecurity and fear to gain and hold audience attention (analyzed in depth in chapter 4).

These dynamics highlight the underlying sentiment and cultural narrative that generate public tragedies. The trauma script resonates because it dovetails with how the modern risk paradox is experienced: the positive gains of modernity are now consistently counterposed with its excesses.

These manufactured risks include such "modern" trade-offs as state expansion and the loss of privacy and liberty, fossil fuel energy and climate change, wonderous chemicals and horrendous toxicity, consumer luxuries and environmental decline, democratic governance and political extremism, wage work and life precarity, free-market expansion and economic crisis, and human rights recognition and the rise of authoritarian illiberalism.

THE LAISSEZ FAIRE STATE AND CRISES

Changes to how the state manages risks and remedies crises have played a crucial role in transforming public expectations regarding who and what is responsible for their well-being (Dauber 2013). At the same time, changes in state actions also reflect changing public attitudes that have increasingly pushed the state toward risk management and risk interventions before, during, and after crises. Changing public attitudes have also led the state to take proactive measures to stem potential threats before they occur.

This contrasts with a previous hands-off approach. Reflexive and routine state risk management and crisis intervention are relatively recent developments. For most of its history, the U.S. federal government has been relatively laissez faire about intervening when disaster strikes and when citizens confront other sorts of less acute risks and hardship(s). Response and recovery were mainly left to victims, who relied on personal networks and local communities. If a disaster was particularly horrific, state authorities may have helped, but that help was not assured and certainly not expected (Roberts 2006). Understanding the emergence of public tragedies therefore requires attention to the transformed role of the state and its surrogates in responding to crises of a range and type, as well as the American public's expectations and reactions to such actions (or omissions).

For its first 160 years, the U.S. federal government had no charter, policy, or agreement with U.S. states or citizens outlining its statutory responsibility for responding to disasters, emergencies, or crises (Platt 1999:1; Painter 2019; Rubin 2012). This was not because crises and the victims they created were unknown or less consequential than they are today (or less "tragic," for that matter). Indeed, infamous disasters such as the New

York City cholera epidemic of 1832, the Chicago fire of 1871, the Johnstown flood of 1899, the Galveston hurricane of 1900, the San Francisco earthquake of 1906, the flu pandemic of 1918, and the great Mississippi flood of 1927 were devastating in terms of casualties, immiseration, and social and economic cost. For example, the Great Chicago Fire of 1871 was an industrial accident. The extreme damage and death it caused were due to the heavy concentration of lumber industry facilities, wood houses, fuel, and other chemicals in a small city area. The 1911 Triangle Shirtwaist Factory fire in New York City caused the deaths of more than 100 garment workers, who died in the fire or jumped to their deaths (McEvoy 2018). In 1918–1919 influenza killed more people than World War I: between 30 and 40 million worldwide. It has been cited as the most devastating epidemic in world history, even more damaging than the plague that ravaged medieval Europe. (The death toll from the influenza pandemic was some 650,000 people in the United States, which was then a country of some 100 million—one-third the size of today's population.)

It would not be until the late nineteenth century that this laissez-faire approach would soften, and it was not until the 1930s and the New Deal that the U.S. federal government (hereafter "the state") would embark on a new governance strategy—the welfare state—and with it, develop its contemporary fixation on risk management. Elements of its new disaster strategies included intervening and providing logistical support, financial assistance, and humanitarian relief in the name of "the national interest." The change reflected evolving interpretations of the law and definitions of the national interest (Dauber 2013), along with growing expectations among the general public that the state should take a greater role in planning, managing, and responding to a broad range of emergencies. Indeed, it also involved redefining what constituted a disaster. Before filling in the details of the new governance strategy, let's examine a case that illuminates an earlier time and a paradigmatic laissez-faire approach to disaster and crisis: the 1890 Johnstown flood.

The Johnstown Flood

The Johnstown flood was a horrific instance of human trauma and loss ostensibly caused by human actions and omissions. While achieving a fair amount of notoriety, it never received the kind of national public outrage or political controversy that would define such an event today. It also sits at a juncture: a time when laissez faire was slowly but inexorably giving way to state interventionism and U.S. federal risk-management practices. On May 28, 1889, heavy showers swelled the Little Conemaugh River, overfilling an artificial lake upstream from Johnstown, Pennsylvania. The lake was formed behind an earthen levee created by the South Fork Fishing and Hunting Club, an association of Pittsburgh plutocrats who had made the private lake, which they reserved for their exclusive use. Their members included many of the famous tycoons of the gilded age, including Andrew Carnegie, Henry Phipps Jr. (Carnegie's partner), Henry Clay Frick, Robert Pitcairn (of the Pennsylvania Railroad), and Andrew Mellon, among others. Johnstown, Pennsylvania, had a population of 10,000 and sat just below the dam astride the river.

The source of the catastrophic flood was a shoddily constructed levee dam made from packed earth, straw, and horse manure. Relief pipes had been installed to control overflow but were no longer operational because they had been sold off as scrap metal (Godbey 2006). Under hydraulic pressure, the earthen dam burst suddenly, disgorging the lake into the valley below in less than an hour. Estimates have put the force of the water at the full strength of Niagara Falls (McCullough 1968). The resulting wave of water flung buildings, factories, homes, trees, and train cars down the valley. The wreckage piled up behind a stone railroad bridge that held, but the rushing deluge of water and wreckage diverted into the city of Johnstown itself. Soon after, the giant debris pile ignited, incinerating an untold number of the already dead persons as well as many who were struggling in the wreckage to survive. Twenty-three hundred residents of the Conemaugh Valley and the city of Johnstown, Pennsylvania, died that day (Godbey 2006).

Initially, the victims of the Johnstown flood were primarily left on their own. Volunteers from nearby cities like Pittsburgh provided assistance as the days and week passed. Neither the federal nor the state government provided recovery resources, nor did they offer significant relief funds to the flood victims or the city (although some funds were donated by private entities and individuals). The state did not declare a state of emergency or send in the National Guard. No significant safety policy was created, nor were changes to the law enacted. And while anger was evident, there was no sustained public outcry or protest and no federal or state investigation of consequence.

This is not to say that outrage did not follow the flood's aftermath. There was a great deal of anger in Johnstown because residents knew the dam was shoddy. According to historical accounts, the outrage was also expressed in some newspapers, in which headlines and a few editorials expressed contempt and indignation over the circumstances. But they mainly focused on an aspect of the flood that harmonized with a brewing public issue in America during that period: those who belonged to the South Fork Fishing and Hunting Club were millionaires who were widely perceived to be richer than anyone ought to be. They were not simply millionaires but, according to the day's press, "aristocrats or nabobs" who were nothing less than rich pleasure seekers (McCullough 1968:249). That rich pleasure seekers were responsible for the flood and the death and destruction fit the zeitgeist of the 1890s. The death and destruction in Johnstown were detestable, not so much because people had suffered unfairly at the hands of society, but because the lake was solely created for "pleasure," not to fulfill a purpose: "The dam served no useful end, beyond the pleasure of a few rich men" (McCullough 1968:250). This violated the tenets of "progress," the emergent justification of that day, something that might have made the town's sacrifice understandable. Pleasure seeking did not. Indeed, not more than three years later, steel strikes would explode in Pittsburgh, and labor unrest elsewhere in the country would turn into open battles between labor and many of these same "robber barons" (Brecher 1997; Destler 1946).

Residents' anger also culminated in a handful of lawsuits filed against the South Fork Fishing and Hunting Club and the Pennsylvania Railroad in a quest to gain compensation for the damages and deaths caused by the flood. Yet "not a nickel was ever collected through damage suits from the South Fork Hunting and Fishing Club or from any of its members" or the railroad (McCullough 1968:258). In the most notorious case, the flood was deemed by judge and jury to represent "providential visitation" rather than human fault. This followed the opinion of many of that time who, in the aftermath, opined in newspapers and church pulpits what the flood represented: a story of fate and sin. This was a prominent cultural

framework at the time. The apocalyptic symbolism of the flood represented an act of the Lord destroying the town for being a place of sin.
Many reasoned that this must be true since only a vile and wicked place
would be subjected to such a horrific catastrophe (McCullough 1968:252).

Reflecting a harder-edged view of trauma, loss, and suffering soon after
the flood, Johnstown became as much a public curiosity and tourist des-
tination as a focal point of public outrage over the injustice of the flood.
Within three days, railroad officials and workers, doctors, preachers, char-
ity workers, and Johnstowners who were out of town at the time of the
flood rushed back to look for victims and supply humanitarian relief. Yet
their return and rescue efforts were obstructed by crowds of sightseers
who had hastened to Johnstown to tour the devastation and observe the
dead and dying firsthand (Godbey 2006:277). In the week following the
flood, the town and flood site became a regional tourist attraction. Ven-
dors sold tours and macabre mementos that featured bloated bodies, or-
phaned children, destroyed homes, and an apocalyptic cityscape.

According to accounts of other crises, this was hardly out of the ordinary.
As Godbey (2006) notes, in the aftermath of Civil War battles and disasters like the Galveston hurricane—America's worst natural disaster[3]—the
Chicago fire, or the San Francisco earthquake, "disaster tourism" was relatively commonplace (Lippard 1999). Until the mid-twentieth century, the
victims of catastrophe—whether human-caused, accidental, or natural
in origin—necessarily engaged in "self-help" and relied on extended kin-
ship and community networks to survive. While the federal government

3. After the devastating Galveston hurricane hit Texas in 1900, city officials and local
plutocrats/philanthropists were almost wholly responsible for the city's rebuilding. At a mini-
mum, 6,000 persons died, and some estimates double that number, in a city of 40,000. Even
more devastating than the Johnstown flood, the entire city and surrounding settlement were
literally washed off the sandbar that is Galveston Island. In response, the city, community,
and hometown philanthropists—very wealthy island tycoons and benefactors—politically
organized, took over local government, and paid with local money to dredge their harbor for
sand, dumping it on-site and raising the entire downtown some 15 vertical feet. They then
built a 16-foot-high, three-mile-long seawall to defend against future hurricanes—all with
locally sourced capital (some $32 million at the time or more than $200 million in today's
dollars). Indeed, historians credit the storm and local expenditures with both saving the city
and also playing a part in its long-term decline. In its aftermath, the storm's costs were
simply too much for any one community to absorb alone, even for a city that, at the time, was
Texas's wealthiest (Cartwright 1991; Green 2000; McComb 1986).

was not entirely removed from disaster response (occasionally dispensing official condolences and modest assistance), the task of response, relief, and reconstruction was organized by local groups and institutions. Reconstruction was almost wholly funded by the damaged communities themselves (through local governments, local churches, and local philanthropy) (Painter 2019; Platt 1999). Even U.S. states seldom intervened in local crises unless the associated trauma and loss were truly catastrophic or unless elite interests had been affected. The response to Johnstown was therefore not an outlier. Like many other major disasters of the nineteenth and early twentieth centuries, the Johnstown flood is an exemplar and point of comparison to contemporary crises becoming publicly tragic. Indeed, it was a crisis event clearly caused by human indiscretions, yet it did not transform into a public tragedy as we might likely see today.

THE U.S. FEDERALIZATION OF RISK

The Johnstown flood exemplified a prior period of a relatively laissez-faire approach to crisis by the state and a cultural interpretation of trauma and loss that strongly differed from that which often animates the state and public in the aftermath of tragedy today. As I've noted, risk management and response to crisis are arguably the primary task of federal and state governments today (Friedman 2019). How did we get to a risk society with hyperpoliticized public tragedies from the laissez-faire state mentality and the fated crisis approach of the nineteenth century?

Throughout the late nineteenth and across the twentieth centuries, the U.S. federal government adopted an expanding and increasingly proactive approach to crisis management that edged it toward social welfarism (Dauber 2013). I focus on the federal role because while states, regions, and cities are important, they do not command the resources, expertise, or authority to respond to and rectify many of the country's crises. I also examine the role of growing public expectations in shaping governmental response. These expectations have led to a contemporary "politics of risk" with significant implications for how we view trauma and loss, as well as how we perceive *who* or *what* is held to account, and *why* they are (or are not) blamed when trauma and loss result.

While several catastrophic disasters near the turn of the twentieth century—such as the Johnstown flood, the Galveston hurricane, and the San Francisco earthquake and fire—pushed the U.S. federal government to reconsider its ad hoc and laissez-faire approach to crises, Progressive-Era ethics of social and political reform would also greatly influence these ideas. Progressive-Era reformers sought to harness the power of the government to eliminate unethical and unfair business practices, reduce corruption, and counteract the negative aspects of the "age of industrialization" (e.g., Sinclair 2003). The Progressive Era would also see the emergence of charitable organizations and philanthropy focused on humanitarian relief, as reflected by the American Red Cross (1890) and Salvation Army (1865) (Hall 1987; Soskis 2020). By the time of the Great Depression in the 1930s, a transformation in crisis preparation and response was evident.

Following World War I, the Great Depression also forced the state's hand. Laissez-faire governance when coupled with an emergent "disaster narrative" was just no longer politically tenable. Catastrophic multistate natural disasters—such as repeated interstate flooding that culminated in the great Mississippi flood (1927) and later, recurrent drought coupled with poor agricultural practices that resulted in the Dust Bowl (circa 1934, 1936, 1939)— threatened the whole country and put the national interest in question. These were not simply local problems caused by parochial interests. In partnership with state governments, the federal government began to progressively embrace a larger role in crisis response, especially by financing crisis recovery while advocating state-level proactive hazards mitigation.

Indeed, Dauber (2013) suggests that at root, the "U.S. welfare state" was legally justified by an ascendant "disaster narrative" that had been percolating for nearly a century before its institutionalization in the New Deal and other welfare state policies. The narrative defined eligibility as claimants being "afflicted by sudden, unforeseeable events over which they have no control and for which they are morally blameless" (Dauber 2013:6). Its correspondence with core elements of the contemporary trauma script is striking. The disaster narrative was used to justify disaster relief in a select number of cases in which the executive branch set up specialized federal bureaucracies to evaluate applications and distribute limited funds according to eligibility requirements. As a legal narrative it was also subsequently used to support and explain aid in a handful of cases in which acute disasters harmed collectives rather than individuals. This was obviously out of line with the presumed liberal consensus of that day and the general laissez-faire approach to disasters and collective suffering. But as Dauber makes the case, because the disaster narrative had justified U.S. federal government aid in a handful of nineteenth-century natural disasters, once the Great Depression was framed as just such an "acute disaster," the precedent of these earlier cases was set. The disaster narrative could be applied, and the New Deal became possible.

Regardless of this looming policy innovation, until the New Deal, the federal role in disaster response evolved gradually and unevenly. Compared to today, it was minimalist. For example, because of the Great Depression, the Hoover administration commissioned the Reconstruction Finance Corporation (RFC) in 1932 to make federal loan money accessible to failing banks to prevent insolvency while stimulating economic activity. In response to repeated and massive flooding along the Mississippi, the RFC would also become the first federal agency to distribute loan dollars in the wake of disasters to promote general recovery. The federal government also funded New Deal–focused public works and disaster relief programs that sought to lessen the chance and impact of future disasters, like the national crises noted earlier. Because individuals, firms, and local and state governments did not have the resources to respond effectively, the Great Depression, combined with regional disaster events, eventually pushed the federal government to act in the name of a newly important response scale: "the national interest." In the process, a governance precedent was set. So too were public expectations.

The great Mississippi flood is a case in point. It precipitated a transformation in how the U.S. federal government responded to disasters, managed the risk of future floods, and paved the way for the federal response to "unnatural disasters" like the Great Depression that began in 1929 (Dauber 2013). Following the flood of 1927, Congress passed the Flood Control Act (1928). The act was amended in 1936 and again in 1938 after repeated catastrophic floods in the Mississippi Valley. The flood of 1927 alone devastated 20,000 square miles of territory in six states, generating considerable privation and commercial loss. The legislation set a precedent for a vastly expanded U.S. federal role in disaster management and federal intervention in what had previously been deemed local affairs. This change would also change the view among the American public concerning the federal government's responsibility in times of crisis (Barry 2007).

Due to its response to the floods and its newfound responsibility for the risk of floods, federal involvement in the planning and management of U.S. waterways down to the local level would rapidly expand in subsequent years. Federal flood control was eventually given to the Army Corps of Engineers in the East and the Bureau of Water Reclamation in the West. This began a half-century surge of federal dollars spent to create and maintain levees, diversion channels, earthen works, and dams to control water flows and avert catastrophic flooding across the United States.

Alongside efforts to mitigate the worst impact of flooding and the Great Depression, the Dust Bowl of the 1930s would also push the federal government deeper into local and state affairs, further solidifying its new twentieth-century role as the country's preeminent risk manager. The government initiated programs that had been unthinkable only a decade or two earlier, to address both general economic issues and the impact of widespread drought and farmer insolvency across the Midwest. Established in 1933, the Farm Credit Administration was created to provide farmers with low-interest refinancing and equipment loans. Yet as drought conditions intensified, it quickly refocused on drought relief. In 1934 Congress approved President Franklin D. Roosevelt's $525 million drought relief program. Soon thereafter it formed the Drought Relief Committee within the Department of the Interior to improve drought response, relief, and mitigation (Butler 2012b:66).

Flood- and drought-control efforts, in conjunction with Great Depression and New Deal–era programs, played an outsized role in the emergence of the federal government's crisis-response function, which became increasingly focused on risk management. The changing federal role was also a function of the changing view many Americans held of the government as they were whipsawed by a combination of both human-caused and natural disasters with devastating impacts. Many Americans also increasingly held the federal government responsible for operational responses to crises, for postcrisis financial and material recovery, and even for proactive risk mitigation to stem potential future risks. This new ideal would be expanded to include humanitarian relief as well. This simultaneously set the stage for the federal government and its surrogates to be blamed when their actions or omissions were associated with significant trauma and loss.

Managing Risks, Both Natural and Human-Made

Following World War II, the U.S. federalization of risk through crisis planning and response would also be driven by concerns about national security. As the range of airpower increased, for instance, federal concerns that the United States was vulnerable to enemy attack led to proactive plans for that eventuality. In 1947, under the aegis of "military readiness" and implicitly the national interest, the National Security and Resources Board (NSRB) was established to prepare U.S. industrial and economic assets in case of war (Kreps 1990:277). Its mandate was to establish adequate reserves of strategic materials, conserve these reserves, and strategically locate assets deemed critical to the nation's continued security. The NSRB embodied a growing U.S. federal "risk management ethic" focused on forecasting and planning, an ethic that would not fully congeal until the second half of the twentieth century.

Events like the Texas City disaster of 1947—an explosion that acted as a "focusing event" (Birkland 1997)—hastened this transition. On April 16, 1947, a freighter carrying 2,000 tons of ammonium nitrate caught fire in the port of Texas City, Texas. The fire set off a blast felt some 40 miles away in Houston. It reportedly shattered windows and knocked people to the ground. Its power rivaled that of an atomic bomb. Soon after, fire from the destroyed ship reached another freighter docked in a nearby harbor, which was also loaded with ammonium nitrate and sulfur, causing it to explode some 16 hours later. The explosions exposed mistakes and misconduct on the part of the harbor authority, the ship's captain, and federal oversight agencies. It led to a first class action suit, filed on behalf of 8,485 victims (Butler 2012b).

While the disaster in Texas City is still considered the single biggest industrial catastrophe in U.S. history, the accident and loss of life were not unprecedented in the United States or elsewhere. Industrial and military ordinance explosions in public ports and storage and containment centers before Texas City were dramatic and well known.[4] The postmortem on the Texas City explosions suggested that it resulted from those in charge downplaying the risks associated with loading and transporting highly flammable and explosive materials. Importantly, as reflected in the class action suit, not only were the immediate administrators of the ship, railroad, and port blamed for the Texas City explosions, but the public also held the U.S. Coast Guard and U.S. federal government accountable for not fulfilling their obligation to regulate the transport of highly hazardous materials properly.

The Texas City explosion was a watershed event and catalyst for the future; the dramatic public blaming redefined and reflected ideas about responsibility and who or what should be held to account. Clearly, public responses to the Texas City explosions were much different from those that had prevailed in the aftermath of the Johnstown flood some 58 years prior. Indeed, 47 years earlier, the Island of Galveston, Texas, which is 20 miles from Texas City, was literally wiped off the map in the great hurricane of 1900. It had to be rebuilt largely with locally generated funds, with little or no federal intervention and no outpouring of national support (Beamish 2015; Cartwright 1991; Green 2000). A new pattern of public response to crisis took shape in the aftermath of the Texas City explosions. As an emergent framework for understanding the causes and the associated losses, the trauma script was reflected in growing public expectations, moral outrage, and political conflict over what was increasingly interpreted as unnecessary harm inflicted on innocent victims.

In addition to natural disasters and industrial accidents, the U.S. federalization of risk in the postwar period was also motivated by concerns about Cold War security. With the Korean conflict and Cold War concerns mounting, Congress enacted the 1950 Civil Defense Act (CDA). The federal government's intention under President Harry Truman was to establish a Civil Defense Administration that could address the potential for

4. A partial list of notorious port explosions during this period includes a munitions ship exploding in a Halifax, Canada, harbor (circa 1917, with 2,000 dead and 9,000 injured); a munitions explosion in a Sayreville, New Jersey, plant (circa 1918, with 100 dead and $18 million in damage); an ammonium nitrate explosion at a storage facility in Oppau, Germany (circa 1921, with 600 dead and 2,000 injured); and a munitions explosion in the Port of Chicago (circa 1944, with 320 dead). Ammonium nitrate and munitions were recognized hazards and were not allowed in many ports. Given the risk they posed, ammonium nitrate and munitions were banned from Galveston's harbor, only 20 miles away from Texas City.

"emergencies or disasters that result from enemy attack, which local forces cannot adequately control" (Bea 2012:85).

Following on the heels of the CDA was the 1950 Federal Disaster Relief Act (FDRA). Unlike the CDA, which was motivated by a fear of nuclear attack, the FDRA recognized the millions spent by Congress to mitigate the disastrous flooding of the Mississippi, Red, and Columbia Rivers in prior decades. The FDRA was intended to avert the risk of flooding by establishing the ongoing authority of the federal government to intervene in the aftermath of disaster without having to wait for Congress to act. It also established the executive branch rather than Congress as the arbiter of the decision to provide aid. While the act paid homage to the laissez-faire ideal in stipulating limited assistance and coordination with state-level authorities, it actually pushed federal governance power deeper into local contexts. Indeed, soon after the passage of these two acts, the two tracks—civil defense and disaster relief—would be collapsed under the FDRA, and federal disaster assistance and recovery would be carried out in coordination with the American Red Cross.

Additionally, congressional policies leveraged executive power to play an increasingly important part and, with time, an increasingly politicized role in federal disaster response. In 1953, Congress amended the FDRA to allow U.S. presidents to declare emergencies and promise Disaster Relief Funds (DRF) to assist recovery. Over time this power and its use have increased dramatically. The frequency and ease of presidential disaster declarations have turned them into de facto political instruments (Roberts 2006). Disaster declarations have averaged 35.5 per year since the policy's enactment (1953), but the number of disaster declarations issued each decade has increased. For instance, since the Reagan administration (circa 1981), each new president has increased the number of DRF claims over their predecessor, with more than 15 of those since 1995 and costing $500 million or more in taxpayer funds (Lindsay 2014). Indeed, from 1990 to 1999, DRF claims rose steadily from 35.5 to an average of 46 a year, and between 2000 and 2009 jumped to 56 claims a year (Lindsay and McCarthy 2015). An analysis of DRF also suggests that the increase is not evenly distributed across disasters, disaster victims, or U.S. regions, nor entirely based on victim need. Who is and is not likely to gain relief is at least partly a function of political considerations, driven by regional voting patterns and party affiliations (Downton and Paul 1998; Reeves 2011), an issue I take up in chapter 2.

Following the devastating 1964 Alaska earthquake and soon after a catastrophic hurricane and several catastrophic flood seasons, the U.S. Congress further expanded the federal government's role in risk mitigation and crisis response. In an amendment to the FDRA, Congress authorized the federal government to provide below-market loans to aid communities, rural areas, schools, and colleges. In 1968, the National Flood Insurance Act was passed to assess flood zones across the country and eligibility for federally backed insurance coverage. These two acts culminated in 1970 with the passage of omnibus disaster relief legislation. The 1970 Disaster Relief Act, which superseded the prior 1950 act, would dramatically scale up and transform U.S. federal responsibilities during disasters and emergencies. Following a decade of disasters, the strength of a centralized U.S. federal system of crisis response and mitigation was clear.

THE FEDERAL EMERGENCY MANAGEMENT AGENCY

Pressure to create a centralized crisis-response system also came from state governments, which wanted a single, dedicated national crisis management organization with which to coordinate state and local resources. President Jimmy Carter responded by forming the Federal Emergency Management Agency (FEMA) in 1979. Federal crisis management is legally referenced as a "partnering" effort with states and local jurisdictions to address disasters that cross state lines and jurisdictions and can only be coordinated by a federal agency. FEMA was thus tasked with directing interstate crisis response when catastrophe strikes. With FEMA, the federal government completed its transformation as the central source of disaster expertise, planning, funding, and responsibility, that is, as a *risk manager* when a significant crisis or disaster occurs. With the new disaster agency, the federal government would also increasingly become a target.

While FEMA was initially conceived as responsible for natural disaster response and recovery and only secondarily as a civil defense asset, this conceptualization and policy priority shifted with Cold War concerns about nuclear attack and response. With the election of Ronald Reagan in 1980, FEMA was tasked with providing plans for "governmental continuity" during and after such an attack. This change and a $4 billion budget increase placed FEMA at the center of Cold War plans to develop facilities and equipment to maintain government operations in the event of a nuclear holocaust. FEMA would develop evacuation plans intended to save a large proportion of the U.S. population (Rubin 2012).

FEMA was subsequently tasked with "disaster mitigation" as a risk-management responsibility. For instance, FEMA led an effort in flood plain management called the National Flood Insurance Program to discourage risky construction. Local governments had to participate for local property owners to qualify for low-cost flood insurance. What is more, FEMA's residential buyouts of high-risk, flood-prone homes echoed both newfound risk-mitigation efforts and also an expanding bailiwick; under Carter, FEMA had also been responsible for buying out family homes at Love Canal, New York, and Times Beach, Missouri, where toxic contamination emergencies had made them uninhabitable.

The new attention to Cold War and civil defense projects initially took focus and resources away from FEMA's work as disaster coordinator, leading to criticism of poor performance in several 1980s disasters (including earthquakes in California and Puerto Rico and hurricanes and floods elsewhere in the nation). Importantly, even given the heavy criticism, the political lesson drawn from dealing with disasters as diverse as flooding and flood insurance to toxic events like Love Canal was quite different: federal response to crises—good or bad—could be a game changer for elected officials.

With Bill Clinton's election in 1992, the political importance of FEMA was further enhanced. Even though its recent performance had not been good, under Clinton, FEMA gained stature with new tasks, a larger budget, and a director with a cabinet-level appointment. As early twentieth-century events pushed the U.S. federal government to reconsider its ad hoc and laissez-faire approach to crises, the federalization of risk and the federal government's transformation into the nation's preeminent risk manager were fully manifest by the century's end. Successive administrations had learned the political lessons of poor response to crises. Carter, Reagan, and Clinton elevated crisis planning and response because their constituents demanded it. The public had embraced this new federal role, a function that has today become an expectation if not an entitlement.

Dereliction in an Age of Manufactured Risks

Even before September 11, 2001, the risk of domestic acts of terrorism and the ability to respond had become significant political concerns. With the

1993 attacks on the World Trade Center, the 1995 Oklahoma City bombing, and the subsequent terror attacks on U.S. assets abroad,[5] security analysts, political elites, and hazard planners warned that further attacks were imminent. In this context, risk management was not about if but when another significant attack would occur in the United States.

The September 11 terror attacks shocked the nation and world, activating political elites in a frantic scramble for answers to why such an event could happen, what would ensure it would never happen again, and how we might prepare for any future attack(s). The attacks promoted another shift in how the United States conceived of crisis response and management: a shift that would have implications for understanding state and public reaction to public tragedies.

Through the application of an "all-hazards approach," George W. Bush embarked on the most comprehensive reorganization of the federal government since the New Deal. The September 11 attacks had exposed missteps, failed communication, and failed coordination among the nation's security establishment. This weighed heavily on U.S. federal risk-management plans. In response, experts believed that by integrating intelligence services, law enforcement agencies, and emergency management functions, the federal government could respond to different types of crises more effectively. In theory, this seemed best. The Bush administration specifically reorganized the crisis-management apparatus and created the Department of Homeland Security (DHS), into which a formerly independent FEMA was placed. Yet the inclusion of terrorism, the restructuring of FEMA as part of DHS, and a highly centralized and top-down approach to crisis management made coordination with local, state, and federal levels of government, nonprofits, and even military organizations extremely difficult. Because crisis response almost always involves multiscalar reaction, coordination, and improvisation, the new agency structure also proved cumbersome and slow. The all-hazards approach, the vertical integration of crisis response functions within DHS, and the inclusion and focus on terror—coupled with the rigid bureaucratic structure characteristic of

---

5. Attacks on U.S. domestic and international assets include the 1993 Twin Towers bombing in New York City, 1996 bombing of Khobar Towers in Saudi Arabia, 1998 bombing of U.S. embassies in Kenya and Tanzania, and 2000 bombing of the USS *Cole* as it was refueled in the Yemeni port of Aden.

DHS—made FEMA less adaptable, compromising its ability to see and respond to disasters as it had as an independent agency.

Hurricane Katrina, which devastated much of New Orleans and surrounding areas, exposed some of these rigidities. Unprepared for a storm and a humanitarian crisis of this magnitude, the Bush administration and FEMA failed. With cameras rolling, cable networks showed people suffering from the failures of government intervention and humanitarian relief. Indeed, Hurricane Katrina became an exemplar as the first natural disaster and, soon after that, humanitarian crisis to receive cable and network news coverage 24 hours a day, seven days a week of the storm and its aftermath. That coverage exposed the suffering of thousands of New Orleanians, especially that of poor African Americans from the 9th Ward of the city, and the role social inequality can play in disaster response and life and death decisions. Intense social and political public outrage followed. Local victims gained widespread recognition due to their neglect, mistreatment, and racial disenfranchisement.

Katrina was a quintessential public tragedy involving accusations and social blame, outpourings of grief and anger, collective action, and a struggle to define the meaning of the event (Birkland and Waterman 2008; Bullard and Wright 2009; Dreier 2006; Gotham 2007; Johnson 2011; Kellner 2007; Pastor et al. 2006; Sze 2006; U.S. House of Representatives 2006). In the aftermath, FEMA's reputation was so politically damaged that many emergency managers left the organization and few qualified emergency planners applied to fill the vacant spots (Roberts 2006).

Indeed, soon after that, with the Deepwater Horizon blowout (2010) and a new administration under Barack Obama, FEMA and DHS were tested again and largely failed to live up to expert or public expectations. The Deepwater Horizon oil platform ("rig") was owned and operated by offshore oil-drilling company Transocean and leased to BP to tap the Macondo oil prospect. Situated over the Mississippi Canyon, a valley some 5,000 feet below the surface, the Deepwater Horizon suffered a subsea blowout that led to a natural gas explosion topside, igniting a fireball visible as far as 40 miles away, that killed 11 crewmen and injured 17. The fire, fueled by a high-pressure gas geyser, was inextinguishable. Two days after the explosion, the Deepwater Horizon sank, leaving the well gushing at the seabed. Over the next 87 days, it became the largest marine oil spill in U.S. history (Freudenburg and Gramling 2011). The federal government's response was perceived as a mixed success. Under intense media pressure to stop the oil gush, the Obama administration's response involved so many federal, state, and local actors that it soon became marred by confusion over who was in charge and who was responsible for what aspect of the oil spill catastrophe (Beamish 2010). The postmortem analysis of spill response that emerged once again suggested that the federal response was inadequate to the task. The National Response Plan, developed after September 11 to direct federal response to human-induced technological, and natural disasters, came up short.

While Katrina and the Deepwater Horizon blowout challenged FEMA and the federal government's crisis-response reputation, the criticisms of their performance in no way suggested that the federal government's obligation to protect the public from risk should diminish; quite the contrary. The idea that the federal government was responsible for public well-being, specifically in times of crisis, was, if anything, reinforced. The U.S. federalization of risk had become an abiding expectation among many Americans and most experts. With an expanded list of crisis types now entitled to government intervention (as well as eligibility for relief funding), the public now largely takes for granted the expectation that the federal government, with help from state and local partnerships, should plan, prevent, and rebuild in the aftermath of crisis. Indeed, for many Americans, it is not a question of if but how much support "the government" will offer when a crisis strikes an individual or the public. Crisis response has, for many, become an entitlement. As I have suggested, it is often the mismatch between public expectations of government response and assistance, on the one hand, and public impressions of government action and omission, on the other, that has become a prime basis for public tragedy, undergirding scenarios in which those harmed frequently feel victimized by the government.

THE EMERGENCE OF "POLITICAL VICTIMHOOD"

As suggested in this chapter's opening, within the context of the welfare state, the emergent social dynamics of risk society have created, among the public, a general fear of being harmed by circumstances that are outside individual control. Such fears, when coupled with an expectation that the government or its surrogates will protect, intervene, and secure one from harm, turn many traumatic events into political contests. Those harmed impugn the authorities for their response (or lack of it), and the authorities, in turn, extol their efforts and seek to avoid blame for any harm that has occurred. (See chapter 2 for an analysis of "politics of blame avoidance" in postcrisis contexts.) This has created a context wherein traumatic crisis events have increasingly become focal points for political recriminations, claims of victimization, and social blame and moral outrage over it. In a phrase, "risk disputes" have become commonplace (Beamish 2015). Yet being a victim and claiming to have been victimized has only recently become politically efficacious (Best 1997; Jeffery and Candea 2006; Ochs 2006). How, then, is the forgoing history and transition from a modern to a risk society linked to contemporary claims of victimization and victimhood, claims whose moral suasion and political power are relatively new? Furthermore, why have claims of victimhood become so politically consequential? And how is it that they can lay the basis for public tragedy? These are important social and cultural questions with obvious political ramifications.

In the Western cultural tradition, we have not historically associated victims with the exercise of political power or social change, but rather with pity and powerlessness (Dunn 2004; Ochs 2006; Ryan 1971). The etymology of the word *victim* originates in the Latin term *victima*, which roughly translates as "sacred thing." In its original Latin usage, *victima* referred to a living creature offered as a sacrifice to supernatural powers. While its earliest usages in English emphasized sacrifice, by the seventeenth century, *victim* was widely used as a specific reference to Christ's sacrifice. In the biblical tradition, Christ was said to have sacrificed himself for the sake of humankinds' sin, not his own, the very embodiment of a victim.

We can also find an early appreciation of victims and the processes surrounding victimization in literary treatments by poets and novelists in traditions like noir fiction, as well as novelists like Franz Kafka, Aldous Huxley, Vladimir Nabokov, and more recently Margaret Atwood. Indeed, by the 1920s, in the aftermath of World War I, modernist writers and artists began to articulate disillusionment with modern conditions and therefore modernity. Works like T. S. Eliot's *Wasteland* (1991) developed the darker aspects of human nature and emphasized self-awareness, introspection, and the cultural decay he associated with modern Western society. In all, the modernists were some of the first to communicate through their art the irrationality at the base of what was supposedly a rational (i.e., modern) world.

By the late twentieth century, the darker aspects of modernity were further being reflected in a contemporary definition of victim: someone who suffered injury by forces beyond their control and over which they had no personal responsibility (OED 1984). Notably, it is not until this time that victims and claims of victimization would gain the political-cultural influence they currently exert. Intersecting events, trends, and movements coalesced and further destabilized public confidence in modern society and the promise of progress. These changes exposed a range of social, political, and technological risks, seemingly out of control and threatening to everyone. Widespread cultural recognition of "victimization" after World War II ascended as the Holocaust narrative diffused, and with it the acknowledgment of "victims' rights," significantly accelerated (Alexander 2002; Best 1999; Dunn 2004; Kleinman et al. 1997; Ochs 2006). By the late 1950s and into the 1960s, the civil rights, antiwar, women's, and budding environmental movements—among others—would unsettle civic life through social protests that prompted a widespread rethinking of the postwar status quo (i.e., modernity and the narrative of progress). The increased awareness of the threat posed by social and material relations—reflected in wars, racism, and sexism—was joined by a growing dread that industrial toxins, unsafe products, and inadequate regulation and enforcement were putting Americans at risk. These movements and the politics they generated raised awareness of the perils of "modern times" that unsettled the general public. They promoted a widespread sense of disquiet and vulnerability that slowly but inexorably undermined the credibility and legitimacy that the notion of progress had supplied the modern project.

These developments also cast light on groups who had been "victimized" in the post–World War II context. The rhetoric of freedom and progress—both political and economic—was sorely tested. For example, during World War II many women stepped into jobs to sustain the war effort. Yet after the war, many of their jobs and freedoms disappeared when male soldiers returned to their prewar positions. The U.S. government repeatedly justified its foreign interventions—in Korea, Vietnam, Iran, Central America, Granada, Panama—as part of a fight against tyranny and for freedom, democracy, and an American-style market system. Yet many soldiers who were poor or persons of color or both returned from abroad, having fought for America and its dream, only to see their domestic chances little changed, despite their service and sacrifices. The contrast between America's social and political rhetoric and the reality of domestic inequality left high-minded ideals of freedom and progress open to criticism from both the left and the right. It also left many Americans feeling unjustly treated by status quo social and political relations.

Crucial to the development of sympathy for and the political empowerment of "victims" was the emergence of the "victims' rights movement" and from it the emergence of the "victim industry" (Best 1997). Initially championed by a conservative movement in response to legal changes made by the United States Supreme Court in the 1960s, the language of victims' rights later would be adopted by the political left. The court, under Chief Justice Earl Warren,[6] enacted several procedural protections for criminal defendants that restricted police powers that the court traced to the Bill of Rights. Social conservatives were outraged that the court would seek to protect "perpetrators" rather than "victims." Soon after that, reflecting conservative unhappiness with criminal jurisprudence, the victims' rights movement surged, focused on criminal justice reform and the perceived mistreatment of the victims of crime (Best 1999; Fattah 2000; Galaway and Rutman 1974; Smith and Huff 1992).[7]

By the late 1960s, the United States was rocked by widespread political protests over the Vietnam War, urban race riots, and shocking political assassinations that undermined public security and confidence in the future. By 1968, half a million U.S. soldiers were fighting in Vietnam, and by the 1973 U.S. withdrawal, 58,000 had died. In a period of heightened political tumult, the discourse associated with victims' rights, while initially a conservative one, entered the left's lexicon with William Ryan's 1971 publication of, *Blaming the Victim*. Ryan argued that the societal focus

6. Circa 1953 to 1969.
7. Victims' rights legal reforms took the shape of victim compensation, victim impact statements, and allowing victims to address the court during the sentencing phase of criminal court proceedings.

on "welfare abuse" and "petty crime" blamed powerless victims of racial and class oppression. As Joel Best (1997) noted, the language of "blaming the victim" soon moved well beyond Ryan's usage to explain the plight of America's "underclass." It became part of the discourse used by the political left to explain any number of societal abuses.

It also became an effective political weapon for both left and right because it did not specify precisely who (or what) was doing the victimizing, outside of blaming indefinite institutional forces, social structures, ideologies, and social categories (like race, class, and gender constructions and biological essentialisms) for inequality (Best 1997:10). The cultural frames characteristic of both victims'-rights and victim-blaming discourses did little to change the conditions and harms they identify, Best argued. However, they did provide explanatory cover for a notable politics of accusation and social blame in which suspected perpetrators—individuals, groups, institutions, society—were accused and denounced for transgressions with little accountability or substantiation of the levied charges.

The close of the ill-begotten war in Vietnam, the proliferation of risky technologies and toxic events, and the general economic instability that followed coincided with the continued push for socially progressive values by social movements. Comprised of second-wave feminists and antinuclear, LGBT, and environmental-justice activists, each suggested that everyday life was not safe, secure, or predictable.

Events like the toxic contamination of Love Canal, New York, and Ralph Nader's story about automobile safety captured these dynamics. Love Canal residents were exposed to toxic chemicals, damaged by the mistakes, misconduct, and outright hubris of public officials, corporate interests, and their surrogates. Modest working- and middle-class homes had been built over a former toxic waste dump without homeowner knowledge. The contaminants sickened some of the residents, forcing their evacuation (Gibbs and Levine 1982; Levine 1982). The plight of Love Canal residents, whose homes and families were contaminated, left many Americans fearing for their own health. And Ralph Nader, in his bestseller *Unsafe at Any Speed* (1965), documented and exposed the resistance of General Motors (GM) to spending money to improve the safety of their automobiles. GM's decisions resulted in the deaths of tens of thousands of Americans every year. In response, GM sought to sabotage Nader's reputation. Nader subsequently sued GM for invasion of privacy and in 1970 won his battle with GM for discrediting and defaming him for writing the book about unsafe American automobiles.

Instances like these represent what became a nearly continuous string of crises, involving middle-class, working-class, and poor communities, that attracted sustained news media coverage about people who had been victimized by frighteningly risky conditions associated with a "modern way of life" and by the governments, industries, and surrogates responsible for such conditions (Brown and Mikkelsen 1990; Bullard 1994; Carson 1962; Szasz 1994).[8] Adding to the angst and insecurity was the seeming disregard from those who were "in charge" for everyday Americans, coupled with the lack of substantial progress on core issues of the day, from environmental decline to poverty and women's rights, even after more than two decades of social movement activity. For many Americans, whether rationally conceived or not, threats to their immediate health and long-term well-being seemed out of control (Mazur 2010; Slovic 2000; Starr 1969; Wildavsky 1988).

By the late 1980s and early 1990s, many investigative journalists, therapeutic professionals, and academics embraced a normative line in their crafts, in which they exposed, theorized, and moralized harm and engaged in victims' advocacy. Their efforts reflected a clarion call to expose inequality and suffering, support human rights, and stop blaming victims for socially induced harms (Best 1997; Fassin and Rechtman 2009; Furedi 2004; Ryan 1971). Through such efforts, many Americans also became sensitized and sympathetic to stories of trauma and loss, likely because of their own feelings of vulnerability to the risks of a contemporary way of life—modernity. As such, the public increasingly viewed themselves as besieged by human-induced conditions and forces beyond their control and seemingly out of control (Bauman 2013a).

---

8. Other toxic events, like the meltdown at Three Mile Island, Pennsylvania, and the catastrophic methyl isocyanate gas leak at Bhopal, India, by an American company, Union Carbide, further exposed the American public to the perils of modern industry and the risks of being victimized by it. In response, risk-management policies like Superfund legislation, or the Comprehensive Environmental Response, Compensation, and Liability Act (CERCLA), were pushed through Congress, directing the Environmental Protection Agency (EPA) to clean up abandoned toxic waste dumps, while the Emergency Planning and Community Right-to-Know Act (EPCRA) required manufacturers to report releases and transfers of toxic chemicals to a publicly accessible database, the Toxics Release Inventory (TRI).

With the opening of the twenty-first century, a politics focused on trauma and victimization emerged as an increasingly conventionalized rhetoric within U.S. political discourse (Best 1997; Campbell and Manning 2018; Fominaya and Barberet 2013; Jeffery and Candea 2006; Lukianoff and Haidt 2015; Ochs 2006). This enhanced the ability of individuals and groups who believed they had unnecessarily, unreasonably, or unjustly been harmed to inveigh against their victimization and, in so doing, cultivate public sympathy. It also changed the shape of claims making and political discourse in the United States. Indeed, scholarship relating to victims, victimhood, and cultural trauma shows that political claims making and the narratives used to explain cases of trauma and loss have had a lasting impact on contemporary political discourses and political outcomes (Alexander 2002; Barker 2007; Best 1999; Dunn 2004; Eyerman, Alexander, and Breese 2015; Jeffery and Candea 2006; Ochs 2006; Rothenberg 2002; Weed 1990).

Again, as noted earlier, these kinds of claims and the conditions that promoted them reflect extant structural inequalities, crisis events, and actual cases of misconduct and wrongdoing. They are also grounded in less tangible changes in the beliefs, expectations, and identified vulnerabilities associated with the conditions of a risk society. Indeed, currently, 4 in 10 Americans fear being the victim of gun violence, while nearly half fear for their children's physical safety at school; three-quarters worry about being the victim of cybercrime; and almost 4 in 10 worry they will be mugged, their homes robbed, or cars stolen, or they will be the victims of a hate crime or even terrorism (Brenan 2021, 2022; Newport 2017). These and other fears are exacerbated by the existential anxieties produced by contemporary political dysfunction; democratic decline; and a range of seemingly apocalyptic scenarios, including climate change, war, the threat of nuclear conflict, and air, food, and water toxicity, among many others. Combined, these beliefs and the politics and political developments at the opening of the twenty-first century help explain why events framed by the trauma script hold more cultural salience and political power than in the past. The move toward self-identification as a victim, that is, *victimhood*, has facilitated the framing and translation of what were, for much of U.S. history, "private traumas" into today's widely resonant "public tragedies."

Alexander's theory of cultural trauma (Alexander et al. 2004) explains how collective identities of this kind came to be. He persuasively argues that collective identities constructed around victimhood involve groups reconstructing memories of past traumas in ways that challenge dominant societal definitions. These reconstructions give rise to collective identities that involve cultural trauma forged in remembered suffering, hardship, and loss. Alexander used historical cases such as the Holocaust, India's partition, and the Japanese slaughter of Chinese in Nanjing during World War II to demonstrate how cultural trauma manifests (or does not) in modern times. Likewise, Eyerman (2001, 2015) has sought to explain the culture of trauma that has resulted from American slavery among African Americans. Sztompka (2000) found that social change and the hardship it promoted in Eastern Europe in the post-Soviet context also resulted in a culture of trauma there. This occurs when a collective believes it has been subjected to extreme distress and builds an identity around it. Therefore, the theory of cultural trauma advances one understanding of how collectively constructed memories of prolonged suffering can manifest in the identity of a group or collective and, once articulated, can be culturally passed along.

Collectively remembered traumas therefore operate at the collective level in ways similar to the individual, psychological level: they injure the collective psyche, leaving collective feelings of distrust and vulnerability from which group recovery is difficult, if not impossible. Cultural trauma even persists over time, these theorists argue, injuring persons intergenerationally as one cohort passes its memories to the next.

Yet cultural trauma is not inevitable. The transformation of individual suffering into collective trauma requires cultural work pursued by "carrier groups" that, through protest, accusation, speeches, meetings, correspondences, stories, and so forth, make such trauma "real." The "truth" of such cultural trauma is not its empirical validation but rather reflects a carrier group's ability to convince others of the suffering they have experienced, as I also argue in chapter 4. This is where understanding the manifestation of cultural trauma and the emergence of public tragedy overlaps with the cultural work pursued by movement entrepreneurs and victims' advocates. Those who seek to cultivate support must do so by promoting a view of those events and conditions that stimulate emotion, concern, and commitment. They exploit rhetorical tools that moralize harm, using examples of trauma, victimhood, and persecution. To do so, they must also gain the sympathy of some significant share of the public, a public that until the second half of the twentieth century neither were readily willing to give their sympathy nor had the means to express it if they had.

How then do cultural trauma and an ideology of victimhood align with and, in some measure reflect, the dynamics I have suggested are characteristic of risk societies? The incongruous beliefs and expectations that currently animate the public's understanding of risk and governance expose a contemporary mentalité that is no longer "modern." Instead, this new mentalité comports with the conditions and vulnerabilities associated with the risks of our day. The social, cultural, and political dynamics and transformations that take shape in and through public tragedies reflect unintended outcomes of modernity's successes: a desire to control, rationalize, and promote progress ushered in not only benefit but an increasingly precarious age of risk that has paradoxically undermined the very control it once promised. Notably, the transformations have not simply been technical, technological, and environmental, as is often stressed in risk society theory.[9] The changes have been broadly social and cultural, too. The pursuit of modernity and successive rounds of development have destabilized "progress" as a justification for support of the modern project (Giddens 1990). This is because modernity's promise has proven to be Janus-faced. The promises of rights expansion, equality, and a better life have frequently been used to justify modern social relations. Yet systemic injustice and repeated *real* and *rhetorical* exposure to claims of mistake, misconduct, and wrongdoing, perpetrated by the very same modern social, political, and economic institutions tasked with securing society and achieving progress, persist. This reality has undermined trust and faith in modernity and the progressive narrative that animates it (see, for example, Jones 2022).

Paradoxically, then, like technological control and risk, social and cultural change has produced commensurate risks that have provided the pretext for conflict and controversy and an increased sense of vulnerability among the general public. The "victim industry" is a case in point

9. For a thorough treatment of the "consequence of modernity" see Giddens (1990), who also writes on "risk society" (Beck, Giddens, and Lash 1994).

(Best 1997); it has emerged out of dissatisfaction with the pace of progress and has sought to expose modernity's failures and excesses. Carrier groups that have expressed a "culture of trauma" in the political domain have likewise effectively leveraged their complaints and concerns (Alexander 2004). The language and rhetoric they have deployed over the second half of the twentieth century has now become a conventionalized political language, whether reflective of actual trauma or deployed as strategic rhetoric (see chapter 4).

Dovetailing with the culture of trauma argument, an ideology of victimhood has emerged that has been expressed through waves of protests over normative assumptions and rules for conduct and claims regarding the mistreatment of women, persons of color, immigrants, LGBTQ+ persons, and disabled persons. These protests have transformed the contemporary social and political environment. They pivot on dissatisfaction with progress—that the modern project has not delivered or not delivered fast enough.

Right-of-center movements have also mobilized, often in response to left-of-center claims making. They speak to a sense that either the state has overreached in its attempts to manage risks or they themselves are the victims of state policies that they claim discriminate against them to advantage others (Hochschild 2018). While animated by different concerns, social and religious conservatives, nativists, nationalists, and the "illiberal" have likewise come to rely on a similar protest trope—the trauma script—founded on a sense of betrayal, persecution, and blameless victimization (Gorski and Perry 2022). They too have come to see themselves as the victims of a society that has forsaken them as they face social, cultural, and political trends that threaten to diminish their standing (Ehrenreich 2020; Gidron and Hall 2020; Hochschild 2018; Kurer 2020).

What has resulted is increasingly strident rhetoric amid zero-sum political competition for representation and resources. As such, the contemporary politics of risk represents a foundational shift away from modernist politics, in which the prior focus was consensus building, integration, and a "melting pot" analogy founded on the promise of prosperity and the distribution of benefit. Politics has moved toward identity, justice, liberty, and a zero-sum competition over allocating societal risks and benefits. In this new context, in which a politics of risk reigns, grievance and victimization have become shared experiences and the basis for movement, political contestation, and upheaval.

Reflecting this epochal social and political context, public tragedies have surged in the twenty-first century. They emerge from a currently ascendant "structure of feeling" (Williams 1961) that features a widespread sense of vulnerability and grievance and an understanding of many traumatic events involving blameless victims who have suffered unnecessarily at the hands of societal factors and social forces. This, of course, is the trauma script: a cultural explanation of harm that centers on a sense of victimization and the assignment of social blame. Again, it contrasts with explanations that predominated in the past, where fate, chance, or individual responsibility were commonly used to explain individual and collective suffering. It suggests that those harmed have been wronged in avoidable ways and that fault and recompense are at issue. Indeed, when guilt and blame are the charges, the harm is moral (Oorschot and Halman 2000). When an event is moralized, anger, outrage, and politicization are sure to follow, and public tragedy is more likely.

CONCLUSION: RISK, VULNERABILITY, AND PUBLIC TRAGEDY

Social and historical transformations in the United States have cultivated a pervasive sense of precarity and vulnerability to risks of a range and type among the public. Risk society reflects paradoxical public expectations of trustee action on a range of social and material risks and growing apprehension about trustee authority and its intentions. These dueling impressions often lead to the widespread blame of trustees (such as elected officials, administrators, and nongovernmental organizations) for actions taken or omitted, fueling public distrust and grievance, resulting in quasi-sectarian claims and movements (Finkel et al. 2020). These fears and expectations help explain *why* the trauma script has come to resonate so profoundly with the American public, regardless of political persuasion. In the preceding, I have analyzed *what* this tells us about public tragedies as a reflection of the structure of feeling of our time (Williams 1961).

In this chapter I argued that the rise of the modern welfare state unintentionally created the conditions for modernity's risk paradox. I focused on the U.S. federalization of risk and, therefore, the U.S. federal government's role in responding to national crises, such as natural disasters and economic depressions. I outlined the institutional agendas that resulted and provided the president, the Congress, and newly created administrative units with the power to intervene to rectify local and regional trauma and loss in previously unknown ways. This contrasts with the first 160 years of U.S. history in which responding to crises was in most cases left to individuals, familial networks, communities, local governments, and occasionally, states. As the federal government increasingly intervened in the lives of Americans to manage crises in the name of national interest, the unintended effect was the cultivation of expectations among those same Americans regarding the role of the state in responding to and preventing trauma and loss of all kinds. And when the government acts, fails to act, or appears ineffectual (or halfhearted), it is likely to be blamed for the harms that befall victims regardless of their cause.

Following my discussion of risk society and the federalization of risk, I suggested that the emergence of a discourse of trauma, victims' movements, and a pervasive sense of grievance and victimization also reflect a darkening mood in the United States and growing cynicism—a lack of faith in progress from which has emerged greater sympathy for those who experience trauma and loss. We see this in the penchant to socially blame harm on social and political forces and therefore society. Indeed, by the 1990s, a "victims' ideology" and "victim industry"—constituted in the work of journalists, therapeutic professionals, counselors, and academic researchers committed to supporting, exposing, and politically leveraging claims of victimization—had emerged, fueling efforts to pursue grievances socially and politically. Collectives and emergent movements expressing "cultural trauma" have likewise been politically influential, leveraging their complaints and concerns in the political domain.

Yet the specification of cultures of trauma and how they socially construct traumatic experiences and identity and seek to right the wrongs done against them reflects more than the cultural manifestation of trauma. Rather, a discourse of trauma has become a conventionalized political language used by both those who have been traumatized and those who have not to make claims and leverage public sympathy and support. As such, the language of trauma and grievance—the trauma script—has gained speed and legitimacy, becoming the preeminent political language of the twenty-first century. This is reflected in now common claims to victimhood, which emerged in the twenty-first century with these developments, and reflects a set of beliefs and expectations regarding personal and institutional responsibility that tracks closely with the rise of the risk-management state and risk society. They are all key to the social and material vulnerabilities now associated with postmodern, risk-based societies like ours. In the following chapters I turn to other domains, including that of political elites, the media, and the victim industry, to understand and explain the culmination of contemporary beliefs and conditions in what have become the preeminent political events of our time, *public tragedies*.

2 The Political Construction of Public Tragedy

CRISIS AND POLITICAL COMMUNICATIONS
IN AN AGE OF BLAME

Responses to crises can involve any number of actions: from little or no assistance to forced evacuation; emergency assistance; urgent triage; search and rescue; deployment of security forces; legal restrictions and curfews; postcrisis support, treatment, and counseling; and even damage assessment and postcrisis restoration. In principle, through one or all of these interventions, the response seeks to ameliorate injury and provide those harmed—the victims of crisis—with assistance to save lives, reassure the afflicted, and moderate their trauma and loss. In truth, the state, as represented by the government—in conjunction with surrogates such as political and commercial elites and nonprofit crisis-relief organizations—also responds for less principled reasons. For instance, as suggested in the prior chapter, governments often try to limit the damage a crisis can have on "broader concerns," such as the national economy and local, regional, and national well-being. Yet they may also be motivated by less honorable calculations, such as political expediency, financial advantage, or favor, or to avoid blame for actions or omissions. Blame avoidance reflects a contemporary political reality in the United States that elected officials and government representatives know all too well. When the public widely views a government's actions or omissions as causing harm to an innocent victim (or victims), we see public tragedy unfold.

This political reality has not been lost on the contemporary political class. Blame avoidance has become a conspicuous feature of governance in general and crisis management specifically (Bovens, 't Hart, and Peters 2002; Kuipers and 't Hart 2014; Weaver 1986). Unlike in the past, when bad luck and "fate" were common explanations for trauma, disaster, and loss of all kinds, today political elites, public officials, and their surrogates actively seek to avoid being blamed for the suffering they are now expected to alleviate. Indeed, in line with the risk paradox introduced in the prior chapter, many Americans believe that the government should be able to prevent most risks or, at the very least, significantly diminish the harms associated with adverse events (Platt 1999; Rubin 2012). And for their part, public officials curry this conception, making promises they often cannot keep; that no one could keep. The public therefore presumes trustee institutions will effectively respond to all actual and potential crises to limit harm and will be held to account—blamed—when they fail to do so.

Clearly this is a very unrestricted set of expectations. One might even say that a deep sense of entitlement anchors twenty-first century attitudes and beliefs about the role and responsibility of the state and governance institutions. Given this social and cultural backdrop of governing, it is little wonder that in the aftermath of many crises, the public blames officials and their administrative actions (and omissions) for causing or worsening the trauma and loss associated with them. Disputes of this kind, in turn, typically reflect competing assessments of what has happened, who (or what) was responsible, who (or what) should receive moral judgment and blame, and what should be done (Beamish 2002, 2015).

In the previous chapter I outlined the expansion of the interventionist state and the rise of risk society. In this chapter I examine the state's role through "government"—by which I mean political elites, public officials and administrators, government agencies, and their surrogates—in shaping the occurrence of public tragedy. I argue that governments respond to and politically manage crisis contexts as they seek to claim success and avoid blame for trauma and loss. I primarily use the term *government* to refer to that multifaceted system through which both "public" and "private" entities provide services. I also use the terms *trustee* and *trustee institution* to capture the responsibilities of both public and private entities to manage risks to the public at large. Specifically, they have been entrusted with some aspect of the general public's safety and security and therefore fulfill a "trustee function" when carrying out this role.

I focus on the rhetoric that government administrators, policy makers and experts, and political elites deploy in times of crisis: the language and discourse they use to claim success or defend their administrative efforts from blame. Revelations that mistakes have been made or of negligence or wrongdoing can, and frequently do, inspire moral outrage among the general public that can quickly escalate, turning into social blame. This outpouring can translate what might have been a "fateful disaster" into a human-made "public tragedy" and can occur even when the initial cause of a crisis is not human (such as when a natural disaster strikes).

I begin by reviewing scholarship that addresses the political aspects of crisis response, including political communications and policy failures. Following this, I compare the political communications and blame-avoidance strategies used by political elites and public officials during and after two devastating hurricanes—Harvey and Maria—in 2017. I explore and contrast news coverage of each hurricane event, focusing on the political rhetoric public officials used to claim success and avoid blame. I also analyze government reports and recent scholarship on official responses to assess and compare the shape of government reaction(s) in each case. While they were objectively similar natural disasters, the political rhetoric used to describe each hurricane event and the government's operational response to them were distinctive. Judging by this rhetoric, one became a political success—Hurricane Harvey—and the other—Hurricane Maria—a public tragedy. The analysis and cases I present are illustrative; they exemplify how public tragedies are accomplished rather than "just happen."

Political communications, then, play an important role in shaping and reflecting public impressions and encouraging (or, by contrast, inhibiting) the emergence of a public tragedy. I conclude the chapter with some reflections on responding to crises in an age of blame, wherein the public presumes that government and its surrogates will provide the remedies to trauma and loss but just as often end up being seen as the cause.

THE SOCIAL CONSTRUCTION OF POLITICAL
SUCCESS AND FAILURE

As I have argued, crisis response historically was carried out by the directly afflicted and their immediate relations. If the scenario was dire enough, an entire community might mobilize with the help of local and regional volunteers. State governments were known to respond if the disaster was genuinely devastating or involved more than a single community. It wasn't until the late nineteenth and early twentieth centuries that humanitarian organizations, such as the Red Cross, began providing crisis relief (circa the 1890s). And it was only after massive floods and environmental catastrophes in the first quarter of the twentieth century threatened the "national well-being" that the U.S. federal government began to respond to crises and proactively plan against future potential crises, thus federalizing the management of risk.

Catastrophic events such as floods, droughts, and the Great Depression, in conjunction with the rise of the modern welfare state, led to the emergence of numerous federal trustee institutions tasked with responding to crises and affording relief in their aftermath. Over time these trustee institutions were progressively entrusted with the public's safety and security. In turn, the public came to both depend on them and hold strong normative expectations regarding their performance. Trustee responses to crises are frequently viewed as either having "succeeded" or "failed." Yet Bovens and 't Hart (2016, 1996) persuasively argue that interpretations of both successful and failed policy outcomes do not typically pivot exclusively on technical accomplishments but often reflect a framing contest among political stakeholders. Paralleling Bovens and 't Hart's studies of "policy fiascos," trauma, loss, and victimization that are explained as a function of trustee actions (or omissions) are more likely to become publicly tragic. They represent "failures" by the government and its surrogates (i.e., trustees) to fulfill their public trust obligations.[10] Damning judgments of trustee actions and omissions can elevate a

___

10. The notion of the *public trust* entails the expectation that in societies with representative government (i.e., democracy), the government manages aspects of society for the well-being of its members. When government fails in this mission, public trust erodes.

Table 1   Interpreting Crisis Response: Success or Failure

Technical dimension	Political dimension	
	Political success	*Political failure*
Technical success	Success, public tragedy unlikely	Discounted success, public tragedy possible
Technical failure	Fictitious success, public tragedy unlikely	Failure, public tragedy likely

Source: See Bovens and 't Hart (2016:654) for a facsimile of table 1.

victim's formerly unfortunate but largely private trauma into a notorious public tragedy.

What does a "successful" versus a "failed" response to crisis look like? First, such judgments can reflect either (or both) *technical merit* or *political accomplishment*. Success based on technical merit hinges on factors that prevent or minimize harm: extant law and policy; rapid response; successful personnel and resource deployment; search, rescue, and property protection; or the passage of new laws and policies to protect against future crises (see "Technical success" in table 1).

By contrast, successful resolution of a crisis can be viewed as a political accomplishment. This depends on how political rivals perceive trustee actions, how the mass media frames the event, and ultimately, how the public understands and remembers the event. Political accomplishment need not be tightly coupled to trustee performance and its technical merits (such as actual social and material outcomes, like saved lives and property). Indeed, an official response to a given crisis might be reasonably effective—technically speaking—but be subjected to damning accusations by journalists, pundits, victims, watchdog groups, policy makers, legislators, and political rivals who influence public opinion and collective memory. (This is referred to as a "discounted success": the resolution of the crisis was technically successful but politically unsuccessful; see Bovens and 't Hart 2016. See "Discounted success" in table 1.)

Likewise, the official response may technically fail due to mistakes or misconduct of public officials and their surrogates and yet may not be labeled as such in the news media because of the promotional efforts of political operatives and sympathetic pundits. Indeed, the presentation of a crisis in the media typically reflects a public framing contest among engaged stakeholders, where the "winning" presentation is the frame conveyed by media that succeeds in delivering a definitive assessment of the event in question (Beamish, Molotch, and Flacks 1995; Boin, 't Hart, and McConnell 2009; Entman 2010; Meyer 1995). As such, when an event is framed as a success, irrespective of technical performance, the public may believe that government has fulfilled their expectations (i.e., a "Fictitious success" in table 1). The political accomplishment of success and failure therefore reflects the way trustee actions and omissions are presented to the public by diverse actors and how these events are then perceived and remembered.

Crisis Response: The Katrina Exemplar

Hurricane Katrina (2005) exemplifies a case of failed crisis response and social blame. Much of the public and many government representatives acknowledge that Katrina was both a political failure and a horrific technical failure that involved a lack of federal hazard preparedness and what appeared to be a racially biased approach to crisis response (Birkland and Waterman 2008; Bolin 2007; Bullard and Wright 2009; Dreier 2006; Gotham 2007; Johnson 2011; Kellner 2007; Pastor et al. 2006; Sze 2006; U.S. House of Representatives 2006). Yet the prevailing lesson learned by subsequent administrators and administrations was not technical or intrinsically "racial" in nature but imminently political and strategic. The Bush administration was lambasted for their technical failures and their racial implications. They also became notorious for their failure to control the political framing of that disaster, especially in its aftermath (Kellner 2007). The specter of Hurricane Katrina has haunted successive U.S. administrations—on the political right and left—when crises occur. Memories and lessons taken from Katrina have also influenced how state and local trustees conduct themselves and have even impacted the field of humanitarian relief generally, such as in contemporary attention to issues of social justice in planning for and responding to disasters (Eikenberry, Arroyave, and Cooper 2007).

Why has the specter of a natural disaster like Hurricane Katrina had such a profound impact on crisis response? When the official response was framed as a failure, people transferred social blame from a fateful cause—nature, God, randomness—to those trustees responsible for the botched response. They were now to blame for profound death and destruction. Failure of this kind can and often does arouse public outrage, inspiring a social crisis: the failure suggests a violation of the public trust. Those in positions of authority failed to follow through on their responsibilities to the public (i.e., they were recreant) (Beamish 2002; Freudenburg 2000; Mitchell 1999). And once lost, trust can be very hard, if impossible, to regain (Beamish 2001; Beamish, Grattet, and Niemeier 2017; Freudenburg 2001; Slovic 1993).

Hurricane Katrina also became an exemplar because of the accompanying media coverage. It was the first such disaster to receive round-the-clock coverage across cable and network news services. Americans watched firsthand as social inequality and social structures like racism and poverty played a role in decisions about who was and was not "worthy" of being saved (Johnson 2011; Molotch 2006). Based on this coverage and the public outrage it provoked, local victims and victims' advocates gained widespread recognition for the trauma and loss they experienced because of neglect, mistreatment, and racial disenfranchisement (Voigt and Thornton 2015). Official disregard and victims' accusations of this kind muddied the distinction between the harms caused by a natural and therefore fateful disaster and those caused by trustee action, omission, and misconduct. Indeed, according to hazards researcher Enrico Quarantelli (2006), Katrina was not just a disaster. Because of its natural attributes in conjunction with official federal, state, and local failures, it was a *catastrophe* (Quarantelli 2006). I would suggest, given how it was understood and responded to, that Katrina was also a significant public tragedy.

In the shadow of both technical and political failures like Katrina, claims of trustee mistake, misconduct, and political disregard have become increasingly commonplace (Littlefield and Quenette 2007). Indeed, blaming the government and its surrogates for failing the public has become a routine aspect of crisis management and response (Platt 1999). Government or governance blame is also an aspect of virtually all public tragedies. In the analysis that follows, I focus on how the government and specific trustee institutions responsible for public safety and security strive to control the framing of their crisis response efforts. Through this framing process they endeavor to avoid blame and appear successful—or at the very least blameless. Yet they do not do so in a vacuum. Journalists, pundits, political rivals, victims, victims' advocates, and watchdog groups, among other stakeholders, also strive to frame and interpret crises and the institutional actors who respond to them. The trustees managing a given crisis must therefore react to both the event at hand and the competing claims made by stakeholders regarding their actions and omissions, all the while pursuing their political survival. The key to political survival and success is avoiding blame, and in avoiding blame becoming embroiled in a public tragedy.

FIASCOS, CREDIT CLAIMING, AND BLAME AVOIDANCE

A characteristic feature of public tragedy is the political controversy that swirls around and comes to define it. Considering the horrific harms and public expressions of sympathy often associated with victims, why do public tragedies predictably involve controversy and political conflict? The short answer is blame. The longer answer is that because blame and accountability are involved, there is almost always a struggle to control how crisis events are framed and which "official memories" prevail. These struggles reflect political attempts to manage an event and its defining narratives. Was the official response a success? If not, who (or what) is to blame? Given the stakes and costs associated with being blamed for harms, whose definition of the crisis ultimately prevails? As case studies of crisis events have found, political narratives are created and contested in their aftermath through rhetoric and dramatic imagery (Anker 2015; Button 2016; Littlefield and Quenette 2007; Simons 2007; Young 2007). I argue that when the conventionalized political narrative I refer to as the trauma script prevails, a public tragedy is much more likely to result.

Like other social and political phenomena, crises also involve active social and political construction (Tierney 2012). That they are "real" and horrifically traumatic events does not diminish the competition that can take place over their symbolic construction. The competition can involve an assortment of stakeholders—victims, advocates, watchdogs, pundits, journalists, experts, political elites, administrators, spokespersons, and political rivals—who strive to achieve their desired social and political ends by controlling representations and interpretations of the event ('t Hart 1993). Literature on the politics of blame and political accountability primarily focuses on policy failures and only nominally on crisis management and crisis-induced accountability rather than on public tragedies sui generis (see Boin and Kuipers 2018 and Kuipers and 't Hart 2014 for exceptions). These scholars have highlighted how framing policy fiascos and avoiding blame are essential to political survival in contemporary representative government. For instance, in studying policy failures, Bovens et al. (2002) showed that when events become notorious "policy fiascos," they typically generate several consistent discursive elements: the public assesses them to be harmful to the public interest, to be the result of official actions or omissions, and to be unnecessary and avoidable.

As such, Bovens et al. (2002) identify elements of policy fiascos that parallel those that are characteristic of public tragedies. Like policy fiascos, discursive claims highlighting preventable harms (had authorities fulfilled their official responsibilities) or that officials played some role in causing the harms at issue typify public tragedies too. Once trustee actions and omissions become a cause, claims of victimization can quickly gain momentum, and the crisis can develop into a moral violation. In this way, claims of not following through on their obligation to serve from this a sense of betrayal can supersede whatever may have initially precipitated the crisis, leaving authorities being blamed for victimizing those harmed. Targeted by the trauma script, authorities can very quickly become the perpetrators. Social blame drives this process, where the actions or omissions of trustees are faulted and violated expectations spur public outrage. The makings of a public tragedy emerge. Accusations of this kind have become so potent and common that blame avoidance preoccupies virtually all political elites, public officials, and industry executives (Roulet and Pichler 2020).

Indeed, the literature on political scandals and policy fiascos enumerates many tactics deployed by political elites to avoid blame for failure(s). As outlined earlier, governmental success or failure can be seen as political or as technical accomplishments. According to the blame-avoidance literature, whether a given interpretation of a policy's success or failure prevails depends on the way the court of public opinion frames, decodes, and judges it (Bovens et al. 1999). However, important questions about how political rhetoric and tactics make (or avoid) public tragedy remain unanswered. Does the use of blame-avoidance tactics by political elites and government administrators make political controversy and public tragedy more or less likely? Do strong claims of success, in the face of blunder and victim suffering, moderate political controversy or exacerbate tensions and further inflame public outrage? And ultimately, does it matter what public officials say or do if victims, watchdog groups, and political rivals label their operational response(s) as a failure (or, by contrast, as a success)? These political questions and their answers are more nuanced and contextual than straightforward and causally predictive. However, the literature on policy fiascos discusses the many ways political elites, public officials, and policy makers seek to avoid blame and gain credit for their actions and omissions. To better understand how crisis response and crisis management can be politicized, I turn to the political and policy accountability literature for clues before comparing two cases of crisis for what they expose about the making of public tragedy.

Credit Claiming

Surprisingly, only a handful of works explicitly deal with political elites and their "credit-claiming tactics." One early example is the work of political scientist David Mayhew (1974), who noted that, along with advertising and staking out policy positions, members of Congress frequently engage in credit claiming while campaigning. When someone engages in credit claiming, according to Mayhew (1974:52–53), they act "so as to generate a belief in a relevant political actor (or actors) that one is personally responsible for causing the government, or some unit thereof, to do something that the actor (or actors) considers desirable." In other work focused on the politics of credit claiming, Schram and Soss (2001) analyzed the political success attributed to U.S. welfare reform in the 1980s and 1990s. They suggested that there was little hard evidence that welfare reform succeeded. Instead, they claim that the contrived political climate of the time privileged some kinds of facts over others, leading to a subsequent label of success (Schram and Soss 2001:50). Building on Gusfield's (1984:37) work on the social construction of problems and "public facts," Schram and Soss suggested that the interpretation of welfare reform as successful was a political accomplishment. This understanding reflected decontextualized truth statements taken from aggregated and reductionist statistical accounts that ignored the hardships experienced by welfare recipients themselves. Political elites and government officials used these socially constructed "truths" to shape public perceptions of welfare, framing welfare cuts as a story of success. This allowed them to further slash programs and benefits without public resistance.

The political success (or failure) of policies and programs, such as claims of successful welfare reform, can also entail the strategic and selective use of evidence. This involves editing out a substantial portion of evidence that contradicts the success narrative (McGraw 1991). Knowing this, when will any given "preferred understanding" of success or failure prevail? What explains the success of one storyline and the failure of another? I argue that a storyline captures the public—becomes hegemonic—when it socially and culturally resonates with the public, or at least with a significant subset of it. The more a story resonates with the extant cultural milieu or zeitgeist of the day (Williams 1961), the more likely it will be broadly accepted as "true" (Gamson 1992). The trauma script and public tragedy are a case in point.

Yet establishing a success story is just one side of a two-sided coin. On the other side we find *failure stories and blame for them*. As Deborah Stone (1997:189) suggested in her groundbreaking book on political decision-making, political conflicts over an issue or event's "causal story" are ultimately fights over who or what controls the assignment of both credit and blame—who (or what) gets credit for success and who (or what) is blamed for a failure. Political actors therefore compete to establish stories that reflect positively on their efforts, stories that if necessary blame their rivals for failure (Mayhew 1974).

Blame Avoidance

While credit claiming might seem the most advantageous means of acquiring and maintaining a political reputation, the evidence suggests otherwise. According to Weaver (1986), in a landmark article on what has come to be called "the blame-avoidance perspective," elected officials prefer blame avoidance over credit claiming. That is, politicians "are not credit maximizers but blame minimizers and credit claiming and 'good policy' satisficers" (Weaver 1986:372).

Why would this be? Weaver and other like-minded policy scholars suggest this reflects both the nature of satisfying constituencies in a representative democracy and voter psychology (Weaver 1986). Any given policy or program cannot satisfy all of one's constituents. Any political action is sure to make some constituents happier than others. Therefore, elected officials will succeed with one group but fail with another. This win-lose scenario is structural and undermines some of the attractiveness of sponsoring ambitious policies and programs and of claiming credit for them. While they are likely to gain political credit from some constituents, they are just as likely to be criticized by others who do not benefit from the policy. I would suggest this dynamic is amplified in a time like the present, when identity politics reigns even within constituent groups and parties, which are also riven by identities that operate according to a zero-sum logic: if "they" get some, "we" do not.

The second issue with credit claiming and constituents involves what cognitive psychologists call "negativity bias," as voters—indeed all humans—are more sensitive to actual or potential losses than real or promised gains (Kahneman, Slovic, and Tversky 1982; Kahneman and Tversky 2000). These structural dynamics encourage limited policy agendas and blame-avoidance tactics like denial, scapegoating, and "passing the buck" over policy and program cultivation and credit-claiming strategies.

Since blame avoidance is the prevailing political concern of officeholders, policy makers, and regulators can be expected to adopt defensive strategies to maintain their reputations. When public officials confront criticism and accusations of mistake and misconduct, what forms do such defensive strategies typically take? Edelman's (1988) classic treatment of political spectacle describes several blame-avoidance tactics that political elites deploy to defend themselves and their activities against outside criticism and to deflect blame. These include suggesting that the failure was not a failure at all but a routine occurrence, or that the failure in fact created a benefit or advantage. Negative outcomes related to the event outweighed the harm done: everyone is better off for it. Bovens et al. (1999), in studying policy fiascos, also identified typical avoidance strategies and forms of rhetoric frequently used by public officials when defending themselves or their programs. They suggest that officials may deny responsibility for an outcome. They may remain silent. They may reinterpret criticism and suggest that the wrong was not wrong at all—or at least not the kind of mistake or misdeed one might think.

Political elites may claim that the failure was not theirs—they acted appropriately even if something went wrong. They can also claim they had no control over whatever occurred or can engage in the "blame game," accusing their accusers, shifting blame to critics, and scapegoating political rivals. Officials charged with wrongdoing often initiate investigations to appear to seek exoneration, all the while actively stalling criticism and accusation. Finally, public officials and political elites accused of misconduct or failure can, if necessary, opt for forgiveness by admitting partial responsibility, apologizing for any harms of which they stand accused, and if need be, simply asking for forgiveness.

THE POLITICAL CONSTRUCTION OF PUBLIC TRAGEDY

Clearly, credit-claiming and blame-avoidance strategies are at the core of the "political game." As a political tactic, blame avoidance also sows political controversy and conflict (Bovens, 't Hart, and Kuipers 2006; Edelman 1988; Stone 1997). Grandiose claims of success can amplify the political stakes and therefore the conflict and controversy associated with an issue or event. Given the evident overlap with policy fiascos, clearly blame-avoidance and credit-claiming tactics also influence the emergence of public tragedy. For instance, the social blame associated with events like Hurricane Katrina and the resulting political fallout for the Bush administration taught political elites that being blamed can be devastating to both an administration and one's career, but also to the policies and programs with which one or both are associated. And since accusations of trustee mistake and misconduct have become commonplace in the aftermath of crises, political elites, public administrators, and industry officials routinely and proactively engage in the same blame-avoidance and credit-claiming behaviors that they rely on when confronted with policy failures. All this would lead us to predict that political communications and therefore the political construction of crisis and governmental response to it likely play a pivotal role in generating public tragedies. Indeed, as illustrated in what follows, this is the case.

To show how political communications work in the political construction of public tragedy, I compared the rhetoric that public officials (and their surrogates) used to operationally respond to crises and to claims levied at them by rival public officials, pundits, victims, and watchdog groups. To do this, I collected trade publications, academic accounts, government reports, and news media coverage of two natural disasters: Hurricane Harvey, which was heralded as a disaster response success, and Hurricane Maria, which became a public tragedy. I then systematically compared news media coverage to explore in further depth how political rhetoric diminished or aggravated, even ignited, criticism and public outrage in the aftermath of each event. In 2017, Harvey and Maria both struck the United States, within a month of one another. And while no two disasters are the same, these two storms had much in common. I also use Hurricanes Harvey and Maria and two other paired cases of crises in chapter 3, where I explore the role of mass media in public tragedy.

First, both storms hit U.S. territory—Harvey hit the southeastern Gulf Coast near Houston, Texas, and Maria hit the island of Puerto Rico. What is more, both were category 4 storms with winds over 130 miles per hour, both involved record-breaking rainfall, both devastated the communities they struck, and both put tremendous strain on the federal government's capacity to respond. And yet each storm gave rise to remarkably different federal relief efforts and political and civic responses to them. The differences are not easily dismissed (or excused), as then president Trump suggested, as the result of Puerto Rico being "an island surrounded by water—big water, ocean water," or because government resources were stretched thin by prior storms (i.e., Hurricanes Harvey and Irma preceded the landfall of Maria; aKarni and Mazzei 2019; Robles 2018a).

Judged by objective indicators like technical merit, FEMA's crisis-management efforts were factually different for each hurricane event (Willison et al. 2019). However, as suggested previously, public tragedies do not simply result from objective conditions rendered by an event. Nor do they purely reflect operational responses and, therefore, the technical successes or failures of the authorities. Rather, they are also social and political accomplishments (Bovens and 't Hart 2016). In this regard, the political rhetoric the president and his surrogates relied on—their effort to politically construct each crisis event—was markedly different too (e.g., Duhart 2019; Einbinder 2018; Vinik 2018). Taking the political construction of crisis and crisis response as my focal point, the remainder of this chapter examines and explores the rhetorical contests that ensued in the aftermath of each hurricane event. The analysis illustrates how two very similar crises were communicated differently to the public and how distinctive communications likely played a significant role in generating praise and political credit in one crisis and a public tragedy in the other.

Managing Crises, Technically and Politically

To compare the event frames and political rhetoric associated with each hurricane, I analyzed national news stories that involved political communications in which political elites, officeholders, and other public officials addressed the general public and one another in the public domain. They sought to describe, defend, claim credit for, and avoid blame for the devastation wrought by each hurricane event. I also coded news stories as examples of political communications if they featured the comments of local victims, victims' advocates, and the judgments of journalists, whether those were expressed overtly as opinions or via journalistic "slant." (By slant, I meant to capture when news stories included directional statements attributed to no one but that conveyed a distinct attitude about the hurricane and responses to it. For example, a story that opened with or repeated the sentiment that the "hurricane response has been heavily criticized" but did not quote or suggest a source of criticism was coded as representing journalistic slant.)

Political communication stories featured claims making by these diverse stakeholders either extolling or criticizing the actions or omissions of political elites, government relief efforts, and those affected by the storms (i.e., the victims). Claims making of this kind often involved references to the timeliness (or tardiness) of humanitarian response; resource allocation and budgeting; praise of operational response (i.e., credit claiming); or accusations and social blame for mistake, misconduct, or mismanagement. In short, my focus was on political claims making, criticism, and rebuttal across a range of actors.

To understand the public political communications regarding the two hurricane events, I immersed myself in news stories, trade publications, academic articles, and government white papers. I then systematically collected and compared news stories of the two hurricanes to better detect and verify patterns I had gained through immersion. To collect a sample of news stories, I searched ProQuest news database using keywords. I collected all the stories available in the year following each hurricane event, which resulted in 245 Harvey stories and 192 Maria stories. Additionally, I collected feature stories from national news magazines and reports (*Newsweek, Politico, Salon, Frontline*), official reports regarding FEMA's humanitarian relief efforts after each storm (Amadeo 2018; FEMA 2017, 2018; Insurance Information Institute 2018; National Hurricane Center 2018; NCEI 2019), and academic studies of each storm (Brown et al. 2018; Duhart 2019; Einbinder 2018; Garcia-Lopez 2018; Kishore et al. 2018; Santos-Burgoa et al. 2018; Santos-Lozada and Howard 2018; Shultz and Galea 2017). Having examined these and other sources as each hurricane event unfolded, I then zoomed in on and sorted the news stories from three major daily news sources: the *New York Times* (*NYT*), the *Wall Street Journal* (*WSJ*), and the *Los Angeles Times* (*LAT*). This allowed me to access the "public domain" and national "discourse" relating to each hurricane event (Calhoun 1998; Fraser 1990; Habermas 1979, 1991; Lichterman 1996).[11] Having read all the collected news stories, I further sorted within the set of hurricane-specific news stories for those that featured political communications among important stakeholders. I distinguished "political communication" stories from other hurricane-related stories to isolate and compare those that explicitly featured political content, including rival claims, political conflict, and controversy, taking form in credit claims, blame, and rebuttal among stakeholders regarding hurricane response.

In Maria's case, 20% of the 192 stories (38 stories) featured such political communications, which parallel the furor that erupted about Maria and the federal response to it across many other news, social media, and

---

11. I explain my justification for using the *New York Times*, *Wall Street Journal*, and *Los Angeles Times* in the Appendix.

academic sources. By contrast, political communications in Hurricane Harvey's 245 stories were comparatively infrequent. I identified political conflict and controversy over hurricane response in only 13 Harvey stories (5%), as indicated by accusations levied against federal, state, or local governments. What is more, of the 13 political communication stories, 6 were not criticisms of the official response to Harvey at all but rather communicated other sorts of political disagreements (see tables A.1 and A.2).

Why did I narrow my search to news stories featuring political communications? My strategy was to explore and analyze the rhetoric relevant actors used during crises to exemplify the process by which crises are politically constructed. I wished to explain whether and how such rhetoric encouraged or inhibited the widespread perspective that an event was a public tragedy. As stakeholders responded to each hurricane crisis and to one another, they sought to control the narrative as they perceived, understood, and tactically approached what had transpired during and after the storms. Was government action depicted as adequate or exemplary? Were the trauma and loss simply chalked up to fate or individual responsibility? Were the injuries sustained in the hurricanes and their aftermath blamed on the government? A political controversy surrounding an event like Maria or Harvey can include social outrage and criticism, disagreement over cause(s), and contention over whether harm might have been ameliorated through the actions of the government (or its omissions). Struggle can also ensue over how an event will be remembered and, therefore, who (or what) might be held to account in the immediate aftermath or in the ensuing years. In figure 1 I show the distribution of political communication stories in the *NYT*, the *WSJ*, and the *LAT* over the year following each storm's landfall. (See tables A.1 and A.2.)

Having pooled the political stories, I then analyzed and coded them along two further dimensions to capture the shape of political messaging and therefore the framing strategies that political elites and public officials used to claim credit and avoid blame. These included statements regarding the *severity and manageability* of each hurricane event and the *rhetorical tactics* deployed by political elites and public officials and their rivals to avoid blame and claim credit. The first code—statements about the severity of each hurricane event by public officials—typically took shape as references to their manageability (or unmanageability) such

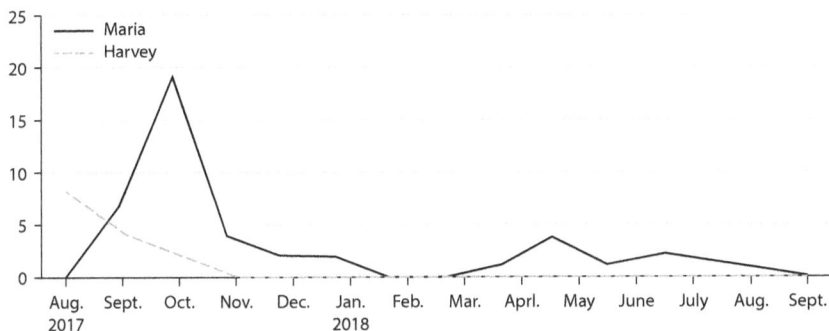

Figure 1. Hurricanes Harvey and Maria: Distribution of political communication stories. SOURCE: See tables A.1 and A.2; data compiled by author.

as in affirming, maximizing, or denying the severity of each storm. Public officials can deny, affirm, or maximize a crisis event based on their political interests and relationships to it (Boin et al. 2009). Generally, affirmation tends to signal support for the victim's experiences, whereas denial suggests that the harm the event caused is at least partly the victim's fault. When public officials engage in hyperbole to maximize the significance of a crisis, they can also be suggesting nothing could have prevented it and therefore that they should not be held accountable for the subsequent trauma and loss. By contrast, when rival stakeholders maximize the significance of a crisis, they are likely suggesting that more help is needed and that political support has been inadequate. The suggestion that public officials, laws, and regulations are flawed also carries at least a hint of social blame for the trauma and loss sustained by victims of the crisis in question.

My second set of codes aimed to track and compare political use of "blame-avoidance" and "credit-claiming" rhetoric in the context of news about each hurricane event. Therefore, I also coded stories for the rhetorical tactics public officials used to address relief efforts and operational responses in each case. These included cases in which political elites tried to claim credit, attempting to paint their efforts as exemplary and lifesaving, or to avoid blame for the trauma and loss experienced by victims of each storm. Blame avoidance often takes shape in statements of denial and evasion, disqualification of critics, disassociation, reinterpretation, and scapegoating (Bovens and 't Hart 1996; Edelman 1988; Weaver 1986). Credit claiming was likewise a catchall category, reflecting the use of grandiose claims of success, downplaying the severity of the crisis, and reframing failure as success (Boin et al. 2009; Bovens, 't Hart, and Peters 2002). I also coded for political messaging represented in "rival framings" of credit and blame, such as those that blamed political elites, public officials, and agencies for trauma and loss stemming from poor planning and a failed operational response to the hurricane. These typically took shape in accusations of mistake, misconduct, and/or mismanagement on the part of the government and its surrogates.

In sum, I wanted to explore the national political construction of each hurricane event and the role this may have played in creating the conditions for political controversy, political conflict, and with that, public tragedy. I specifically wanted to explore how communications regarding Hurricane Maria, a de facto tragedy (Brown et al. 2018; Garcia-Lopez 2018; Joseph et al. 2020; Straub 2021), differed from those related to Hurricane Harvey, a hurricane response that would become an exemplar for successful federal and state relief efforts (Einbinder 2018). Was it simply a matter of "real" technical deficiencies in the official response to Maria and, therefore, a surfeit of suffering that explains the different public and political reactions to each storm? Or might the political rhetoric deployed by political elites and public officials and their rivals also have played a vital role as political interests battled for control of each storm's causal narrative?

The blame-avoidance literature suggests that while real suffering and a deficient relief effort can be the basis for public outrage, it is just as likely that public outrage requires both actual material conditions and the active political construction of a crisis event for the general public to understand and remember it this way (Bovens et al. 1999). In the case of Hurricane Maria, there were plenty of both; there were failures in federal and state operational responses and alarming political rhetoric used by political elites and public officials to defend themselves as their efforts lagged and the island's inhabitants suffered in the aftermath of the hurricane.

By "official" (as in "official response") I mean federal and state actors as well as their surrogates (i.e., nonprofit relief and subcontractors, among others) and their efforts at hurricane relief. The official response involves both political communications and technical-operational actions, such as search and rescue efforts and humanitarian relief. Through political communications, public officials frame their technical operations as successful while defending themselves against accusations of poor performance. In this context, the technical-operational response took shape through the efforts of FEMA and its state counterparts and can be materially compared using established disaster response metrics such as response timeframes, deployed personnel, and dedicated resources, which I take up below.

As for the rhetorical tactics used by political elites during and after hurricane events, public officials responsible for operational responses to each crisis sought to control the disaster narrative and did so in competition with others, including political rivals, victims and victims' advocates, and other stakeholders. In the brief comparative analysis that follows, I illustrate how the political construction of Hurricane Harvey and Hurricane Maria differed in the national news and how this difference helped Maria become a public tragedy. I supplemented the news stories and analysis with analysis of trade publications, academic studies, and government white papers and reports, showing that the narratives expressed in the news cohered across these different media types.

THE STORMS

Hurricane Harvey made landfall as a category 4 storm on August 25, 2017, striking the southeast Texas coastline and, soon after that, Houston, Texas, the nation's fourth largest city (with a population of 2.4 million). Harvey clocked cyclonic winds over 132 miles per hour, which spawned tornadoes and a 10-foot-plus storm surge. Yet its landfall is most notorious for the rain event associated with it. Rather than moving further inland and away from Houston, Harvey stalled over southeast Texas for days, dumping 50-plus inches of rain and generating massive flooding that pushed 40,000 persons from their homes. In all, Harvey killed over 100 people and directly affected 13 million more across five states. It damaged more than 200,000 homes, ruined one million automobiles, reduced the nation's petroleum output and refining capacity by 5%, and ultimately caused $125 billion in damage—the second highest hurricane damage total in U.S. history after Hurricane Katrina (Amadeo 2018; National Hurricane Center 2018).

Nonetheless, while Harvey caused catastrophic damage that trauma-tized tens of thousands of residents (Shultz and Galea 2017), the official response was widely proclaimed to be an operational success, especially by U.S. federal and Texas state officials (FEMA 2017; TCEQ 2018). As the opening of the FEMA press release *Historic Disaster Response to Hurri-cane Harvey in Texas* proclaimed: "Neighbors, strangers, nonprofit or-ganizations, and governments at all levels joined together to mount an extraordinary effort to save lives and meet the needs of thousands of people who suffered from the storm and subsequent flooding. It was Tex-ans helping Texans, aided by people who came to Texas from all parts of the nation" (FEMA 2017).

Three weeks later, the federal response to Hurricane Maria in Puerto Rico received a much harsher verdict and was roundly criticized as an op-erational failure. Maria made landfall as a category 4 storm on Septem-ber 20, 2017, striking the southeast corner of the island of Puerto Rico (Robles 2018a).[12] Maria brought sustained winds as high as 155 miles per hour and involved massive rain and catastrophic flooding. These knocked out virtually all of the island's electric power and blew down most cell-phone towers, leaving Puerto Rico's 3.3 million U.S. citizens without elec-tricity or communication. According to Kishore et al. (2018), because of Maria, the average household on the island went roughly 41 days without cell-phone service, 68 days without municipal running water, and 84 days without electricity. Maria caused $90 billion in damage, making it the third most expensive hurricane in U.S. history after Harvey. The island's suffering did not last days or weeks but months, and for some, it contin-ued for years. Many of the island's elderly and infirm were forced to forgo medicine or health care for months, which resulted in many casualties.

Because U.S. federal response was slow and because President Trump's rhetoric was both bombastic and dismissive, island residents understand-ably questioned whether the neglect revealed an intentional disregard for them. This led stakeholders on the island to question official statements and official numbers. One number that stood out and began to generate controversy was the island's official mortality rate in the aftermath of the

---

12. Maria struck just two weeks after Hurricane Irma, which had skirted the island just to its north. Nonetheless, Irma caused extensive damage and also depleted many of the island's emergency relief stockpiles (Robles 2018a).

storm (Kishore et al. 2018; Santos-Burgoa et al. 2018; Santos-Lozada and Howard 2018; Willison et al. 2019). For nearly a year after the storm (up through fall 2018), Maria's official death toll of 64 continued to generate political controversy, both on and off the island. Indeed, then-president Trump used the low death total to claim credit, suggesting it showed how successful his administration's relief efforts were. Yet for many, the low mortality rate belied their experience; the undercount was perceived as another example of the federal government's disregard for the victimization of Puerto Ricans. Many thousands of Puerto Ricans suffered for months after the storm without necessities. At the same time, the president's political communications (and those of his surrogates) expressed not only a lack of concern but an active dislike, at times actively impugning Puerto Rico and Puerto Ricans while claiming that relief efforts were a success (Baker 2017; Baker and Dickerson 2017; Karni and Mazzei 2019; Robles 2018b; Vinik 2018).

In response to the controversy, several research groups set out to estimate the number of deaths caused by Hurricane Maria, to resolve the issue (Kishore et al. 2018; Santos-Lozada and Howard 2018).[13] One of the first to do so was a widely quoted Harvard study by Kishore et al. (2018) that put the number of "excess deaths" at 4,645, highlighting the problematic official count. Under pressure to produce an official and plausible number of casualties, the Puerto Rican government commissioned an independent study from the Milken Institute at George Washington University, which relied on official actuarial statistics, not estimates as used in the Harvard study (estimates were also used in another widely cited study; see Santos-Lozada and Howard 2018). The Milken Institute study suggested that the storm, and the humanitarian crisis that followed, accounted for 2,975 excess deaths (Santos-Burgoa et al. 2018). Nearly a year after the storm made landfall, Puerto Rican officials accepted this number as the storm's official count, cementing the storm and its aftermath as one of the worst human catastrophes in U.S. history. It also exposed the federal government's relief efforts to further scrutiny since the vast majority of deaths came from what many critics claimed was a prolonged

13. Estimates were generated by comparing mortality rates for the same months in non-hurricane years to those that occurred in the aftermath of Hurricane Maria. This allowed researchers to estimate "excess deaths" resulting from Maria's landfall and the dearth of available water, food, and medicine in its aftermath.

and underresourced relief effort and lack of access to medical care, clean water, and food.

Consequently, the federal government was heavily criticized for what appeared to be its official indifference (Einbinder 2018). Indeed, the confrontational public relations strategy of the president and his surrogates had never been observed in any other contemporary U.S. disaster response. Comparing official responses to Harvey and Maria, based on equivalent metrics—both operational responses and the forms of rhetoric deployed—provides a view of why the furor erupted in Maria's aftermath and why it became so much more than simply a "disaster." It would become a disaster framed by the trauma script and emerge, with that framing, as a public tragedy. My comparison begins with operational responses and the technical dimensions of disaster relief in each hurricane crisis.

COMPARING OPERATIONAL RESPONSES

Judging from salient disaster response metrics, federal efforts to operationally address Hurricane Harvey were rapid, extensive, and urgent (FEMA 2017; Willison et al. 2019). Within one week of the storm's landfall, FEMA had dedicated 73 helicopters to search and rescue and supply delivery (in the aftermath of disasters that destroy critical infrastructure, helicopters are essential technology). By day 9, the federal government had approved $141.8 million in individual assistance; deployed 30,000 federal personnel; and delivered 5.1 million meals, 4.5 million liters of water, and 20,000 tarps. It took FEMA just 10 days to approve permanent disaster infrastructural repair work for Texas and the southeast Gulf Coast.

Employing the same technical metrics to assess the official response to Hurricane Maria reveals that federal action was slower, involved fewer personnel, and was less well resourced. For example, FEMA took three weeks to supply a number of rescue helicopters (70) comparable to the number deployed in Houston in the first week (73). Using the same 9-day metric for comparison, FEMA distributed just one-quarter ($6.2 million) of the individual assistance, a third of the deployed federal personnel (10,000), a third of the meals (1.6 million), half the water (4.5 million liters), and half the tarps (10,000) to the victims of Maria as were deployed in Houston and the Gulf Coast. This was the case even though the needs of the island's population after Maria were by all accounts much greater: more structures were destroyed; more critical infrastructure was devastated; more people were impacted; and island residents were more isolated, had fewer resources available to them, and had higher rates of poverty. Finally, it would take FEMA four times as long to begin infrastructural repair work: 43 versus 10 days (Einbinder 2018).

The response to Maria was objectively less effective than the response to Harvey. While some of this surely reflects Puerto Rico's remoteness, this cannot completely explain away the lapses in federal disaster response. As we will see, the president (and his surrogates) used distinctive political rhetoric, mirroring the overall performance of federal relief efforts in each case.

Comparing Political Communications

If the differences in operational and technical response were surprising, the disparity in political communication was shocking. With strikingly different terms, tones, and forms of political rhetoric, officials from federal and state governments responded in starkly different ways to the two hurricane events. In simple terms, Harvey's operational and political response was less conflictual, as reflected in the rhetoric used to discuss and describe the hurricane event and the damage it dealt. Indeed, there was a dearth of stories dedicated to rival claims or angry public denunciations of official hurricane relief efforts in the news media. Again, only 13 of Harvey's 245 stories (5%), over nearly a year of coverage, involved political communications that conveyed "political conflict" over hurricane response. By contrast, 38 (20%) of Hurricane Maria's 192 news stories focused on such political communications. This highlighted political controversy and conflict over federal efforts, to which then president Trump and his surrogates responded in surprisingly antagonistic terms.

Overall, my analysis of the limited number of news stories with political communications published in the aftermath of Harvey showed that White House political messaging was overwhelmingly positive. For example, in the coded subset of political contest articles, public officials in charge of hurricane response—including the president—tactically focused on credit claiming while also affirming the severity of the hurricane in half or more of these stories. Officials also suggested in a third of these stories that the trauma and loss experienced had been "uncontrollable," maximizing the severity of the storm; by extension, it was not their fault (see table A.1). What is more, in more than a third of political communication-focused stories, the president, his surrogates, and their supporters also praised federal and state efforts at storm relief and the victims of the storm for their "volunteerism" and "self-help" spirit. For example, in the following quote from an opinion piece, the Editorial Board (2017) at the *WSJ* both chides rival (liberal) political views while giving credit for the hurricane response to local, state, and federal efforts:

> Who says progressives don't believe in religion? They may not believe in Jehovah or Jesus, but they certainly believe in Old Testament-style wrath against sinners. . . . Witness the emerging theme on the media left that Texas, and especially Houston, are at fault for the devastation of Hurricane Harvey. This has happened even faster than usual, perhaps because the Katrina II scenario of emergency mismanagement didn't pan out. The state, local and federal governments have done a competent job under terrible conditions, and stories about neighborly charity, racial goodwill, the heroism of rescuers, and Big Business donating money and goods don't fit into any agenda.

To express his support, the president visited the region four days after the storm made landfall, conveying to all that his attention was focused on their hardships. At worst, he was chided for avoiding hurricane-devastated areas and not meeting directly with storm victims. He would remedy this critique with another visit within the week, making it a point to serve food to families housed in recovery shelters (Nussbaum 2017). The president's tweets were also indicative of his administration's political communications regarding Harvey. In his initial tweets, while Harvey was still battering Houston and the Texas and Louisiana coasts, Trump shared with the nation the following (Politico Staff 2017):

> "Great coordination between agencies at all levels of government." "Continuing rains and flash floods are being dealt with. Thousands rescued." That same weekend Trump would also Tweet, "Many people are now saying that this is the worst storm/hurricane they have ever seen. Good news is that we have great talent on the ground"; "I will be going to Texas as soon as that trip

can be made without causing disruption. The focus must be life and safety";
and "Wow—Now experts are calling #Harvey a once in 500-year flood! We
have an all out effort going, and going well!" And finally, "Major rescue
operations underway!"

The first week after the hurricane hit, the president tweeted 24 times,
lauding federal personnel, Texas state officials, and the storm victims for
their fantastic response (Politico Staff 2017; Vinik 2018). On its face, while
this political attention and claims making may not be surprising, when
compared to the attention and response to Hurricane Maria, the differences are stark.

Comparing Rival Claims

While the president lavished praise on federal recovery efforts and the
victims of Hurricane Harvey, his response to Hurricane Maria and Puerto
Rico was at best ambivalent and at worst callous, insulting, and bombastic. Indeed, across the year of coverage, the president did not provide his
unequivocal support to either Puerto Ricans or their government. In the
aftermath of Maria, as conditions materially deteriorated, the federal government's response was hesitant and lackluster and failed to address or
remedy those conditions forthrightly. As hurricane victims suffered ap-
palling conditions on the ground, victims' advocates and rival political interests began to agitate for government relief efforts. Critics increasingly
blamed government mistakes, misconduct, and mismanagement for the
island's suffering. As President Trump's rhetoric escalated, critics added
accusations of political partisanship and outright racism to their frame
about the hurricane response gone awry (Garcia-Lopez 2018; Lloréns
2018; Rozsa 2017).

   In response to public accusations, the president and his surrogates
further ramped up their political rhetoric, airing allegations carried in
a quarter of the news stories that sought to avoid blame by maximizing
the storm's magnitude and unpredictability, while claiming credit for
what they repeatedly claimed were very few deaths (see table A.1). For
example, when Carmen Yulín Cruz, mayor of San Juan, Puerto Rico (the
island's capital and largest city), criticized federal efforts for their slow

and inadequate response, she was met with denial and then outright derision. President Trump lashed out in several tweets, calling her "crazed and incompetent," while suggesting Puerto Rico's lawmakers were "grossly incompetent" (Baker and Dickerson 2017; Karni and Mazzei 2019). In subsequent tweets, he also accused the victims of Hurricane Maria of lacking initiative: "They want everything to be done for them when it should be a community effort. . . . 10,000 Federal workers now on Island doing a fantastic job. The military and first responders, despite no electric, roads, phones etc., have done an amazing job" (Baker 2017).

Indeed, in the first week after Maria, the president tweeted about the plight of Puerto Rico just eight times, preferring to focus his tweets (and hence his attention) on a controversy over professional football players kneeling for the national anthem (Vinik 2018). His 8 Maria Tweets were a threefold difference from the 24 he devoted to Harvey. His tweets regarding Maria and Harvey differed qualitatively in their tone and target as well. Unlike Harvey, about which his tweets heaped praise on Texas, his tweets about Puerto Rico lambasted the incompetence of its officials, castigated its high levels of government debt, highlighted the poor quality of the island's infrastructure, and even suggested that its citizens lacked grit and self-sufficiency. This understandably outraged many Puerto Ricans and the wider general public, creating a highly charged political atmosphere (Baker and Dickerson 2017; Einbinder 2018; Vinik 2018). The president's rhetoric was a defensive tactic intended to avoid blame and claim credit while holding his political rivals responsible for the damage and losses. However, it also helped stimulate a sense of victimization among islanders; they had been neglected at best because of partisan politics and at worst because of a racist president and his federal government.

Comparing Crisis Stories

The comments of the president and his surrogates did not occur in a vacuum. Prior research clarifies that during crises, authoritative social, political, and administrative explanatory discourses and structures of authority can be strengthened as people rally around them. On the other hand, they can be subverted if the assumptions and beliefs that animate them and their efforts are exposed, tested, and criticized (Beamish 2002, 2015). In the cases of Hurricanes Harvey and Maria, public officials responsible for hurricane response had to contend with rival frames of reference that were advanced by victims, watchdog groups, pundits, the media, and other stakeholders, whose explanations did not necessarily comport with the official storm narrative. Therefore, to understand the shape that political communication took in the aftermath of each hurricane, we must also account for the rival frames that competed for dominance in each case.

In analyzing the news stories focused on political communications in the aftermath of Hurricane Harvey, again, the first thing that stands out is that there were very few of them—13 total. None involved direct attacks on federal or Texas state relief efforts. I also found this to be the case when I searched other sources such as news magazines and expert reviews. Even if there was little or no accusation that state and federal hurricane responders were to blame for the trauma and loss delivered by Hurricane Harvey, the political communication stories I collected did include references to "mistake, misconduct, and mismanagement during the crisis." If not criticisms of federal or state hurricane relief efforts, what were these references about? This is where numerical quantification must be supplemented with qualitative interpretation.

Of the 13 political communication stories, 6 were not criticisms of the official response to Harvey at all but rather communicated other sorts of political conflicts. Of those stories that were critical, 2 were editorials. One focused on the continuing dispute associated with planning for climate change and the lack of planning for hurricanes (Kristof 2017), and the other discussed flood insurance and congressional budgeting for storm relief (Welch 2017). Two other stories focused on a running political conflict between Houston's mayor, a Democrat, and the governor of Texas, a Republican, over dueling evacuation orders just before Harvey hit land.[14] Two further stories were more apropos of institutional blame for

14. The mayor had asked Houston residents to shelter in place, whereas the governor suggested evacuation from Houston was the safest bet. While this was indeed a political contest, neither suggested the other was to blame for the hurricane or trauma and loss that resulted from it. Rather, it was a dispute over jurisdiction and appropriate crisis response, not over any damage or suffering that occurred as a consequence of the storm or relief efforts.

trauma and loss. One focused on an Army Corp of Engineers water release from a reservoir upstream from Houston that flooded several Houston area homes. Homeowners claimed they had not been forewarned of the flooding and that it was unwarranted (Randazzo 2017). They intended to sue the federal government for damages. The final story showcased the lack of posthurricane resources made available to the city of Port Arthur, Texas—a predominantly working-class, lower-income community with a sizable African American and Latino presence. The story suggested that racism may have explained the lack of adequate relief funding (Carlton and Elliott 2018). Largely missing from Harvey's 245 stories and disaster narrative were, therefore, accusations of trustee mistake, misconduct, or mismanagement. Harvey's crisis narrative never became politicized in the national media.

By contrast, of the politically focused stories about Hurricane Maria, 35 of the 38 political communication stories I assessed involved direct references to mistake, misconduct, or mismanagement. For example, the island's indebtedness, its shoddy infrastructure, and the failure of its power authority—Puerto Rico Electrical Power Authority (PREPA) (Autoridad de Energía Eléctrica, AEE)—were repeatedly derided for incompetence, cronyism, and worsening the storm's impact on the island. Indeed, the Trump administration regularly tried to avoid blame when defending its efforts at hurricane response by mentioning PREPA and the island's poor fiscal shape. For example, in a story titled, "In Battered Puerto Rico, Governor Warns of a Humanitarian Crisis," President Trump and his surrogates emphasized the unmanageable difficulties of hurricane response given the island's "broken infrastructure" and "massive debt," while praising federal efforts as "unprecedented":

> After facing criticism for a lack of public support for Puerto Rico, President Trump on Tuesday said he would visit the island next week. The announcement followed a series of tweets he posted on Monday that tied the natural disaster to the island's already fragile economic situation. He said that while Florida and Texas were coping well with hurricane damage, "Puerto Rico, which was already suffering from broken infrastructure & massive debt, is in deep trouble. . . . Its old electrical grid, which was in terrible shape, was devastated," he continued. "Much of the Island was destroyed, with billions of dollars owed to Wall Street and the banks which, sadly, must be dealt

with. Food, water and medical are top priorities—and doing well." The White House rejected criticism of its response. "The federal response has been anything but slow," said Sarah Huckabee Sanders, the White House press secretary. "In fact, there has been an unprecedented push through of billions of dollars in federal assistance." (Robles, Alvarez, and Fandos 2017)

In framing political rhetoric like this, references to mistake, misconduct, and mismanagement were embedded in most political communication stories. The president, the head of FEMA, the governor of Puerto Rico, PREPA, and their surrogates all used this kind of political rhetoric to control the storm narrative and rebut responsibility for trauma and loss in the aftermath of Hurricane Maria. In half of the political communication stories I coded, public officials relied on blame avoidance and credit claiming while "maximizing the crisis conditions" to suggest that someone or something else (such as the storm) was to blame for trauma and loss, not them.[15]

While only detailing the first year of coverage, the hurricane cases I compared illustrate the shape that highly politicized communication processes can take. Harvey's narrative reflected a political rhetoric that emphasized credit claiming and success and very little political conflict. Maria's narrative, by contrast, highlighted a political rhetoric of blame avoidance, whereby those in positions of authority sought to distance themselves from accusations of government failure: not just any kind of failure, but moral and political failure. The dominant storyline that emerged in the aftermath of Hurricane Maria communicated public judgments of official actions and omissions that linked them to unnecessary and avoidable trauma and loss. The suffering of Puerto Rico and Puerto Ricans was frequently framed as a consequence of governmental negligence or worse. As hardship on the island continued without significant relief, accusations quickly accelerated into claims that the real crisis was the absence of aid and concern on the part of (mainly) federal disaster responders and the standing administration (i.e., the president of the United States). This represented a violation of the public trust and abandonment of U.S. citizens. The perceived needlessness of those harms transformed

---

15. Of 38 political communication stories, 19 featured blame-avoidance rhetoric, 16 featured credit claiming, and 15 maximized crisis conditions.

them into a moral afront. If the president, FEMA, the governor of Puerto Rico, and PREPA had been prepared—had they responded and importantly showed that they *cared* as they should have—local trauma and loss would have been greatly diminished. This therefore reflected a blameworthy instance of wrongdoing on the part of partisan political interests and racist disaster relief decision-making (Garcia-Lopez 2018; Lloréns 2018). Maria was not a natural disaster but a socially founded public tragedy.

CONCLUSION

Crises, by definition, disrupt social order and with it authority, opening it up to scrutiny and criticism. This is because crises reveal risks and dramatize vulnerabilities to the social order while exposing societal trustees—those individuals, organizations, and institutions responsible for maintaining order—to criticism. Very little political conflict was evident in the news and press coverage of Hurricane Harvey. With Hurricane Maria, there was a good deal. The political controversy surrounding a crisis event suggests how deeply it shook the existing social and political order. Indeed, in the aftermath of devastating crises, violations of public trust can even emotionally supersede whatever ostensibly precipitated the crisis—like a hurricane—leaving only the authorities to blame for the trauma, loss, and victimization experienced in the aftermath. In the contemporary moment, events like these can quickly become publicly tragic.

As exemplified by Hurricane Maria, a core element of public tragedy is that regardless of its source, social and institutional forces are deemed to be the "ultimate cause" of human suffering and victimhood. We see this in the claims and accusations that governments, surrogates, or other societal institutions have failed to fulfill their obligations to the public. Because many Americans believe the government and its surrogates should significantly diminish, if not wholly prevent, risks to their health and safety, they often experience societal disruption as a social affront. As a consequence, because they believe that the harms they have experienced are preventable, these harms can feel unwarranted and unfair. If the social institutions—government, industry, science, technology, education, the police, the military—had performed as expected, no one would have been harmed. At the very least the trauma and loss would have been greatly diminished. Trustees and the institutions they represent are increasingly held accountable when they (or their proxies) appear to have failed to fulfill their responsibilities to the public adequately or when their efforts are viewed as unfair, misguided, or wrong. In such cases, their failure(s) are often experienced as immoral.

In Hurricane Harvey's case, the federal government was perceived to have defended social order and therefore was given credit for saving lives and ameliorating the trauma and loss associated with that hurricane event. In Hurricane Maria's case, the prevailing view, expressed in the news media and elsewhere, was that federal efforts failed to protect the public and therefore were to blame for the tragedy that befell the island. The juxtaposition of relief efforts for Hurricane Harvey and Hurricane Maria and the political rhetoric used in both cases notably diverged. While Hurricane Harvey was often held up, in news accounts, opinion pieces, and scholarly studies, as a successful crisis response, it was also used to emphasize how tragic the federal response was to Hurricane Maria (Baker 2017). The extreme level of suffering in Puerto Rico, coupled with the sitting administration's reaction to appeals for quicker and more intensive humanitarian relief, was astonishing (Robles 2018b). In the end, the story of Hurricane Maria, like that of Katrina before it, has become an iconic instance of trustee failure and victimization. It would not be the hurricane but the federal response to it that would render it a public tragedy.

The political process by which a crisis, disaster, or catastrophe becomes a public tragedy begins with an event that deviates from and transgresses the expected or the norm. While a hurricane can be incredibly destructive, sowing death and trauma in its wake, it need not transgress expectations and will not necessarily be viewed as a deviant crisis event. Deviance emerges when a crisis occurs and the trauma and loss represented in it seem to represent a violation of trust. When attributions of responsibility suggest the harms done stem from "official" choices—not the impersonal forces of nature, God, chance, or bad luck—those harms appear avoidable, unnecessary, and ultimately unfair. The harms are quickly moralized, and those harmed become framed as the victims of official acts or omissions. The preventability of the harm done suggests a betrayal from which moral outrage, accusation, and social blame quickly emerge, further politicizing crisis events and responses to them. Involved stakeholders wage a battle over who or what ought to be blamed for the trauma and loss, what ought to be done for the victims who have unfairly suffered, and what sort of punishment should be apportioned to those guilty of violating their obligations to the public.

As is clear in the preceding analysis of political communications, the media plays a critical role in framing crises and in the processes that characterize the construction of public tragedy. This role also involves and reflects a new media logic and communication ecology that emphasize and promote specific aspects of crisis to gain and hold public attention. Indeed, as I will show in the next chapter, a new media logic and communication ecology can quickly supercharge a crisis by highlighting accusations, conflicts, and political controversies associated with an issue or event that can make public tragedy more likely.

3 The Media's Role in Public Tragedy

A NEW COMMUNICATION ECOLOGY, TRAUMA SCRIPT, AND TRAUMA REPORTING

Over the last three decades, 24-hour cable, online news, the internet, wireless smartphones, and social media platforms have changed the relationship between communication formats, information technology, and public discourse. They have fundamentally transformed the communication ecology, reshaping how information is distributed and diffused to the public and by the public. These emergent technologies and services have pushed news, entertainment, and social media-generated content deeper into everyday life than was possible with earlier forms of mediated communication (which included network television, film-based cinema, radio programming, fixed-line telephone service, and very early on, the printing press; Altheide 1994; Gencarelli 2000; Lum 2006; Margetts et al. 2015; Postman 1980; Stoycheff et al. 2018; Tarrow 2011). Indeed, the level of media penetration achieved in the twenty-first century through cable, the internet, smartphones, social media, and related communication technologies was impossible before their invention and broad adoption by the public. Because it can rapidly scale up issues and events and persuasively spread information about them, twenty-first-century mass media has intensified its influence over local meanings and emotions in ways that scholars and policy makers still incompletely understand (Chadwick 2017).

Public tragedies are, in part, a manifestation of this new communication ecology. Their emergence and proliferation as transformative social and political events rest partly on the power of mass media to mediate experience. The media's ability to influence and cultivate the conditions for public tragedy exposes a new and distinctive media logic and communication ecology and, as suggested in previous chapters, the sentiments and sympathies of contemporary audiences. Altheide (2013:225) defines *media logic* as forms and processes of communication through which media transmits and conveys information. Moreover, as I develop it in this chapter, communication ecology concerns the larger information environment within which such media logics operate. Borrowing from Postman's (1979, 2005) classic treatment, this includes how new technologies and communication techniques shape the form, content, quantity, speed, and distribution of information and how, in turn, such information influences people's perceptions and attitudes (see also Gencarelli 2000). In this regard, public tragedies both involve and reflect a contemporary media logic and environment characterized by how the news and entertainment are produced and consumed. This contemporary logic also provides insight into how journalistic professionalism shapes news reporting: journalists strive to provide compelling, indeed "entertaining" information, presenting shocking stories that feature spectacle and melodrama (Anker 2014; Kellner 2003; Ritzer 2010).

What is the general public's relationship to the trauma and loss it regularly consumes? This relationship is almost entirely mediated. Via mass media, the public routinely learns about horrific events people do not experience directly. Nor do they initially learn about them through trusted networks, where experience and common sense can play a more substantial role in their decoding (Entman 1989). Referenced as the media's "default function," events and issues for which viewers have no personal information mainly depend on mass and social media sources to frame and provide meaning (Entman 1989). An investigation of the media's role in cultivating the conditions and sentiments associated with public tragedies is therefore crucial to understanding their emergence as a socially and politically transformative event.

Mass media refers to information sources and technologies that reach a broad audience via communication technologies, channels, and strategies.

As a grouping, mass media includes both broadcast media—such as film, radio, recorded music, or television news and entertainment—and internet media—such as email, social media platforms, websites, and internet-based radio and television programming. While seemingly vast, a limited number of commercial organizations (social media platforms; movie studios; publishing companies, including newspapers, magazines, and books; radio and television stations; and cable news programming) control the overwhelming majority of these media services and technologies. What is more, the media frames and tropes used to structure the content of news and entertainment programming are limited in number and type. They are also relatively predictable (Altheide 2013; Burke 1973; Hall 1980; Semetko and Valkenburg 2000).

As a soures of content, mass media shapes popular culture and therefore "public understanding" by providing event narratives that create conscious and unconscious comprehension. Through repetition and association with events and issues, media frames and discourses become "common knowledge," both shaping and reflecting the zeitgeist of the day (Schudson 2018). News formats are deliberately created to select, organize, and present "evocative, condensed, thematic, easy to digest, and familiar" information that the audience will easily and steadily consume (Altheide 2013). Television news, for example, relies on standardized presentation formats that, through iteration, have become universal and anticipated by audiences: an anchor (or anchors), sitting at a desk, notes in hand, introduces and concludes news stories in a standardized format for live broadcasts in television, cable, and internet news. Indeed, the public expects this. It means "news."

The frameworks and formats used to organize media narratives also rely on the repetition of specific words, themes, arguments, and frameworks that, when assembled, take the form of a discourse. *Discourses* are modes of organizing knowledge, ideas, and experiences into a meaningful whole. Producer-driven media discourses are used repeatedly to convey the meaning and significance of targeted issues and events to the audience. These repetitive media discourses can (and do) become conventionalized, appearing as commonplace tropes and expectations that are then associated with audience emotion and even thinking. Significantly, issues and events that become conventionalized through media iteration can then shape how many other societal problems and issues in daily life are understood and "felt" (Benson 2004). In this way, media programming can shape public thinking and feeling about issues and events featured in news coverage and entertainment programming.

In developing consistent frames of discursive reference to promote products and commercial interests, the mass media also intentionally and unintentionally shapes the public's political views, cultural outlooks, and emotions. The media exercises its influence by relying on institutional sources and opinion makers. Government officials, professionals and experts, commentators, pundits, and political candidates who represent powerful societal institutions commonly appear on the news to explain events and justify official actions (or omissions), thus framing them for the public (Gans 1980; Schudson 1989). Through dispensation processes like these, media discourses become *de facto* conventionalized narratives common to popular culture and, therefore, common to everyday thinking (Hall 1975). As such, news and entertainment media has come to play a central role in "encoding" the world around us, making it consumable: entertaining, engaging, and easily understood. It promotes cultural modes of interpretation and conduct that the public internalizes and tacitly uses to make sense of events, independent of the media channels from which they originate. These modes of interpretation and conduct then become taken for granted as common knowledge.

What I have labeled the trauma script is just such a conventionalized discourse: a political explanation and now, through repetition, a "social heuristic" used time and again to make sense of the causes, sufferings, and outcomes associated with trauma and loss. Again, social heuristics are shared rules of thumb that aid in interpretation and decision-making by aligning decisions with collectively recognized and conventionalized understandings of routine problems and issues (Beamish and Biggart 2009, 2011, 2015; Biggart and Beamish 2003; Marsh 2002). The conventionalized narrative that underlies the trauma script features a victim who has suffered unprovoked, crippling harms that are moralized as wrong and that therefore require political redress. The core elements of the trauma script—claims of perpetration and victimization—are staples of news and entertainment discourses; they supply the shock value contemporary programming uses to grab and hold audience attention.

Importantly, in the United States political elites regularly invoke the trauma script or its elements—for instance, a focus on cases of victimization, social blame, and moral panic—to promote policies, political candidates, and resource outlays that support their interests. For example, when the media links the day's events to trends in crime, terrorism, economic precarity, and other "sources" of insecurity and fear, this promotes a public expectation that danger and victimization at the hands of dangerous perpetrators of all kinds—criminals, terrorists, immigrants, corporate villains, the police, self-interested government officials, and partisan, even sectarian political movements—are now an inescapable aspect of everyday life (Altheide 2013; Anker 2005; Fishman 1978). This primes the public to emotionally self-identify with and respond to news events framed by the trauma script.

In this chapter I analyze the mass media's role in generating public tragedy. I explore news media logics because "news makers" play a pivotal role in alerting the public and in framing and sustaining public attention to issues and events that might otherwise remain peripheral to their consciousness (Stoycheff et al. 2018). As outlined in the previous chapter, the media is a primary conduit through which political communications occur and, therefore, where issues and events are prioritized or disregarded. As such, the news media's hand in preconfiguring the conditions for public tragedy—by emphasizing spectacle and exposé and relying on the trauma script to frame and explain instances of trauma and loss—helps to explain the latter's emergence and proliferation.

As a chronicler of events, the news media is an especially important catalyst for political controversy. Yet controversy is as much a product of news media routines and biases as it is something the news media "finds" in the world and simply reports about. For example, the journalistic priority and bias placed on portraying "two sides" to any issue can intensify issue polarization and skew public understanding because presenting two sides—even when the evidence suggests more than two sides or does not support them as equivalent sides—promotes a false dichotomy and a false equivalence. Termed the "objectivity bias" (Tuchman 1972) in journalism, a glaring contemporary example is journalistic accounts of climate change, which routinely give equal weight (i.e., truth value) to climate experts concerned about a warming climate and a small cadre of denialists

(Oreskes and Conway 2011). Important also is the frequent manipulation of the news media by political elites and campaign strategists. Because journalists rely on institutional sources and objectivity biases, they frequently fall prey to opportunistic political elites who use both their relationship with the media and their stance on specific issues to cultivate concern, fear, and moral panic. Having sown fear among their constituents, the same political elites will then gain favor with them by promising to protect them from whatever boogeyman they have invoked (Fishman 1978; Goode and Ben-Yehuda 2010).

To address how issues of media framing and discursive explanation might influence the frequency and intensity of public tragedies, I relate several significant changes in news making, journalistic practice, and technological innovation that help explain their emergence and that increased their political influence. I argue that these changes reflect a new media logic characteristic of current news and entertainment venues. Having discussed media trends, a new media logic, and emergent communication ecology that cultivates the conditions for public tragedy, I then explore the news coverage of six paired cases of trauma and loss for what they reveal about contemporary crisis coverage. I explore topics, rhetoric, and news frames to distinguish events that achieve widespread public notoriety, outrage, and political controversy to become publicly tragic from those that do not. My analysis is illustrative, suggesting that when media relies on the core elements of the trauma script—perpetration, victimization, moral failure, social blame, and political controversy—the events in question are much more likely to become notorious and publicly tragic.

THE MEDIA AND THE MAKING OF A PUBLIC REALITY

The "mainstream" news media changed significantly with the advent of cable news, the internet, and social media platforms. Even so, there remains ample evidence that across these domains—print, cable, and the internet—the "traditional" news continues to play an important, if not the lead, role in cultivating public impressions and connecting them to concerns regarding the day's events (Schudson 2018; Tewksbury and Rittenberg 2009; Nielsen and Schrøder 2014). Research suggests that through its agenda-setting power, traditional journalism and the news media continue to influence the public's sense of what is and is not significant (Schudson 2018; Gaskins and Jerit 2012). We observe this in the way that newscasters emphasize some issues over others (Vliegenthart 2019) and in the consistency, continuity, and repetitiveness with which topics and issues are featured across news media types and social media domains (McCombs and Valenzuela 2014; Tewksbury and Rittenberg 2009; Vliegenthart 2019). The power to shape the publics' agenda, Entman (1989) suggests, is that on many issues it provides the public with a view by "default." Since much of the public would know nothing of the events or places reported on and about, the view they receive by default is the only view they have. The power to shape popular impressions also resides in the news and entertainment media's ability to set the public agenda. This is termed the media's "agenda setting function," and scholars have shown that media doesn't so much tell the public what to think, but rather shapes what the public thinks and argues about (Entman 1993; Gamson 1992; Gitlin 1980; McCombs 2014). As such, one can say the news media plays a lead role in shaping popular understandings of virtually all public issues and events (Entman 1989; Hall 1975; McCombs and Valenzuela 2014; Schudson 2018; Stoycheff et al. 2018).

The news media also plays a pivotal role in defining the social problems that gain sustained political attention and therefore the "issue-environments" within which such social problems compete for public attention (Best 1999; Gusfield 1980; Hilgartner and Bosk 1988; Stoycheff et al. 2018). Because time and attention are zero-sum qualities, if one issue or problem takes up a majority of the media's attention, another cannot. The practical significance is that while people may choose "what side of an issue they are on," in many cases, the issues on which they hold opinions are not of their choosing. What is more, because political elites and social movements require access to the media to gain the public's attention, they are often forced to pursue strategies and actions that conform with media conceptions of newsworthiness and entertainment. At the same time, they must avoid strategies and actions that either violate media routines—casting them as outsiders—or risk being ignored (Beamish, Molotch, and Flacks 1995; Gitlin 1980; Molotch 1979).

Research on media influence has also exposed the impact that media routines, styles, genres, and frames have on how the public understands and "decodes" issues and events (Gamson 1992; Graber and Dunaway 2017;

Hall 2001). For instance, news editors and journalists learn to compose news stories that reflect standardized media frames. Journalists routinely use these frames to structure their stories in ways that are both familiar and immediately understandable to their audience(s). Such standardized media frames include the human interest frame, the conflict frame, the morality frame, the economic frame, and the responsibility frame (Semetko and Valkenburg 2000; Seon-Kyoung and Gower 2009).

Once conventionalized, however, media frames do more than simply structure news stories for easy consumption; the general public uses these frames as conceptual tools to sort out and evaluate issues and events in everyday experience and to convey them to its social networks (Chadwick 2017; Semetko and Valkenburg 2000). Similarly, media sources and the frames they rely on shape political attitudes and emotions that viewers associate with specific issues and events (Semetko and Valkenburg 2000). This includes heightened levels of partisanship and a sense of precarity and fear now common among much of the U.S. public (e.g., Dunn 2020; see also Altheide 2017; Bude 2017; Finkel et al. 2020; Glassner 2009). The broadcast and internet news media therefore plays an integral role in shaping popular social and political consciousness, imbuing social and political issues with both understanding and affect.

The content and style of news and news making have also changed dramatically over the last half century, such as in the reporting standards to which journalists adhere and the topics and issues editors choose to feature in their newsfeeds. These changes have likewise played a crucial part in the emergence of public tragedies as socially and politically transformative events. But before answering questions concerning how changes to news making and journalism have encouraged public tragedies, we must first address what news making looked like before these transformations reshaped the news.

TWENTY-FIRST-CENTURY NEWS MAKING

The need for news media producers to gain public attention has clearly played an important role in the shape, style, and formatting of news reporting and has inspired the *media logic* of our day. I suggest that contemporary media logics play a central role in facilitating public tragedies—they reflect current media formats, styles, and frameworks. Contemporary news media formats emphasize visual drama, action, and brevity. They play up horrific news content, relying on oversimplifications, limited vocabularies, restricted ideas, and polarized political depictions.

Internet news and social media platforms are relatively new entrants into our communication ecology. The interaction among and between broadcast and internet forms of communication is still new enough as to be incompletely understood (Chadwick 2017). What we do know, however, is that a dynamic broadcast-internet media "feedback loop" can super-charge an issue or event, quickly giving it widespread attention. That is, hyperbolic news formats and story content are amplified through a social media "feedback loop" on X (formerly Twitter), Facebook, Instagram, Tik-Tok, and other social media platforms on which posts are read and shared by hundreds, thousands, and sometimes millions of people. Attention to an event can then trend and explode across multiple media formats, feed-ing yet further waves of coverage and attention, and even spurring collec-tive action.

Likewise, storylines on social media that feature spectacle and involve overt exaggeration, hoax, and falsification can, yet again, create feedback and queue news media outlets to a topic or issue that is "trending," accel-erating its diffusion to millions more (Stoycheff et al. 2018). This dynamic characterizes public tragedies, in which "outrageous cases" of trauma and loss go viral and are viewed by thousands and then millions, who see in them not fate or accident but purposeful mistakes, misconduct, and wrongdoing—a view that is often reinforced in journalistic accounts. This framing then sets off subsequent rounds of accusation, moralization, and social blame, resulting in political controversies and conflicts.

Propaganda, News, and Exposé Journalism

Reflective of new media logics and resultant changes in the communica-tion ecology, Americans share a significant dread of being victimized by criminals, terrorists, and other risks of all kinds (Altheide 2017; Anker 2005; Calhoun 2004; Chevigny 2003; Fishman 1978; Simon 2007). Ac-cording to Gallup, for example, nearly half of Americans fear being a victim of terrorism or a mass shooting, and more than half say that crime in the United States is "extremely" or "very" serious (Brenan 2019a; McCarthy 2020). Sentiments like these reflect and reveal a general sense of unease and insecurity among the public (Gallup 2021; Poushter and Fagan 2020). This insecurity has also encouraged identification with and empathy for those victimized by what are perceived to be dangerous conditions. The constant drumbeat of terror, crime, and risk lends itself to a sense of vulnerability that readies the public to interpret and respond to the elements at the center of the trauma script: perpetration, victimization, social blame, moral failure, and political controversy. This is an inescapable aspect of everyday life in risk society. Indeed, it defines it.

Given the central role that news and entertainment media plays in cultivating fear, one must ask if it has always engaged in overstatement and superlative, featuring spectacle, scandal, and the horrific while playing on (and playing up) political polarization to sell news and entertainment programming (Adut 2008; Anker 2005, 2015; Kellner 2003, 2015b). One way to answer this is to compare how *newsworthy* has come to be defined by news organizations and journalists over time. Before the civil rights and Vietnam War eras, trauma and loss associated with social crisis, war, and natural disaster went largely uncovered and were certainly not featured in entertainment venues as they are today. What is more, while in the 1960s and 1970s the first televised foreign war occurred and culminated in a highly visible protest movement and civil unrest, institutional wrongdoing, grievance, and collective action were still far less visible then than they are today, when they have become a mainstay of news and entertainment programming (not to speak of their inescapable presence in online commentaries, blogs, zines, and social media posts; Margetts et al. 2015). It may be surprising that the exhibition and spectacle associated with human suffering and the trauma script is a relatively new focus for news programming, given its current ubiquity across contemporary media types. But this is the case.

According to Seaton (1996), during World War I in Britain and the United States, the salacious use of war atrocity propaganda to dehumanize enemies and legitimize state violence provoked deep cynicism among social and political elites. Consequently, reporting on the horrific became strongly associated with "politicized news," which was widely viewed as propagandistic and led the public to question its truth value. In response, the print media of that day began to strongly hew toward a media logic that emphasized "independent, impartial, and balanced reporting" that rewarded a restrained style of journalism and storytelling. Journalists played down or failed to cover extreme events, instead emphasizing the "facts" in descriptive accounts of the everyday. Apropos of the deliberate neglect of events deemed too horrific, news reporting during World War II almost entirely avoided covering the "horrors of war," instead featuring a decidedly quotidian war discourse featuring standardized vocabularies, ideas, and frames. The news tended to emphasize the banality of war and, when possible, featured acts of heroism.

The conveyance of war sans its horrors would falter at the close of World War II, as pictures and films of the allied invasion of Germany and the opening of the Nazi concentration camps (and other war atrocities) began to circulate following the victory.[1] Especially important was the moral outrage that emerged with documentation of the Holocaust, with its tragic scenes of extreme deprivation and torture and the apparent lack of Allied efforts to stop it. The explanation that quickly gained ground in Western Europe and the United States was that of a "hidden horror"—that no one knew or believed it could be true.[2] This was, of course, untrue—through espionage, the Allies had learned of Nazi plans to exterminate Jews, political dissidents, and disabled persons because anti-Nazi collaborators had been actively smuggling Jews and others out of Nazi-controlled territories since before the war began (Lipstadt 1993; Niewyk 1992; Wyman 1984). Yet with time, and through news media repetition, the hidden horrors Holocaust trope became common knowledge (Seaton 1988, 1996). This treatment was also given to other war atrocities committed on both sides. The pretense that news was independent and balanced and that journalistic reporting was impartial had at times led professional reporters and editors to present "just the facts" at the expense of those facts. This amounted to a cover-up: the sanitizing of war often left its horrific costs hidden from public view.

---

1. There was, for example, a film commissioned by the British Parliament and directed by Alfred Hitchcock on the Holocaust and Nazi attempts at genocide (see Seaton 1996:66).
2. See Alexander's (2002) treatment of the Holocaust as a postwar moral construct.

By the 1970s, the emergence and proliferation of visually oriented news media brought a new era of journalism, with a particular style and bias. The press embraced the role of watchdog, and journalists at this point were determined to uncover all manner of "hidden horror," from civil rights abuses to military atrocities. In the United States a new generation of journalists was committed to exposing institutional and authoritative overreach and societal wrongs in all their forms. Journalists' role in this era was to generate news based on "the truth" that would alert the public to act on newly exposed information to promote change for the better.

This new sort of exposé journalism represented a professional social movement that paralleled the civil rights, women's, and environmental movements of that day. All these groups sought to expose corporate wrongdoing, government crime, and police abuse, as well as more diffuse sorts of discrimination like sexism, racism, and other kinds of abuses. The underlying coda of the journalists was to shock the public into action by exposing mistakes and malfeasance. Vietnam War coverage exemplified this sort of exposé journalism. Embedded wartime correspondents were uncovering the truth behind the war effort and, in doing so, exposing immoral U.S. military tactics (and the tragic outcomes associated with them, such as the My Lai massacre) to the American public (Hallin 1989; Hammond 1998; Pearson 2018). These journalists exposed the war effort as a horrific disaster rather than a heroic fight for freedom, as political elites had sought to sell it to the American public. Events and issues that previously had been omitted from the news and therefore obscured from Americans (based on a professional journalistic prohibition against "unbalanced" and "political" news) were mainstreamed. As journalists sought to expose the American public to the sources of power and wrongdoing and promote social and political change (Hammond 1998), they depicted horrific scenes of human suffering and commentary and articulated claims about who was to blame for the carnage.

Risk Reporting: Crime, Terrorism, Fear

In the 1980s, the 24-hour news cycle and further changes to the prevailing media logic of the day moved the news media well beyond the stylistic changes of the exposé era of journalism in the late 1960s and 1970s.

Indeed, with the Reagan administration's repeal of the Federal Communications Commission's fairness doctrine in 1987, the news media was no longer mandated, however weakly, to show the "sides" of controversial public issues. The original purpose of the doctrine was to ensure that U.S. news consumers were exposed to diverse viewpoints. The news could now present singular accounts of ideologically inflected information without referencing other views or limitations. Critics have since suggested that repealing the fairness doctrine has encouraged media "tribalism" and with it increased political polarization (Kruse and Zelizer 2019).

What emerged from the crucible of 1980s-era news was a fixation on crime reporting and, with it, an abiding fear of crime on the part of the American public. Amplified by stories of horrific crimes, reportage of public safety risks helped fuel anxiety, even dread, among Americans (Altheide 2002; Bude 2017; Furedi 2007; Kellner 2015b). With the founding of CNN (1980) and its coverage of the 1990 Gulf War, cable news set news journalism on a different path while eroding the dominance of conventional broadcast news. This accelerated in the 1990s with the emergence of competitive cable news providers such as Fox News and MSNBC (circa 1996).

By the mid-1990s, the shock value of exposé journalism waned with at least some Americans, leading to what has been variously referred to as "compassion fatigue," "media malaise," and growing "public cynicism" about social and political institutions like the media itself (Earl Bennett et al. 1999; Moeller 2002). Twenty years of programming intended to expose the public to the facts and the truth, to shock people into action with stories of egregious official mistakes and misconduct, instead seemed to promote public cynicism, ultimately diminishing the effect associated with the spectacle of official wrongdoing (Cappella and Jamieson 1996). Yet far from moving away from the exposé news format, in the new era, cable programmers intensified their efforts to promote audience shock and outrage to maintain viewership numbers. As 24-hour news channels searched the country and world for ever more horrific events in the form of disaster, conflict, and political crisis, programmers continued to scare and appall their audiences and, in doing so, capture and maintain their attention.

The September 11, 2001, attacks proved pivotal (Altheide 2009; Anker 2005; Kellner 2004). In their aftermath, news media attention to trauma

and loss, and with it the cultivation of audience fear, became more frequent and intense (Altheide 2006; Anker 2014; Bude 2017; Glassner
2009). The competition to attract audience attention and present around-
the-clock commercial news led to a heavy reliance on spectacle, hyperbole,
and melodrama. Media coverage before and after September 11 played on
similar qualities to cultivate fear and lock in audience attention. Events
such as the Columbine High School shootings of 1998; the anthrax attacks
(2001); the wars in Afghanistan (2001) and Iraq (2003); the Minneapolis
bridge collapse (2007); Hurricane Katrina (2010); the Deepwater Horizon oil spill (2010); the Boston Marathon bombings (2013); the Orlando,
Florida, nightclub shooting (2016); the Las Vegas concert shooting (2017);
Harvey Weinstein's sexual assault scandal (2017); and George Floyd's murder (2019), among many, many others, have transformed news making,
not to mention the impact that other national and international tragedies occurring over the same period and often simultaneously have had as
well. Audiences in this context are compelled to live in fear of events that
might happen but have yet to be experienced. Horrific events, the kind of
coverage they garner, and the public response to them have transformed
news making (i.e., encoding) and news consumption (i.e., decoding) in
ways that dovetail with and have preconfigured the conditions I argue are
associated with the emergence of public tragedies.

Hyperbolic news formats work to focus the public's attention on the
sensational aspects of a story to appeal to and provoke audience emotion
(Loren and Metelmann 2016). Whether the focus is a local crime, an international act of terrorism, ecological collapse, election news, or pundit
commentary, journalistic attention has, over time, increasingly featured
intentionally alarming stories of actual or possible trauma and loss. These
stories prime the public, acting as implicit warnings meant to provoke
angst and fear as well as a desire to follow a story to its resolution (Altheide 2002).

But fear reporting did not begin with the events of September 11, 2001;
instead, the event marked a high point. Fear reporting as a news phenom-
enon began with journalistic attention to crime and crime waves in the
1970s (Best 1999; Fishman 1978). While fear of crime sells news, its gen-
esis also reflects the structure of news making and the ambitions of political elites—that is to say, the focus on crime was also driven by institutional

relations as much as news makers' desire to feature fear in their columns. The relationship between news reporters, police departments, and the government is partly the by-product of journalistic needs and institutional routines; to meet afternoon deadlines, "beat reporters" rely on institutional sources to generate timely news reports (Gans 1980; Tuchman 1978). As a consequence, journalists often rely on political and institutional elites—politicians, government institutions, professional experts, and public personalities—to supply the content they require to produce a story (Altheide 2017; Tuchman 1978). Elites routinely and opportunistically use this relationship with news outlets to cultivate fear and manipulate public emotion. For example, as developed in chapter 2, politicians routinely use a "crime mythology"—in which they promise to protect middle- and upper-class voters from criminal predators, dangerous strangers, and random acts of violence—to gain favor and win elections (Best 1999; Chevigny 2003; Fishman 1978; Newburn and Jones 2005). Indeed, cable news programming's willingness to feature pundits and political operatives who frame social issues and events through hyperpolitical lenses has also intensified the emotions associated with traumatic events and the real or imagined trends that link to them (Kellner 2014; Letukas 2014). Politicians and social control agencies have therefore also played an essential role in propagating fear and vulnerability through warnings and overt fearmongering that, distributed via the news media and social media, read as factual news content (Altheide 2006; Best 1997; Bude 2017).

In the aftermath of September 11, fear of terrorism was frequently used by the political establishment and state security apparatus to promote policies, political candidates, and resource outlays that supported their interests: more research, more facilities, more personnel, more weapons, and so forth (Anker 2005; Beamish 2015; Sparks 2003). The linkage of fear of crime with fear of terrorism and the further connection with all kinds of insecurity, precarity, and worry has promoted a public perception that danger and victimization at the hands of perpetrators—criminals, terrorists, and immigrants, on the one hand, and self-interested government officials, the police, and partisan political rivals on the other—is a now-pervasive aspect of everyday life.

Embedded journalists routinely present events from the "victim's perspective," providing in situ coverage from natural disasters, war zones, terror attacks, police shootings, protests, and riots, and from courtrooms and detainment centers where horrendous events unfold live. According to Altheide (2006, 2013), this "discourse of fear" has resulted from a media logic that relies on visually dramatic, action-oriented, brief, and highly polarized media formats. Such formats condition the public, making it more politically malleable (Altheide 2013). This is at least partly a cultivated sense of vulnerability and fear, which readies the public to self-identify and respond emotionally to instances of trauma and loss when framed by the trauma script.

A NEW MEDIA LOGIC, TRAUMA REPORTING, AND PUBLIC TRAGEDY

The focus on trauma and loss reflects both late twentieth-century journalistic professionalism and new media routines. Cable and online news routinely present spectacles of unfolding crises to anchor round-the-clock news cycles. The media logics characteristic of print, 24-hour cable, and online news rely on media frames that feature victims who have suffered at the hands of a perpetrator (or perpetrators). Stories focus on dramatic twists and turns and nearly continuously report as live streams of "breaking news." The plot-like formula is meant to keep viewers captivated with recurrent updates on the latest "terrifying" news developments. This simultaneously occurs in overlapping print news coverage and push notifications, social media feeds, talk shows, bulletin boards, blogs, and documentaries. Interviews with victims, victims' advocates, pundits, and politicians can further politicize, even polarize, these events: advocates, pundits, and "influencers" try to "win" the competition to provide the most compelling explanation of "what it means," "who/what is to blame," and "what should be done." Indeed, the media can and increasingly does turn information flows about events into a kind of "chaotic pluralism," in which moralization and even moral panic can quickly result (Margetts et al. 2015).

This in turn can either reflect or promote further online activity through social media searches and feed "shares." As the viewing public seeks more information on a given crisis and victims' advocates and political elites seek to share and frame the trauma, loss, and suffering, sympathetic audience attention can intensify. The news media also reacts to such social media trends to generate new and compelling stories. It tracks celebrity and grassroot posts to report on and enliven event coverage broadcasts; find new subplots to a crisis; or discover entirely new cases of trauma, loss, and victimization on which to pivot and report, generating another plot-like line of breaking stories. In this way, news media and social media, through an entwined process of story construction and dissemination, have generated a new communication ecology that takes shape through successive recursive loops in what is now best conceived as a hybrid system of messaging. This new communication ecology features storylines that grab the public's attention with exaggerated spectacle and hyperbole while also accelerating the pace of issue generation and politicization (Chadwick 2017).

Altheide's (2006, 2013, 2017) theory of media logics and what he claims is a mediated discourse of fear suggests another reason the trauma script resonates so intensely with the American public and why public tragedies have become such an indelible aspect of the twenty-first century. He suggests that media amplification of trauma and loss currently saturates everyday life. Personalized technologies like smartphones, iPads, personal computers, computer assistants (i.e., Google Voice, Alexa, Apple Talk), and internet service providers now use algorithms to tailor their streams toward "viewers" based on personalized consumer behavior, expressed identities, and political commitments (Zuboff 2015, 2019). This even permits coverage of a fearful issue or event to be targeted at the groups and individuals most likely to react. The nearly continuous coverage and chatter about threats to personal and collective security has promoted generalized angst, pervasive fearfulness, and high levels of social distrust among the public (Beck 1992, 2002; Beamish 2015; Freudenburg 2001; Giddens 1990, 1999).

The current media logic and the overarching and transformed communication ecology have increased the likelihood of fear, moral outrage, and collective action (Chadwick 2017; Margetts et al. 2015; Tewksbury and Rittenberg 2009). Therefore, outside of the immediate trauma and loss they exact, public tragedies can also influence millions who vicariously experience them via news broadcasts and internet media sources and who, in turn, respond to them by communicating their sense of fear, violation, and outrage on their personal social networks (Williams and Carpini 2011).

Why does the public respond so viscerally to public tragedies as moral affronts? What about them generates so much notoriety and outrage? Again, public tragedies remind people of their vulnerability, that their world is at risk, that they too could be victimized, and that they should be fearful (Bude 2017; Füredi 2006; Glassner 2009). In this way, the new communication ecology both dovetails with and cultivates the conditions characteristic of risk society, from which public tragedies have proliferated.

But fearful of what, precisely? In risk society, the risk is a failure of humankind that takes innumerable forms, including civic unrest, economic decline, technological catastrophe, environmental decline, climate change, terrorism, police brutality, sexual assault, drug overdose, and teen suicide, to name but a few. Perception of these social problems mirrors a widespread belief that these ultimately reflect a failure of too much or not enough governance. This would seem almost totalizing in nature. And it is. It is the failure of progress to buoy hopes and allay fears. Put another way, while many issues and events could be destructive, those explained as human failings that result in human harm—those that adhere to the trauma script—are currently more likely to gain public attention, rouse public concern, and provoke public outrage. Again, the trauma script is an ascendant and conventionalized cultural story that explains trauma and loss as involving a victim (or victims) who must cope with unforeseen, unprovoked, human-caused, and crippling harms. Social blame lies at the center of this storyline, where societally produced forces and factors are the perpetrator. Social blame of this kind channels collective fear and anger because it suggests that the harm done was avoidable, unwarranted, and wrong. By moralizing harm, the trauma script cultivates a deep sense of injustice, encouraging collective action to right wrongs committed by society. And news media's use of the script, even reliance on it, has helped to cultivate a kind of trauma-based populism in which fear, moralization, and moral panic have become normal political responses to crises of virtually any kind.

A COMPARATIVE ANALYSIS: NEWS MEDIA FRAMING OF PUBLIC TRAGEDIES

The contemporary news media relies on the trauma script, or the elements that comprise it, to call attention to its stories and their narratives. News media reliance on the trauma script to frame events also encourages fear and outrage, and from emotions like these, public tragedies. Objectively similar cases of trauma and loss that are not framed in this way are far less likely to gain the same public attention, provoke emotion, and attain notoriety, and therefore become publicly tragic.

To explore how the news and related media help to preconfigure the conditions for public tragedy, I conducted a comparative content analysis of news stories documenting several crisis events.[3] I specifically examined online and print news coverage of six paired cases of trauma and loss: two catastrophic hurricane events, two mass school shootings, and two community toxic events. Using "face validity," I deliberately chose and paired cases in which one had achieved "national notoriety" and the other, an objectively similar case, had not. I sought to identify patterns in news coverage associated with that public notoriety and with it the claims of perpetration, victimization, moral failure, social blame, and political controversy that occurred in the aftermath of these events. I speculated that the more nationally notorious cases of trauma and loss would involve more sustained public attention and of a specific kind. I further hypothesized that they would more frequently involve claims of victimization, refer to the moralization of harm, involve social blame, and consequently would involve heightened levels of political conflict and controversy in the aftermath.

To make comparisons, I examined news stories for each of the six cases in three leading U.S. national news services: the *New York Times* (*NYT*), the *Los Angeles Times* (*LAT*), and the *Wall Street Journal* (*WSJ*). My search for news stories relating to the six cases resulted in an initial sample of 1,141 news articles. After sorting and analyzing the selection of stories for relevance and duplication, 830 news stories remained for analysis and coding.[4] I specifically compared the media frames and story content for each case, contrasting those that had not achieved public notoriety with those that had become social, moral, and political dramas. The more notorious cases were de facto public tragedies.

---

3. I pursued a qualitative content analysis of news stories (Altheide 1987, 1996, 2004). See the appendix for further detail on news story search, selection, and analysis.

4. Print and electronic versions of the same story are often titled slightly differently and therefore are at times duplicated in database searches of this kind. Stories that might mention the event, but only in passing or in a way irrelevant to my investigation, were also passed over and deleted from the final tally of coded stories.

Natural Disasters and Catastrophic Losses

For the paired cases of natural disaster, I used the same sample of news stories for Hurricane Maria and Hurricane Harvey that I used in chapter 2 but subjected them to a different coding scheme based on the distinctive focal argument and analysis taken up in this chapter. Here, I focus on how the media framed each crisis and communicated it to the public (in contrast to my previous focus on how political elites sought to frame such events in order to avoid blame). Because I provided a great deal of detail on Hurricane Harvey and Hurricane Maria in chapter 2, I omit a detailed account of those cases here.

Intentional Harm and Mass Shootings

The mass shootings I explored and compared occurred within three weeks of one another and involved dozens of grievous injuries and deaths: Benton, Kentucky's, Marshall County High School shooting (January 2018) and Parkland, Florida's Stoneman Douglas High School shooting (February 2018). Marshall High School involved 18 injured and 2 killed. Stoneman High School involved 17 wounded and 17 killed. In each case, a student or former student opened fire at the school as students went about their daily routines. The Marshall High School shooting never gained national media attention, public notoriety, or significant political interest. This is born out in news media coverage, in which a very low volume of national news stories left the tragedy at Marshall High School largely unknown outside local and regional contexts. Following the event, students at Marshall High School attacked the recurrent nature of school shootings in the United States. They blamed negligent government officials for doing little to stop gun violence at schools through gun regulation. However, local gun rights advocates quickly met those claims with derision and counterclaims stoking local resistance, which undermined the efficacy of the student protests that had initially been planned in the shooting's aftermath (Healy 2018).

By contrast, the Marjory Stoneman High School shooting became a nationally notorious event. Some of the reasons are obvious. Parkland is within the greater Miami-Dade, Broward, and Palm Beach metropolitan areas, the nation's seventh largest. This makes it a media market in its own right. It was also a horrific instance of death and injury, involving 17 deaths and 17 injuries. Yet geography and the number of deaths alone can't explain why Stoneman would become a public tragedy and Marshall High School would not. The attention the Stoneman High shooting achieved in conjunction with the character of the coverage and how the event was cast in the news also clearly played a part. The news coverage consistently featured aspects of the shooting that cohered with the trauma script. The news framed it in a manner that elevated its notoriety and highlighted the political conflict that would animate it. This included frequent expression of social blame by the aggrieved for the shooting; frequent moralization of the harm; and frequent political conflict, wherein student activists charged political elites with failing to make schools safe for kids. This fed back into the event's aftermath, generating more political conflict and controversy around the shooting and more coverage of those who had been harmed, who used their status as victims to seek social and political change.

Student protestors from Stoneman High School, some of whom had survived the shooting or had friends or siblings who did not, gained extensive media exposure. They aired their feelings that more should be done to stop school shootings; that these events reflected a moral-political failure; and that politicians, political parties, and "government" were to blame because of their collective unwillingness to regulate guns and stop gun violence at schools. While a mentally unstable 19-year-old shooter was the perpetrator, he was typically not the focus of accusation and moralizing in the shooting's aftermath. The focus of student accusations and protests was that the government had failed to keep "American kids" safe at school (Burns and Turkewitz 2018; Letters to the Editor 2018).

In response, gun rights groups also mobilized. They, too, focused on institutional failures. They blamed a school deputy for failing to fulfill his responsibility to confront the shooter because he was a coward. They blamed politicians and regulations that prohibited administrators and teachers from carrying guns on school campuses to protect students from shooters. They suggested that better mental health screening and earlier intervention by schools to identify potential shooters would likely have prevented the shooting. However, both sides tended to agree: government and governance were ultimately to blame.

A Municipal Debacle and Toxic Water

The final pair of case comparisons involved the contamination of municipal drinking water in two communities: Flint, Michigan, and Newark, New Jersey. Each community's municipal water supply was contaminated with lead and heavy metals from aging infrastructure and leaching water pipes. In Flint, the decision to switch water sources was not made by a locally elected official but by the governor-appointed ward of the city in 2014. The emergency manager and ward of Flint reportedly pushed through the switch to force the financially strapped city to save money. In Newark, the lead had been leaching into municipal water supplies for many years, but officials failed to act to stop it or to warn residents that their schools and even their home tap water might be contaminated. In both cases, children (and adults) tested positive for elevated levels of lead in their bloodstreams. Also, in both cases the most affected neighborhoods were poor and majority African American.

Flint became notorious in 2016 during the presidential campaign. While residents had complained of foul water—there was even a Legionnaires' disease cluster and several deaths as early as 2014—nothing of substance was done until a doctor found that local children had elevated levels of lead in their blood. An outside expert confirmed that its source was the local water (Hanna-Attisha et al. 2016). Social blame and moral claims quickly took on a distinctly partisan and racialized hue since the decision to switch water sources was made by an emergency manager appointed by the Republican governor rather than by a duly elected city manager or mayor in a strongly Democrat-leaning city. As the case unfolded, it became a nationally notorious public tragedy involving accusations of governmental negligence, intentional cover-up, and environmental racism (Clark 2018). Flint continues to garner headlines (Rio 2021).

In Newark, as early as 2014 high concentrations of lead were found in as much as 10% of the tap water samples taken in its water service areas. By 2016, 30 local public schools were found to have drinking fountains and faucets with lead levels exceeding federal standards. Local homes received water from the same delivery system as the schools, leading to general concern over tap water contamination as well. The results from 2017 tests revealed that 22% of Newark's water samples exceeded federal standards and required state action. In October 2018, even as the problem persisted the mayor proclaimed the city's water safe (Leyden 2018). Poor results from another engineering study pushed the city to suddenly change course, warning that children under six should not drink tap water. The city soon distributed 40,000 water filters and bottled water to residents. Yet Newark's lead water problem gained little outside attention, remaining primarily a local and state issue. It never became a nationally notorious public tragedy.

FRAMING PUBLIC TRAGEDY

To explore each case further, I engaged in comparative analysis and assessed how the media communicated trauma and loss in each event. Again, I sought to better understand the role of news media framing in reflecting and/or cultivating the conditions for public tragedy. Overall, the paired case comparisons of news coverage confirmed that the more notorious cases were more likely to highlight the elements associated with the trauma script. The framing of the publicly tragic events was more likely to involve claims of victimization in which social blame and moral-political failure were the principal explanations given for the events. News stories of the more notorious events highlighted political conflict, the predictable outcome of accusations of wrongdoing and social blame, and the moral failure the event came to represent. Public concern and sympathy were also featured in personal testimonials; memorials and commemorations; and collective demands for official recognition, investigation, and legal and regulatory action (cf. Doka 2003a; Jorgensen-Earp and Lanzilotti 1998). Except for Hurricane Harvey, the cases framed by the trauma script also resulted in many more stories and therefore a good deal more public attention.

A qualitative interpretation of the news stories was critical to understanding the differences in coverage and event framing. For example, while more stories were published about Hurricane Harvey than Hurricane Maria over a similar period, Harvey was far less "notorious" when we account for the kind of coverage each event received. As suggested in my analysis of political rhetoric and blame avoidance in chapter 2, more articles on Maria focused on the trauma script than was true for Harvey. Comparing stories that featured "social blame" (when news story content inferred or explicitly blamed the hurricane's trauma and loss on human accident, intention, or negligence), 55% of Maria stories referred to one or more of these social "causes" of suffering. Only 7% of Hurricane Harvey's stories did so. Illustrating how blame was cast, in an *LAT* story outlining the Trump administration's slow response to Hurricane Maria, the headline shouted, "'Aid Isn't Getting to People Fast Enough'; Puerto Rico Residents Suffer as Help Comes Slowly: After So Many Storms, Can a Thinly Stretched FEMA Come Through?" As the *LAT* story continued: "For many in Puerto Rico, Hurricane Maria's aftermath has been even more harrowing than the mighty storm itself. Amid growing warnings of a potential humanitarian crisis in the Caribbean island territory that is home to 3.4 million U.S. citizens, federal relief efforts were ramping up Wednesday, even as criticism mounted" (Hennessy-Fiske, Vives, and Etehad 2017).

My analysis demonstrates that the cases of trauma and loss that achieved national notoriety featured the elements of the trauma script in their descriptions and explanations of those crisis events. My findings also indirectly confirm that when the news media relies on the trauma script to frame a crisis event, the event is more likely to gain and hold public attention, elicit sympathy, provoke moral outrage, and sow social and political conflict. In the cases I explored that did not achieve sustained media attention, the elements of the trauma script were noticeably absent, as were public outpourings of anger, outrage, and political controversy. The stories carried fewer references to victimization, social blame, moralizing, and political controversy and conflict. Whether this began with media attention or was picked up on later by movements and advocates is difficult to say. At the very least, I would suggest they reinforce one another in ways that amplify a crisis, issue, or event.

Note that I am not making a causal argument about the construction of public tragedies. Rather, in exploring the discourses associated with each crisis event, I point to a relationship between the news media's encoding of such events and the public's decoding of them (Hall 1980). Again, how issues and events are framed in the news media helps shape perceptions of them and, just as importantly, reflects how they are perceived, received, and reacted to on the ground. This has accelerated with the entrance of social media (Margetts et al. 2015). This makes the news and related media an ideal target for research on societal machinations involved in events, since it represents both a source of influence and a proxy measure of sorts (Altheide 2002; Gitlin 1980; Letukas 2014; Tuchman 1978; Williams and Carpini 2011).

However, while admittedly important to the formation of public understanding, the news media is ultimately only one aspect of an encoding and decoding dialectic. How a given public encodes and decodes an issue or event can vary by source, belief, political ideology, and the timing and context within which the event occurred (Margetts et al. 2015; Tewksbury and Rittenberg 2009). That said, I approach the news media with the supposition that how it frames an issue or event remains an essential and influential source for categorizing and an analytic proxy for interpreting the events and issues of the day. To assess the public discourse regarding each case of crisis, I compared news stories using three general analytic classifications that correspond with core elements of the trauma script and public tragedy. They include the amount of *media attention* achieved by each crisis event, the prevalence of *social blame* in explanations of each event, and the association of *moral and political failure* with each event.

Media Attention

Because sustained media attention is significant to general awareness and notoriety, an event or issue must achieve it to become a shared experience (Hilgartner and Bosk 1988). Even if the trauma script is present, the event is unlikely to become publicly notorious without sustained media attention (Hoffman and Ocasio 2001). However, sustained media attention is a necessary but insufficient condition for producing a public tragedy; Hurricane Harvey provides a case in point. From the six months of coverage following its landfall, I retrieved 245 stories relating to the storm's impact(s) on southeast Texas, Louisiana, and the nation, the second-highest number of stories of the six cases I investigated. However, very few news stories about Harvey framed the storm and operational responses to it using the elements of the trauma script. For the most part, Harvey's news coverage neither blamed state or federal officials for victims' suffering nor moralized about the outcomes. What is more, accusations of moral failure and calls for social and political change were largely absent from the sample of news stories I analyzed regarding Hurricane Harvey. Hurricane Harvey was indeed a disaster, but not a public tragedy.

To assess and compare media attention to each case, I tallied the number of stories dedicated to an event, separately coding each story as either primarily (i.e., "primary") or secondarily (i.e., "secondary") about each crisis event. It was a primary story if the event in question was the central topic of the news story and a secondary story if the event was mentioned but was not the main focus. Both are important metrics since they suggest how disruptive an event or issue has become. Put another way, direct, sustained media in conjunction with indirect mentions of an event or issue are proxy measures of an event's "social impact." The distinction of primary and secondary also permitted a better sense of how much "direct, sustained attention" an event received versus "indirect mention." The more primary stories media outlets carried, the more significant an event was likely to be. So, for example, Hurricane Harvey, while having more total stories than Maria, had fewer primary stories (137 of 245 or 56%, versus Hurricane Maria with 144 of 192 or 75%). Maria, by contrast, had more primary stories than secondary stories, and a majority of the primary stories made politically charged references to federal, state, and local hurricane responses.

As expected, the cases that received greater media attention and a higher volume of primary stories were also more likely to encode those stories using elements of the trauma script. That is, the events framed as public tragedies received more attention and attention of a certain kind—they emphasized their tragic aspects as moral-political failures. For instance, the Marshall High School shooting (10 stories) and Newark water crisis (12 stories) received the fewest national stories of the six cases and far fewer stories than their comparative cases[5]—the Stoneman High School shooting (251 stories) and the Flint water crisis (120 stories). While comparing the paired cases is challenging given how few stories were devoted to events at Marshall High and in Newark, I suggest that the dearth of national news stories dedicated to them helps explain why neither became "public experiences" and therefore "publicly tragic" stories.

5. See table A.4.

Across the cases, those relying on elements of the trauma script to explain and describe suffering received the most primary stories and therefore more significant news media attention. The exception was, again, Hurricane Harvey, which received a great deal of news media attention, but accounts of the storm were not reliant on the trauma script. For instance, while Harvey received a higher volume of stories (245) than Hurricane Maria (192), none of those stories used the trauma script or relied on elements of it to describe or explain hurricane damage. Indeed, most of Harvey's stories focused on national business issues and the financial implications of the storm's disruption. They said little else about the storm. In fact, a significant number of the news stories regarding Harvey were also economically framed and related to the storm's impact on regional and national business interests. More than a third of Harvey's 245 stories were framed as business/economic stories, whereas only a tenth of Maria's 192 stories were framed as such. While this had a good deal to do with Houston's position as a U.S. petrochemical hub, it also reflected the way the media framed Harvey as a socially and politically unproblematic disaster.

By contrast, while few stories regarding Hurricane Maria were framed as business or economic affairs, many relied on trauma script elements to explain the suffering experienced on the island. These stories often featured claims of victimization and social blame for it. The suffering on the island was also more often moralized as unnecessary and avoidable, with the federal response being roundly criticized as a failure. Journalists and victims of the storm frequently took note or framed their comments by noting the president's Twitter tirades, which featured rants, racial and ethnic enmity, and political conflict. For example, in a story that featured one of then president Trump's Twitter screeds entitled "Trump Slams 'Ingrates' and Media for Not Recognizing Puerto Rico Relief Progress," the story related how Trump responded to criticism by San Juan's mayor, Carmen Yulin Cruz, that the administration was not doing enough for Puerto Rico: "'(They) . . . want everything to be done for them. . . . Such poor leadership ability by the mayor of San Juan, and others in Puerto Rico, who are not able to get their workers to help,' Mr. Trump said. 'They want everything to be done for them when it should be a community effort.' Ms. Cruz in turn accused the Trump administration of 'killing us with the inefficiency' and asked to 'make sure somebody is in charge that is up to the task of saving lives'" (Mauldin and Bender 2017).

When comparing media attention regarding the two high school shootings, news stories about both emphasized the injuries and associated trauma. Yet there was a clear difference in the volume of media attention paid to each shooting in its aftermath. The Marshall High School shooting was given only 10 national stories over six months. Stoneman High School garnered 251 stories over an equivalent time interval from across the three news services.

While statistical comparisons and generalizations are not possible when one case has such a small sample size, qualitative differences in coverage were notable. The attribution of "cause" in each shooting—about what or who was to blame—diverged considerably. In Marshall's case, as suggested already, tensions emerged among community members, blunting local expressions of political outrage by the victims and their families. For example, some students at Marshall High School intended to mobilize to protest the shooting at their school and, by extension, gun violence across the country. Yet unlike their peers at Stoneman High School, where student-victims mobilized a nationwide anti-gun-violence campaign just weeks later, Marshall students were locally challenged by other student-victims and even their own families, based on strong pro-gun-rights sentiments among the latter. A story entitled "Gun Country Backlash When Rural Students Speak Out for Limits" featured local reactions against students mobilizing against gun violence. As a consequence, student plans to mobilize were stymied:

> The teenagers in rural Kentucky decided they were fed-up after a 15-year-old with a handgun turned their high school into another killing ground, murdering two classmates. Like so many other students, they wrote speeches and op-ed essays calling for gun control, they painted posters and they marched on their State Capitol. The blush of activism made them feel empowered, even a little invincible. Then came the backlash. It started with sideways looks and laughter from other students in the hallways, they said. Friends deleted them from group chats and stopped inviting them over. On social media, people called the teenage activists "retards" and "spoiled brats," and said they should have been the ones to die during a shooting in Marshall County High School's student commons four months ago. In a more liberal city like Parkland, Fla., or at a rally in Washington, these students might

have been celebrated as young leaders. But in rural, conservative parts of the country where farm fields crackle with target practice and children grow up turkey hunting with their parents, the new wave of student activism clashes with bedrock support for gun rights. . . . Republican leaders expressed no desire to pass gun restrictions. Many residents and students agreed with them, saying that gun control would not stop the bloodshed at America's schools. "If we had more guns on campus with more teachers armed, we'd be a lot safer," said Layton Kelly, 17, a student who hid in a night-black classroom next to the scene of the shooting in Santa Fe. (Healy 2018)

This muddied the collective action context in Benton, suggesting that the local public was hardly unified regarding "who or what was to blame"— guns and lax gun laws or the school system and current gun restrictions. On both sides, however, the blame was squarely placed on the government and politicians either for failing to regulate guns and keep them out of the hands of unstable persons, on the one hand, or for overregulating guns and not allowing teachers to carry them to stop mentally ill shooters, on the other. This proved divisive enough to obstruct advocacy efforts and discouraged collective action on the part of students who felt victimized by the shooting but who believed gun laws and the government's inaction or action were at least partly to blame. Their lack of consensus and inability to generate a local protest movement also undermined sustained media attention, and the Marshall High School shooting quickly faded from public view.

Finally, the municipal water crises in Flint, Michigan, and Newark, New Jersey, also presented a robust set of contrasts, differences that were both quantitative (in terms of story volume) and qualitative (in terms of predominant story frames and story content). My story search revealed 120 stories over two years following Flint's toxic water event, beginning with local complaints about water quality when Detroit changed its water system to the Flint River and a local water purification system. In Newark's case, I gathered 12 stories over two years, beginning with the public announcement in 2016 that lead had been found in 30 public school water fountains, faucets, and spigots (Associated Press 2016; Ivers 2016). Like the comparisons of high school shootings, quantitative comparisons are difficult given Newark's small sample of 12 national news stories over six months. Newark, like Marshall High School, simply received too few national news stories to become a nationally notorious public tragedy, even though some of those stories did feature elements of the trauma script.

Social Blame

In addition to the volume of media attention, blame is a core aspect of the trauma script that both encourages sympathy for those harmed and imbues that harm with intention. As such, it also encourages outrage over cases framed as involving victimization. But the trauma script doesn't suggest simple blame, rather it suggests *social blame*. Social blame attributes harm to social and relational forces rather than relying on victim blaming, blaming an individual perpetrator, or blaming superordinate forces like fate or bad luck (Oorschot and Halman 2000). Social blame often also takes shape in association with moral criticism. The actions or omissions attributed to the government or to societal institutions are experienced as transgressions since they involve a perceived failure that unfairly harmed someone or something (Malle, Guglielmo, and Monroe 2014). In other words, those harmed have been victimized, and the perpetrator is society. Social blame lies at the emotional and moral center of the trauma script as a cultural framework for interpreting trauma and loss. It provides a compelling basis for the arousal of sympathy and outrage among a public.

Initially, to capture social blame in story content, I coded articles for their references to two general types of causation. The first type was fate: direct or indirect references to "God's plan," personal misfortune, the arbitrariness of life (i.e., nature), or simple bad luck. The other was human cause, which can be accidental, negligent, or intentional. An individual person, social relationships, or institutions may be blamed for wrongdoing. Even when the fault is placed on a person, their wrongdoing can be linked and even attributed to societal factors. The individual may be a stand-in or proxy, representing collective responsibility or "social blame." For instance, in the high school shooting cases, the individual shooters were clearly the "cause"—they intentionally shot the victims. Yet in none of the stories I coded were they held exclusively responsible. Indeed, in most stories the shooters were not presented as the primary cause. Instead, news stories targeted missed trustee opportunities to stop individual shooters before the incidents, neglectful parents and guardians, teachers and school counselors, the mental health system, the police and FBI, and the lack of strictly enforced gun laws. Therefore, while there were individual shooters, government, governance, and society in general were ultimately at fault, and social blame frequently explained "why" the shootings happened.

Apart from stories about Hurricane Harvey, social blame was the most frequently used explanation of trauma and loss across the other five cases of crisis. While stories that featured social blame often included references to individual perpetrators, without exception they also commented on the failure of societal institutions to stop the incidents. Again, even in the school shooting cases, the search for why and what happened rarely focused on individual shooters as individuals who made discrete decisions to shoot. Instead, stories discounted the perpetrator's agency, referring instead to their (assumed) mental illness and/or how the system had failed them. Institutions or their trustees failed to flag and therefore stop them before the shooting, or failed to respond and stop them once they engaged in the shooting. (See table A.4.)

In the Stoneman High School shooting, 90% of the 251 news stories addressing the cause of the shooting relied on "social blame" to explain it, while in the Marshall High School case, only half the news stories did so. These percentages may seem odd since it was indeed an individual shooter who "intentionally" caused the mayhem, injury, and death in each case. Two issues germane to the news coverage of these events help to make sense of this. First, many of the stories I analyzed did not identify a "cause" per se (outside of describing the shooting incident and leaving the shooter and his intentions largely unaddressed). Indeed, 44% of these stories conveyed the "cause" of the trauma and loss in the Stoneman High shooting as reflecting trustee negligence. In this framework, the school, counselors, the police, the FBI, or others had failed to act and stem the threat that the shooter or shooters like him posed to schools and schoolchildren. For example, in a story entitled "Parkland Shooting Survivors Not in Mood 'to Play Nice': Young Gun-Control Activists Reject Critics Who Call Them Disrespectful," students emphasized that they blamed government officials, the gun industry, and the National Rifle Association for enabling the shooter and school shooters in general. The shooter and his intentions were not developed in this story:

Since the shooting massacre at Marjory Stoneman Douglas High School on
Feb. 14, a student there named Sarah Chadwick has amassed a Twitter following of more than 150,000 people. On Thursday night, Chadwick decided to share a thought with them. Was it time for a message calling for
thoughts, prayers and privacy? Hardly. It was time to dunk on one of Florida's U.S. senators for taking donations from the National Rifle Assn. "We
should change the names of AR-15s to 'Marco Rubio' because they are so
easy to buy," Chadwick wrote, earning 45,000 retweets. This is what politicizing a tragedy looks like, and the kids are more than happy to keep doing
it. With 17 of their classmates and faculty shot to death, the students of the
school have become celebrity activists, whom many left-leaning Americans
have embraced as the new leaders of the nation's gun-control movement.
The students have been bold, confrontational, and even abrasive, rarely
holding back their anger, even if it means disrespecting their older, establishment opponents. They say what they mean. "Honestly, just using brutal
honesty—that's it," said student David Hogg, one of the movement's most
prominent voices. "I know people are saying it's intense. I would argue the
opposite. We're fighting for these kids that died because they can't fight
anymore. We're really trying to get justice for them." Hogg added: "Everybody deals with grief in a different way. For me, it's anger, and wanting to
prevent whatever caused it from happening again." The students' stridency
has added pressure on lawmakers and kept the shooting from fading from
the headlines. It has also insulted the feelings of right-wing adversaries at
several points, including by implying gun-rights supporters have the
17 deaths at Stoneman Douglas on their hands. "Sen. Rubio, it's hard to
look at you and not look down a barrel of an AR-15 and not look at [sus-
pected shooter] Nikolas Cruz," student activist Cameron Kasky told Rubio
at CNN's Wednesday night town hall with students, parents, and lawmakers. (Pearce 2018)

If a news story did not explicitly identify the shooter and the reasons
they carried out the shooting—that the shooter intended to hurt students
to satisfy a grievance, settle a score, gain notoriety, etc.—I did not code
it as an "intentional" frame. While in each case the shootings could have
been wholly blamed on an individual shooter, this did not occur. Even in
stories that accounted for the individual shooter and his intentions, the
stories framed the shooter's actions as having to do with larger social issues. Such stories recounted shooters' mental state as insular, troubled,
and angry and their upbringing as unsettled, characterized by negligent
parental figures. Therefore, even in events as individual and intentional

as the mass shootings at Marshall High and Stoneman High, social blame was consistently advanced as the chief cause behind each catastrophe.

In the news coverage, even those who mobilized to stop new gun regulations from being enacted did not simply blame the shooter. The gun rights establishment responded to student claims regarding failed political will and gun regulation by focusing on law enforcement at Stoneman High. Specifically, they focused on a sheriff's deputy who failed to intervene in time to save lives, labeling him in dereliction of his duty as an officer and a coward. Critics of calls to regulate guns also blamed policing and mental health counseling for missing early signs of the shooter's mental illness and advocated for more aggressive mental health checks to ensure that the mentally ill would be identified before becoming dangerous shooters. Like those calling for gun regulation, these claims and accusations were also social and institutional, targeting government and governance and relying on social blame rather than individual blame to explain the shooting.

News media coverage of Hurricane Maria and Harvey also greatly varied by how much social blame appeared in stories relating to the trauma and loss represented in each case. The proportion of news stories about Hurricane Harvey that conveyed social blame was the lowest of all six cases, with only 7% (18 of 245 stories) blaming groups or trustee institutions (i.e., the government or industry) for the trauma and loss associated with its landfall. Indeed, 4% of Harvey stories (10 of 245 stories) suggested directly or indirectly that southeast Texas had suffered an injury because of fate—that the cause of the storm and the trauma and loss that ensued could not be foreseen or averted and therefore no one was to blame. For example, a story titled "New Assault Douses Coast; Houston Sees Sun, but Nearby Cities 'at God's Mercy' as Heavy Rainfall Moves East" suggested that the storm left everyone in its path at "God's mercy": "Mayor Pro Tem Cal Jones estimated that at least 80 percent of the city, 90 miles east of Houston on the Gulf Coast, was underwater.... 'I'm helpless as the rest of them,' said Jones, who was trying to get to a store to obtain supplies for diabetic residents. 'We got caught by surprise. We weren't expecting this kind of flood. We didn't even get a command center because we weren't expecting this kind of outcome. Right now, we're at God's mercy'" (Jarvie, Hennessy-Fiske, and Pearce 2017). While comprising a small percentage of stories, this was the highest "fate" tally of the six cases I compared. And therefore, while personal loss, social blame, moral outrage, and political conflict were largely absent from coverage of Hurricane Harvey, so too were fate and chance as explanations. By comparison, 55% of Hurricane Maria stories (105 of 192 stories) suggested that social blame explained the suffering in Puerto Rico. Only 1 story of 192 regarding Maria suggested that fate had played a role in the damage suffered by the island. Social blame was expressed primarily in accusations against what many Puerto Ricans and their advocates believed was an abysmal federal and, to some extent, territorial government response reflective of callousness, political partisanship, and even racism (Leonhardt and Philbrick 2018).

Finally, Flint and Newark represent a contrast in how the story of community contamination was framed in the news. Social blame appeared in every single story about Flint's toxic water crisis. All of Flint's stories referenced one or more of the three social causes—intention, accident, or negligence—to explain local harms. (In fact, all the coded news stories relating Flint's toxic water crisis had one or more of these explanations embedded in them.) By contrast, coverage of Newark relied on social blame in 7 of 12 stories I collected. Negligence was the most prevalent explanation for the lead contamination of Flint's local water, with 85% (103 of 120 stories) suggesting governmental disregard. Indeed, among the Flint stories, 20% (25 of 120 stories) went so far as to suggest that lead in the water was a criminal act that was the product of "intention." Initially, residents shared a view that administrative neglect explained the contamination of local water. But once outside experts proved that lead and other contaminants were present in local water and public officials still failed to respond, some residents began to believe local and state officials were lying to residents and intentionally covering up the contamination. Adding to the outrage, media coverage held the federal government responsible for standing by and not intervening as residents were further sickened by contaminated municipal water. For example, a mother whose children had been contaminated by local water suggested that the actions of local officials went well beyond "telling white lies" and involved an intentional cover-up: "Ms. Loren, the mother of four, said her sons' skin remained irritated, and she is worrying obsessively about their lead levels, particularly that of her 11-year-old, who has learning disabilities. 'My trust in everybody is completely gone, out the door,' she said. 'We've been lied to so much, and these aren't little white lies. These lies are affecting our kids for the rest of their lives, and it breaks my heart'" (Goodnough, Davey, and Smith 2016). And in another instance, a resident called what officials did "criminal": "But many residents remain unsatisfied. 'Their one job was to make sure our water was safe,' Melissa Mays, a Flint resident, said of Michigan environmental officials. Ms. Mays, who has helped organize protests and been among the most outspoken critics of the water situation, said she worried about how the water might be affecting her young sons' health. 'They cut every corner,' she said. 'They did more to cover up than actually fix it. That's criminal'" (Smith 2016).

Overall, news of Hurricane Maria, the Stoneman High School shooting, and Flint's toxic municipal water had a much higher proportion of stories that used the social blame frame to explain what ultimately caused harm in each case. While social blame was present in the news coverage and explanations of trauma and loss for Hurricane Harvey, the Marshall High School shooting, and Newark's toxic municipal water, it appeared in a much smaller share of those stories. The emphasis on social blame to explain harm coheres with the culturally ascendant trauma script in which society is held responsible for victimizing those who have suffered. It is more likely to provoke public sympathy, outrage, and moral-political conflict. Put another way, in my limited sample of stories, the events that more frequently referred to this core element of the trauma script—innocent victims for whom social blame explained their injuries—generated more public attention, more outrage, more notoriety, and more political conflict than did the other cases. In short, events with explanations that pivot on social blame are more likely to become infamous, politically charged, and consequently publicly tragic.

Moral-Political Failure

If social blame lies at the emotional heart of the trauma script, moralized harms set the stage for social and political conflict. When sympathy, social blame, and moral outrage coincide, public tragedy is likely to result. As Luker (1984) documented in her landmark study of abortion politics, once an issue or event becomes a "moral concern," negotiation among stakeholders becomes nearly impossible. So it goes with other social crises too.

In contemporary society, when trauma and loss are moralized as reflecting failure or wrongdoing rather than bad luck, fate, or individual responsibility, social outrage and political conflict almost inevitably ensue. This is because when trauma and loss are moralized, they are cast as reflecting something that is immoral and wrong. The harm done was not random, accidental, or fated but appears unnecessary, unfair, or even deliberate. And when moralized, political conflict is inescapable. This appeared in the news stories as disputes among major stakeholders over how the crisis was explained and why it went so "wrong."

To capture moralized political strife in the news stories I collected, I coded for both "moralized harm" and the "political conflict" often associated with it. News stories that moralized harm typically posited that the damage was "bad," "heartless," and "meant to victimize," and therefore was immoral.[6] For instance, in the aftermath of the Stoneman High School shooting in Parkland, Florida, public comments conveyed its immorality, indeed its "evilness":

> Jeb Niewood, president of the Friendship Initiative, said two of the victims—Jaime Guttenberg and Gina Montalto—volunteered at his center, where they spent time weekly reading, playing music and doing yoga with children with special needs. . . . Both girls had volunteered with the Friendship Initiative for more than a year, he said, dedicating time each weekend for months at a time. "The kids learn how to socialize, and our student volunteers learn lessons in humanity" . . . he said. . . . "That's what both Jaime and Gina believed in, that you can change the world through love and friendship," he said. "The only answer to evil is through love and understanding, and that's what these girls believed in." (McWhirter and Bauerlein 2018)

The cases with the highest percentage of news stories with moral characterizations linked to victim suffering were also the more notorious cases I explored. Again, Hurricane Maria, Flint's toxic water problem, and the Stoneman High School shooting all involved more frequent moralizations and the kinds of partisan political conflicts typically associated with them. And while Marshall High only had 10 national news stories and therefore never achieved national notoriety, half of those stories moralized the shooting too. This is understandable given the shocking nature

---

6. See table A.5.

of school shootings: a teenager shooting and killing other teenagers at a high school. One reason for such moralization is that events like this defy rational explanation and provoke reference to the sacred and profane while also eliciting questions about the integrity of society (Douglas 1966; Durkheim 1951; Kellner 2015a). When events are this upsetting, people look at society and ask what is wrong with "us" that we would "allow them to happen." They blame systems of authority and oversight for not having been vigilant enough. Another reaction could be to blame atrocious acts on "insanity" to avoid taking responsibility altogether. The carnage might have been averted if "they" had only done more.

As for the more notorious cases of crisis, the highest proportion of moral claims making and political conflict was in news coverage about Flint, where lead-tainted municipal water poisoned residents over a prolonged period of time and understandably generated extreme levels of fear, social blame, and moral outrage among residents. Public outcry resulted in criminal charges being levied against the local and state officials in charge of Flint's transition to Flint River water. But it also spread fear to other U.S. communities, who began to question the cleanliness of their water systems (Fortin 2017). Nearly half the news stories about Flint's water crisis included moralized references to city and state actions in explanations of why the water became contaminated and why residents were not informed or protected for so long. Community activists and advocates initially accused local and state governments of wholesale disregard and negligence. Over time, claims and feelings hardened as evidence mounted, as did increasing references to an intentional cover-up. Indeed, three-quarters of Flint's stories in my sample contained both moral claims—for example, references to "criminal conduct" or "evil" intentions—and mentions of political conflict. In the following example, the story joins the comments of a lawyer representing Flint residents to those of a city councilman from Flint who opines that this was a man-made crisis "like Katrina"—another racialized public tragedy—that was far from over for his city:

> "We are asking a federal court to step in because the people of Flint simply cannot rely on the same government agencies that oversaw the destruction of its infrastructure and contamination of its water to address this crisis," Dimple Chaudhary, a lawyer with the Natural Resources Defense Council, said in a statement. Scott Kincaid, a city councilman, said Flint was still in

"triage" mode, far from a permanent solution. "This is a man-made disaster," he said. "It's like Katrina." He added, "I'm suspecting that there are areas in our community that are still going to be recovering years from now." (Bosman 2016)

The public discourse about Hurricane Maria took a similar direction. Initially, news about the hurricane focused on describing the damage done by wind, rain, and an ocean storm surge. But weeks after the storm's passage, Puerto Ricans were still mostly without power in the countryside, in villages, and even in main cities. Many islanders had little or no access to food, water, or reliable shelter. Especially for the elderly and infirm, these became deadly times. As the situation on the island deteriorated and the federal response floundered, the news discourse also changed from simple descriptions to personalized accounts inflected with allegations of poor response and organization and descriptions of the toll on Puerto Ricans.

Not a month before Maria, Hurricane Harvey had been used to trumpet how the Trump White House could successfully manage a crisis. Yet in the aftermath of Maria, Harvey was used by journalists, political elites, and those who suffered on the island as a point of comparison in their evaluations. The comparisons were not flattering:

Increasingly desperate local officials have demanded more help from the federal government and faster delivery of what aid is coming. "They're going very slowly, the aid isn't getting to people fast enough. We seem to be losing a lot of time in jurisdictional trifles," San Juan Mayor Carmen Yulin Cruz said in an interview Wednesday. "People are dying," she said. "We don't have time for that." The White House has fought back hard against complaints that the federal government's response in Puerto Rico has been less robust than in hurricane-hammered Texas and Florida. "We've gotten A-pluses on Texas and on Florida," Trump told reporters this week. "And we will also on Puerto Rico." (Hennessy-Fiske et al. 2017)

In the aftermath of the storm, as the federal response dragged on, the discourse regarding Maria was also shaped by the contrast: the quick and concerted response to Harvey and the slow, ineffectual federal response to Maria reflected something more than chance, island inaccessibility, or simple negligence. The response reflected a lack of concern, political partisanship (Puerto Rico overwhelmingly votes Democrat), and even racism, given the island's predominantly Latin population and the president's derisive comments. These are explicitly moral claims. In Maria's case, a quarter of the 192 news stories "moralized" the trauma and loss experienced on the island. Half "politicized" those harms by linking failure to political actors and their governmental surrogates. As such, nearly half of all the news stories about Hurricane Maria either moralized, politicized, or moralized *and* politicized the harm inflicted on Puerto Ricans. By comparison, only 2 of Harvey's 245 stories moralized the harms associated with that storm or criticized governmental or industry response to it. And only 6% of Harvey stories politicized, in some manner, the government's response to it—a stark contrast to reporting on Maria.

Finally, as suggested in the discussion of media attention, an act as horrific as a mass shooting lends itself to moralizing and therefore to political conflict and controversy. Over time, the ongoing gun rights versus gun regulation fight in the United States has narrowed the issue to a two-sided affair, with both sides putting forth moral arguments to support their claims (cf. Luker 1984). What is more, both sides of this issue are now well-represented by an established messaging apparatus ready to activate politically when an event of this kind occurs—indeed, the sides prepare in advance for its inevitability (Kellner 2015a).

Reflecting the fraught and now overtly political character of the issue, the news stories on Marshall County and Stoneman High School both carried such moralizations. They also discussed political conflicts over gun control regulations or loosening restrictions to allow teachers and administrators to carry firearms on school campuses. Again, half of the 10 stories relating to the Marshall County High School shooting moralized the death and injury caused there. But only 1 of the 10 stories politicized the shooting, noting that gun regulations would be taken up at Kentucky's state house. By comparison, nearly half of the 251 news stories regarding the shooting at Stoneman High School discussed political conflict and controversy related to the shooting, and 13% contained moral explanations for the injury and death caused there. These news stories often recounted the efforts of Stoneman High School students, their parents, and gun regulation advocates to change federal and Florida state laws and the laws of other states to restrict access to guns. This led to predictable political resistance as gun rights activists and gun advocacy groups mobilized, fomenting a national clash over access to firearms and gun rights, victims' rights, and the treatment of student victims in the political arena (Victor 2018).

CONCLUSION

Broadcast and internet news and social media now cue one another in a hyperaccelerated media cycle that amplifies the urgency and emotion associated with many stories and issues (Allcott and Gentzkow 2017; Castillo et al. 2014; Stoycheff et al. 2018). The contemporary communication ecology, therefore, appears as a recursive loop exposing a hybrid system of relations between mainstream news and social media sources. This system of relations accelerates the pace of issue and event coverage while opening it to new levels of spectacle, hyperbole, and politicization (Chadwick 2017). These are all crucial ingredients in the making of public tragedy.

Print, broadcast, and internet news also remain essential to this new communication ecology. "The news" continues to play a central role in informing the public about events and issues about which it would otherwise remain largely unaware (Stoycheff et al. 2018). The news media informs the public by encoding issues and events, relying on spectacle and melodrama to grab audience attention and make the news easily consumable (Adut 2008; Altheide 2002; Kellner 2003). Four of the five news frames that the media typically relied on to motivate and convey the news—the human interest frame, the conflict frame, the morality frame, the responsibility frame, and the economic frame (Neuman, Just, and Crigler 1992; Semetko and Valkenburg 2000)—strongly cohere with the trauma script and tend to support and even reinforce the conditions that define public tragedies as social and political events. Therefore, to understand public tragedy, one must address the contemporary news media's role in cultivating the public sentiments from which they emerge and that predict their growing social and political importance.

In this chapter, I explored the news media's role in framing crisis events and the trauma and loss associated with them to expose what sets publicly tragic events apart from the sad but routine disasters of the day. I accounted for the historical transformation leading to today's reigning media logic and compared how the news media framed six cases of crisis. In so doing I exposed how consistently contemporary news frames cohere with the trauma script and thus help to cultivate public understandings and emotions associated with public tragedy. Why? Because when journalists are professionally committed to exposé, and news outlets frame events by relying on spectacle and melodrama, they also tend to emphasize aspects of the trauma script. The script emphasizes the unjustified suffering of a victim (or victims), where hapless, disorganized, unresponsive, or malfeasant political elites, government administrators, corporate managers, civic interests, and social movement groups, or even general social and cultural elements, are socially blamed for the harm they have done. A crisis scenario is more likely to capture the public's attention and gain its sympathy while sowing political controversy when cast in this manner. This in turn heightens the probability that an event will gain further notoriety and become publicly tragic.

The cases I compared across three mainstream news media outlets indicate that this held whether the initial cause of harm was "natural," as in the case of hurricanes, or "intentional," as in school shootings carried out by individuals. Three of the six paired cases I investigated were nationally notorious, partly because the harm they caused was attributed to the actions or omissions of such trustees. In each case, the trauma and loss were quickly labeled moral-political failures and condemned as tragic, which led to yet more national notoriety, social and political accusation, and collective action in the name of those victimized. In a phrase, they became publicly tragic.

While I maintain that the trauma script is both a cultural construct and a means of understanding risk and harm, I am not suggesting that *public tragedy* itself is "just a social construct," only partly or wholly accurate, or even inaccurate. Instead, in this chapter I have highlighted how the news media emphasized story frames that comported with the trauma script. In so doing, it fanned the flames of public tragedy as a social and cultural construct that comports with our epoch's "structure of feeling." Indeed, the trauma script is only one of several possible cultural explanations that could be used to explain the causes of trauma and loss. Again, these could include God's hand or fate, bad luck, unintentional mistake, random accident, or personal responsibility. Public tragedies also reflect the increased frequency with which the media and the general public emphasize the unwarranted, blamable, and moralized nature of injury. This encourages the politicization of harm as those blamed are held to account. Blaming someone or something for harm is likewise routinely contested by those being accused (or those who politically support them). Therefore, the trauma script pushes instances of trauma and loss toward moral interpretations that tend to polarize political discussion and response.

Having explored how a prevailing journalistic ethic, media logic, and communication ecology preconfigure the conditions for public tragedy, I now turn to the role of victims and victims' advocates in the construction of public tragedy. Those who have suffered significant harm lie at the center of this process. Understanding why public sympathy manifests for some victims and not others is essential to understanding the emergence of public tragedy. Events of this kind pivot on the public emotionally connecting and identifying with the victims of what is seen as unnecessary and avoidable harm.

4 Advocating Public Tragedy

SYMPATHY, CELEBRITY, AND TRAGIC HARMS

At the center of public tragedy are those subjected to trauma and loss: the victims. The perceived wrongs inflicted on them supply public tragedies with their center points: claims of perpetration and victimization, moral failure, social blame, and political conflict and controversy. As developed in prior chapters, contemporary societal dynamics have sown a widespread sense of vulnerability and amplified sensitivity to and sympathy for the victims of trauma and loss. As I've argued, sympathy is especially likely when those harmed are held to be the blameless victims of injuries perpetrated by societal actions or omissions. Indeed, I argue that the ascendancy and conventionalization of the trauma script, the proliferation of claims to societal victimization, and the valorization of "victimhood" as a claim type and political identity are distinctive sociopolitical features of the early twenty-first century (cf. Best 1997; Jeffery and Candea 2006; Ochs 2006).

And yet while claims to victimhood have become politically efficacious, such claims are fraught with personal and collective risk. To gain public sympathy and support, a victim (or victims) must forge an emotional connection with the public or some significant share of it. To develop that connection, the public must see a victim as blameless and their suffering as worthy of support. Yet the ideal victim in the Western cultural tradition is weak and vulnerable, which is just as likely to provoke pity and stigmatization as compassion (Goffman 1963). Therefore, while claims of victimhood can be politically efficacious, they continue to be double-edged (Dunn 2004; Ryan 1971). Understanding why public sympathy manifests for some victims and not others is therefore essential to understanding the emergence of public tragedy, since events of this kind pivot on the emotional connection between the public and those who claim to have been harmed.

In this chapter I explore claims of victimhood and the role they play in cultivating public attention, sympathy, and support for those who claim to have experienced trauma and loss of some kind (Ott and Aoki 2002). Integral to claims making and politics of any kind are communicative processes—formal, informal, scripted, and unscripted. In chapter 3 I documented the media's role in framing crises and promoting sentiments associated with public tragedy. When media coverage captures the public's attention, it can promote concern and sympathy for those harmed. As also demonstrated in chapter 3, the news media and journalism, through a heavy reliance on several standard news frames and an exposé ethic, frequently draw attention to and emphasize aspects of any given crisis that cohere with the trauma script. The news media often portrays, for example, the unnecessary suffering of victims at the hands of hapless, disorganized, unresponsive, or even malfeasant political elites, government administrators, corporate managers, and civic and social movement groups. Perceptions that those affected have not only been harmed by circumstance or accident but victimized by uncaring, negligent, or criminal trustees can stoke scandal and public outrage and, from that, political crisis, on the one hand, and sympathy and support for the victims, on the other.

Clearly, perceptions and attributions of harm and victimhood play an integral role in whether victims gain public sympathy and support. Furthermore, whether trustee institutions, through their actions or omissions, might have stopped the threat or done more to prevent it and whether they are judged partly or wholly responsible also plays a significant role in encouraging public tragedy. It therefore matters how victims of trauma and loss explain, express, and narrate their harms as they pursue recognition, sympathy, and support. Prior research shows that victims' advocates and social movements play a vital role in cultivating that sympathy through their public framing of victims and their injuries and what they suggest caused them (Best 1997, 1999; Dunn and Powell-Williams 2007; Rothenberg 2002). What is more, because the mainstream news and entertainment media now frequently features stories told from the perspectives of victims and survivors that initially trended on social media, one can see how its influence over public perceptions has recently and dramatically expanded (Margetts et al. 2015). This is significant because victims' advocates' political narratives and claims-making practices have a lasting impact on subsequent political discourses (Dunn and Powell-Williams 2007). They also shape political outcomes, as reflected in victims' recognition and support (Barker 2007; Dunn 2004; Fominaya and Barberet 2013; Lamb 1999b; Ochs 2006; Rothenberg 2003).

In the chapter that follows, I relate the role that victims' claims making, victims' advocacy, and victimhood play in the emergence of public tragedy sui generis. I begin with a historical accounting of their critical aspects, including the meanings of *victim* and *victimhood* as cultural constructs and why they have emerged in the twenty-first century as both publicly resonant and politically consequential. This also involves analyzing how suffering and victimization are evaluated presently and examining what is required for public sympathy to manifest as recognition and support or, in contrast, why it does not. I relate how the victim industry (Best 1997) emerged and why it relies on the trauma script to gain public sympathy and political recognition. Finally, I show how victims and victims' advocates use the trauma script to deepen the general public's identification with their causes and promote a new kind of renown, which I term "tragic celebrity." I use news coverage of George Floyd's murder and, a year later, the trial of his murderer, Derek Chauvin, to illustrate the current role of tragic celebrity in promoting sympathy for and identification with the victimized, and indeed, in generating public tragedies. I conclude with observations regarding what the ascendance of "political victimhood" suggests about contemporary social and political relations and their manifestations as public tragedy.

THE RISE OF POLITICAL VICTIMHOOD

As developed in chapter 1, in the aftermath of World War II a steady flow of issues, events, and social movements began to undermine public confidence in "the modern project," revealing risks that were the outcome of contemporary social, political, and technological forces that were seemingly out of control and that could victimize anyone at any time (Beck, Giddens, and Lash 1994). As the state consolidated its authority and set itself up as the ultimate arbiter of societal well-being, it increasingly became the target of criticism, accusation, and blame when things went awry. Public cynicism has also intensified over time as the state has been repeatedly exposed as a partisan interest based on its support of elite concerns and capital accumulation over nonelites and the common good (Habermas 1975). This has propagated a structure of feeling that has undermined both governance authority and trust in the state and its surrogates as levels of uncertainty have intensified with accelerated social, political, and economic change (Beamish, Grattet, and Niemeier 2017; Beck 1992; Habermas 1975; Harvey 2014; see also Pew Research Center 2019).

Consistent with the current structure of feeling and a growing sense of vulnerability and distrust, many journalistic, therapeutic, legal, and academic professionals had, by the 1980s, professionally and ideologically committed themselves to "exposing" powerful institutional machinations for the victims harmed through institutional mistakes, misconduct, and malfeasance. In what Best (1997) terms the "victim industry," professional advocates of this kind have worked assiduously to uncover, represent, and even benefit from identifying the dangerous trends and unjust social and political relations that have injured and victimized innumerable persons. Formulaic narratives of trauma and loss, while used to publicize harm and gain public support, can also serve those who have been harmed as accounts of "the self," mediating how they come to understand and feel about their personal experience(s). Indeed, they can result in new retrospective interpretations and, arguably, new memories (Davis 2005a, 2005b). Motivated by various interests, from the conservative victims' rights crusade to progressive civil rights movements, an unfortunate consequence of the emergence of this "industry" has been its cultivation of an increasingly cynical and fragmented public with a newfound penchant to blame "society" for virtually any sort of personal hardship as reflecting collective suffering.

This further reflects in part the success of this industry in persuading the American public that many of people's "personal troubles" are not theirs alone. Rather, as C. Wright Mills (2000) exhorted in *The Sociological Imagination*, personal troubles also reflect societal forces and factors that make them eminently "public issues."[1] Aware that their problems often reflect public issues, Americans increasingly hold trustee authority and institutions accountable. Indeed, connecting individual experience and suffering to "American culture" and to governance institutions such as Congress, police, industry, and education has become relatively common. The shift toward social blaming for personal and collective hardship has also played a part in diminished trust in civic and societal institutions of a range and type as well as citizen trust in one another (Dimock 2020; Gallup 2022; Jones 2020; Pew Research Center 2019). This increased distrust and cynicism has in turn promoted a mounting sense of vulnerability among the American public, while also sensitizing them to the plight of victims and processes of victimization. This has opened the door to what Best labels an "ideology of victimization" (1997:10). The ideology of victimization is a political narrative generated by victims' advocates and the victim industry in the 1970s to address America's disregard and neglect of victims. Its basic elements include a belief that victimization is a shared experience, that it represents a life-crippling malady, that it is morally unambiguous—perpetrators are wrong, the violated innocent—and that it requires active exposure. Moreover, due to the fragility of the victimized, their claims must both be declared and uncontested so that they will be protected from further harm. And finally, because of the potential for victim stigma—that is, pity, powerlessness, and victim blaming—victims' advocates suggest that more appropriate labels other than "victim" be used, such as "survivor" and "recovering" (Best 1997:13; Davis 2005b).

Prior research like Best's that focused on victims, victimization, and victimhood (Best 1999; Barker 2007; Dunn 2004; Jeffery and Candea 2006; Ochs 2006; Rothenberg 2002; Weed 1990) parallels more recent research documenting the twenty-first-century rise of victim-centered moral cultures (Alexander 2004; Campbell and Manning 2014, 2018; Eyerman 2001; Lukianoff and Haidt 2015). These moral cultures have taken shape in contemporary movements that self-consciously use victimhood as a

---

1. For Mills, public issues were matters that transcended "the local" and the range of one's private life (2000:7–8).

means of political empowerment. These and related authors have documented such moral movements, labeling them as involving "cultural trauma" (Alexander 2004), "vindictive protectiveness" (Lukianoff and Haidt 2018), and "victimhood culture" (Campbell and Manning 2018).

As detailed in chapter 1, cultural trauma theory seeks to explain how and why collective memories of trauma and loss shape the collective identities of specific groups, ethnicities, and nations. Alexander (2004), for example, theorized "cultural trauma" using the Holocaust and several other horrific historical events that, through active cultural reconstruction, became the basis for group identities. Likewise, Eyerman (2001) sought to explain the cultural trauma that resulted from American slavery. Like Alexander's treatment of the Holocaust, Eyerman's recounting of the cultural trauma resulting from slavery emphasized the role that socially constructed collective memories play in the formation of group identities and trauma-based solidarities.

From such memories, Alexander and Eyerman argue that an ongoing intergenerational "culture of trauma" can result (see also Sztompka 2000). Yet cultural trauma is not natural or preordained. The transformation of individual suffering into collective trauma reflects cultural work pursued by "carrier groups"—the agents behind the culture of trauma process (Alexander 2004:11). Through protests, accusations, speeches, meetings, correspondence, and storytelling, carrier groups make cultural trauma "real" by framing and even generating new memories that can become articles of faith among the "victimized" and their supporters. Therefore, the "truth" of such cultural trauma is not its empirical validation but the carrier's ability to convince others of the suffering they advocate against.

Reflecting the actions of such carrier groups, Lukianoff and Haidt (2015) recount a nationwide movement that has taken shape on U.S. college campuses that relies on claims of victimization to limit speech and expression in the name of protecting vulnerable students from psychological and social trauma. Lukianoff and Haidt suggest that the contemporary campus victims' movement represents an emergent cultural orientation they term "vindictive protectiveness." The movement has sought to restrict speech deemed hurtful to vulnerable groups while also challenging the scholastic canon to include marginalized voices in campus offerings. Carrier groups use the claim of victimization to justify new guidelines in academe such as limiting emotionally damaging curricular "triggers" and providing safe language and role models.

According to Lukianoff and Haidt (2015), activists work with several presumptions. In particular, they are motivated by a belief that students (and people in general) are vulnerable and have fragile psyches that require protection. In this view, psychological trauma is a form of victimization that can permanently harm those subjected to it (Sue et al. 2007). Those who justify the movement's policing of speech and social expression claim that the university and, ultimately, the nation must provide more safety for people hurt by words, ideas, and actions that threaten them and make them feel disregarded or erased (Sue 2010).

Vindictive protectiveness relies on emotional reasoning that is intensified by partisan thinking and the emergence of social media platforms. Via social media, advocates and carrier groups communicate grievances and impassioned pleas to sympathetic others. In so doing, they strive to recruit like-minded people while also accusing and denouncing "perpetrators" for acts of victimization. Lukianoff and Haidt (2015) track the roots of vindictive protectiveness to a cultural change in parenting in the 1980s. Child safety became an obsession, reflecting a surge in fear-based news media reportage of child abductions, school bullying, and by the 1990s, school shootings. This provoked fear and mounting distress among a generation of parents, prompting them to communicate to their millennial children that "life is dangerous and adults will do everything in their power to protect you from harm" (Lukianoff and Haidt 2015:44). According to Lukianoff and Haidt, this further promoted efforts to control talk and behavior judged to be harmful, psychologically traumatic, and therefore dangerous to one's health.

In parallel research, Campbell and Manning (2018) studied the emergence and manifestation of a "culture of victimhood" on American university campuses. For them, it represents a means of social control that, like vindictive protectiveness, is also achieved by policing speech and personal expression. They document an increasing number and type of harmful speech claims, which have accelerated over the last two decades as the internet and social media have exploded. Aggrieved individuals have increasingly used social media resources to publicize personal grievances (including accusations of racist, sexist, gendered, and ableist language and behavior) to which they have been subjected at school, work, and home. In counseling and therapeutic circles, these are referred to as "micro-aggressions," intentional and unintentional verbal, behavioral, and environmental indignities that harm a person or group (Sue 2010; Sue et al. 2007). Advocates claim microaggressions cause short- and long-term psychological distress and even trauma. As more websites, blogs, YouTube videos, TikTok posts, Facebook posts, and X (formerly Twitter) hashtags have focused on microaggressions, they have sowed public concern, sympathy, and moral outrage. The amplification of social media content, news articles, op-eds, pundit columns, and academic studies has pushed the concept of microaggression, the types of claims being made, and their perceived legitimacy further into the mainstream (Campbell and Manning 2014:694).

According to Campbell and Manning (2014), victimhood culture builds from but breaks with prior cultural orientations. It demonstrates the penetration of the state and the rule of law into everyday dispute resolution, supplanting the "self-help" ethic that characterized culture in premodern contexts with a focus on "honor" (Black 2011; Campbell and Manning 2018; Cooney 1998, 2014; Leung and Cohen 2011). Victimhood culture also involves moving away from modern culture's admonition to "turn a cheek" to insult, supplanting it with extreme sensitivity to slights. Insult is treated as a significant trauma and therefore an instance of victimization. However, because victimhood culture does not value violence to recoup honor or exact revenge, it relies on accusation, blame, and public shaming as its social control mechanisms. Therefore, through public appeals for recognition and sympathy, often pursued through personal testimonials and exposé videos posted on social media platforms, those who feel victimized seek sympathy and demand that authorities address the trauma to which they have been subjected.

VICTIMHOOD AND PUBLIC SYMPATHY

How do people outside the movement or carrier group come to recognize those claiming to be harmed? What role does sympathy play in this kind of victim recognition and support? And what role does sympathy for a victim (or victims) play in the emergence of public tragedies as volatile political events?

Victimhood is the state of self-identifying as a victim, a condition of having been hurt (whether fatally or not) because of the actions or omissions of someone or something else. Admittedly, victimhood can also be the outcome of "chance." Yet as I have argued, God, nature, and bad luck as explanations of trauma, loss, and misfortune do not comport with the contemporary notion of victimhood that underlies public sympathy and public tragedies. Understanding how victimhood is evaluated is essential: the status and the power of victims' claims pivot on whether the public or some significant proportion of it feels sympathy for them and their cause. Likewise, public tragedy hinges on public acknowledgment of and sympathy for the victims of tragic circumstances. When positively judged (see table A.6), sympathy can result in—even spur—admiration for those who have suffered through or survived an ordeal. But trauma and loss can also be negatively evaluated: victims can be held personally responsible for the harm done to them or they can be portrayed as blameworthy and be stripped of public support (Lamb 1999a). The capacity of those who have suffered to gain public sympathy reflects contemporary cultural beliefs and expectations about what (or who) has harmed them, what (or who) is to blame, and whether the victims share responsibility for their harms.

Contemporary social relations further shape these beliefs and expectations about victimhood and have encouraged sympathy for victims when the story of their suffering coheres with the trauma script. Again, the trauma script lends suffering both more emotional salience and political heft. Put another way, when people see themselves reflected in those who have become the victims of a public tragedy, they are more likely to empathize with their trauma and loss. This has facilitated the reframing of many formerly "private traumas" into "publicly tragic" events. And again, while sympathy may be more likely, it is not automatic even in today's social and political environment.

How then do victims and their political advocates communicate their losses in a way that commands moral legitimacy and evokes public sympathy? First, sympathy for victims and cases of victimization is not automatic but involves culturally informed moralizing that further reflects a discrete set of "feeling rules" (Bellah et al. 1996). Second, we also know from prior research that when claims of victimization are perceived as morally legitimate, they receive more "political empathy" and resources than do claims and claimants that do not (Barker 2007; Dunn 2004; Fominaya and Barberet 2013; Ochs 2006; Williams 1995). Research on victims of crime and domestic abuse, among other groups of victims, is instructive. It has shown that sympathy for a victim reflects how closely their biography and the circumstances of the harms done to them cohere with a Western cultural ideal of "the victim." To gain full sympathy, the victim must not have been engaged in behavior that would provoke harm nor be in a place or situation where injury might be expected (Christie 1986). The more a victim conforms to this cultural ideal and therefore the feeling rules for sympathy, the greater the moral legitimacy their claims command. Without moral legitimacy, neither public recognition, sympathy, nor support are likely to emerge (Barker 2007; Dunn 2004; Fominaya and Barberet 2013; Ochs 2006; Williams 1995).

Reflecting the Western cultural definition, when we evaluate victims, we focus on their perceived agency or passivity, subsequently creating positive or negative judgments. Dunn (2004) suggests a fourfold table of ideal-typical "victim constructions" (see table 2). When we view victims as agents and view their claims positively, we view them with admiration and respect and hold them to be "survivors" rather than passive, vulnerable subjects. By contrast, when we cast victims as agents but negatively judge them, we often blame them for their victimization. This was the case in early accounts of domestic violence, which frequently held that women precipitated their own victimization (Dunn 2004). When people view victims as passive recipients of harm and victimization but judge them positively, we are more inclined to view them sympathetically if they are vulnerable. This coincides with the "ideal victim" in Western culture (Christie 1986). Finally, when we view victims as passive recipients of harm and victimization due to their own weakness, we tend to negatively judge them as contemptible and therefore stigmatize them for the harm they have experienced. This is consistent with Ryan's (1971) classic work on stigmatized poverty in the United States in which he coined the phrase "blaming the victim." See Dunn (2004:237–44) for the original of table 2.

An important lesson from this and related research on victim constructions is that the status of a victim and claims to victimization are

Table 2   Ideal Victim Constructions

	Positive judgment	*Negative judgment*
Agential	Admired/respected	Blamed/responsible
Nonagential	Sympathized/empathy	Pitied/shameful

Source: See Dunn (2004:237–44) for the original reproduced here.

frequently subject to competing political-cultural renditions. In the aftermath of crisis, victims and their advocates seek to frame their suffering as admirable or noble, while their detractors suggest that they should at best be pitied and at worst ignored or even blamed. Which victim typification prevails plays a significant role in how the public views a victim (or victims), leading to evaluations of whether their injuries deserve sympathy or scorn (Dunn 2004).

This process of evaluating and labeling a victim's harm as worthy (or unworthy) of sympathy plays an important role in the construction of public tragedies. In victimhood discourse, victims desiring sympathy must frame their harms to cultivate political empathy while avoiding the pitfalls of being blamed for the injuries they are declaring. Cultural constructions of victimhood, are therefore, fundamental to understanding public tragedy since acknowledgment, sympathy, and moral outrage (rather than denial, pity, and blame) hinge on political empathy for the harms a victim or victims have endured.

In addition to fulfilling sympathy rules, however, victims and their political advocates must also contend with a public with an exceedingly short attention span and media outlets committed to a model of news and entertainment featuring a constant search for fresh spectacle and trauma (Meek 2016; Rothe 2011). The media and public attention tend to move on quickly to the next traumatic event before those harmed receive the attention or care they may require. This can push the victims of trauma into the political domain as they seek relief, justice, or both and mobilize to have their suffering be socially and politically acknowledged. This intersection has consequences for understanding how and why some losses are recognized as publicly tragic while others are not. It also exposes the difficulties victims confront when trying to reach a "breakthrough" and gain public recognition for their suffering.

Therefore, even when victims gain a measure of attention, sympathy, and support, they are often subject to a foreshortened cycle of issue attention. The "issue-attention cycle" supplies a heuristic that helps explain public response, such as initial public support and a tendency for that attention to fade quickly. This also explains why the victims of trauma must often mobilize and seek aid (Gottlieb 2015; Henry and Gordon 2001; Kinnick, Krugman, and Cameron 1996; Zhang et al. 2017). According to Downs's (1972) classic account of the issue-attention cycle, the public's ability and willingness to focus on any social issue or event reflects the nature of the problem and media communications about it. Downs identifies the attention cycle as involving a discrete sequence of stages, including the preproblem phase, alarmed discovery, cost realization, declining interest, and the postproblem stage. In the preproblem stage, the issues provoking the crisis usually go unacknowledged. While experts and victims may be aware, the public is typically naive about the issues and the scale, scope, or intensity of it. During alarmed discovery, the public is shocked by the problem. Soon thereafter, with heightened attention, the public becomes increasingly aware of the costs associated with its resolution. This typically involves realizing that resolution will be expensive and that its cause is at least partly the result of extant social, economic, and political relations. Therefore, resolution cannot be achieved without significant sacrifice; the victims cannot be protected without it. Realizing that the problem is expensive and requires self-sacrifice, the public's attention typically declines. The decline reflects "resolution costs"—both material and emotional—which take shape as discouragement, threat, and boredom: discouragement because the problem seems impossible, threat because the issue endangers the status quo and requires sacrifice from those benefiting from it, and boredom because by this point the issue has come to dominate public discourse. Consequently, public interest and focus often quickly wane.

What is more, some kinds of problems fade from public attention more quickly than others. Issues that impact a small minority can follow this attention cycle. Likewise, resolutions to problems that do not benefit the majority, or at least a powerful elite minority, are also likely to fade more quickly. These last aspects of attention largely reinforce and reflect the media's role in news selection, creation, and agenda setting (see chapter 3). When the commercial media realizes that coverage upsets or worries important stakeholders, it will often shift attention to a new storyline and spectacle to gain audience share and sell advertising space. It leaves behind the issue and the victims who have suffered in it. Finally, the issue-attention cycle is more than simply an ephemeral aspect of victimhood or a gambit for support; attention or its deficit directly affects the well-being of the victims of trauma. Indeed, the rise and then drop in public attention, and with it trustee responsiveness, can result in a "second wave of victimization" or "revictimization," wherein those initially harmed experience further feelings of neglect and indifference (Smith and Huff 1992; Symonds 1980; Weed 1997).

The issue-attention cycle therefore typically involves an attention gap between the onset of an issue, public attention to that issue, and the media's search for another traumatic event on which to focus its programming. For victims, this is often discouraging, especially if the problem has yet to be resolved or the harms have yet to heal. Recognition of post-traumatic stress disorder (PTSD) and the proliferation of other trauma-associated maladies echo the emotional toll that victims often experience in the aftermath of tragedy when media programming and public attention dwindle. Indeed, claims of PTSD have now become a routine aspect of the postcrisis context, where once they were actively denied by administrators and allied health professionals (Fassin and Rechtman 2009). Over time, the victims of crises (now well represented by a "victim industry") have successfully lobbied for health infrastructures that can better address the different causes and conditions of postcrisis contexts. With such infrastructures, the injured can receive emergency care, on-demand psychiatric services, postcrisis counseling, and other forms of victims' assistance.

Mobilizing for Political Recognition

As suggested in the preceding discussion, because media and public attention often move on before victim grievances are addressed, victims may feel compelled to mobilize to gain the political recognition and support they require. This can be a challenging period for the traumatized. As they seek to cope, victims of crises as varied as natural disasters, acts of terror, and sexual assault can become isolated or experience economic disruption and other hardships while being stigmatized for their claims of victimization. To convince the general public—or some sizable share of it—that the harms they have suffered are worthy of sympathy, victims and advocates apply pressure to the political domain to gain recognition.

Again, sympathy is not automatic, even when an event is shocking or even horrific. Advocates must cultivate sympathy and avoid pity while sustaining public awareness, knowing that the public both has a limited attention span and might blame the victim for their hardships (Downs 1972; Gottlieb 2015; Henry and Gordon 2001; Kinnick et. al 1996; Zhang et al. 2017). The narrative used to express the story of victimization helps to cultivate that sympathy and support. It must resonate with the public by encouraging commiseration while forestalling counterclaims and denunciation (Benford and Snow 2000; Dunn 2004; Fominaya and Barberet 2013; Gamson 1990; Ochs 2006; Rothenberg 2002; Williams 1995).

The trauma script supplies just such a conventionalized cultural narrative. As a narrative, it identifies victims' suffering as unnecessary and avoidable. It locates cause, and therefore blame, in societal forces, factors, and relations beyond the victim's control, which further marks them as innocent. When framed via the trauma script, the harms that befall a victim (or victims) thus appear to suggest perpetration, such as reflected in mistake, negligence, or even intentional wrongdoing on the part of society or a societal proxy. This perception of wrongdoing can stimulate moral outrage. Had those responsible acted as they should have—or been compelled to act as they should have by laws, norms, and cultural expectations—they could have diminished or altogether prevented the victim's suffering. The moralization of harm—the injustice and depravity of it—therefore arouses strong feelings, reflected in surprise, fear, sadness, anger, and disgust, that are then directed through accusation and protest at persons, institutions, or social forces (Eyerman 2015; Goodwin, Jasper, and Polletta 2001; Jasper 1997; Polletta 2006).

In this way, the trauma script cultivates sympathy while encouraging a moral-emotional connection between victims and a public who sees in their suffering a warning: everyone is endangered by the conditions that victimized the victims. The linkage reflects but can also engender moral community and an identity that embraces the story of cultural trauma, strengthening acceptance of the claims to victimhood and support for the grievances that animate their claims (Alexander 2004). A moral community ethically connects people with bonds of compassion and feelings of obligation to protect, shelter, and safeguard (Morris 1996). Public recognition therefore requires that victims and their advocates engage in political performance, moralizing their harms to cultivate sympathy, generate an ethical connection, and mobilize the social and political support required to gain assistance and create social and political change (Gamson 1995). Sympathy, ethical connection, and social and political support are also the basis for an issue or event becoming publicly tragic.

Paradoxically, when victims mobilize to gain political recognition and support for their suffering, their efforts often also reflect an attempt to depoliticize their suffering as well. *Depoliticization* means that claims and accusations concerning neglect, discrimination, cruelty, abuse, and injustice are outside the scope of political challenge (Jeffery and Candea 2006). According to Jeffery and Candea, depoliticizing claims to victimhood "is a way of suspending or attempting to suspend the political through an appeal to something non-agentive and 'beyond' or 'before' politics such as poverty or suffering . . . (victimhood) poses itself as a neutral or indisputable starting point from which discussion, debate, and action—in a word, politics—can and must proceed" (2006:289). Depoliticizing claims to victimhood therefore renders them a priori to extant political relations—its rhetoric, strategies, and beliefs. It is a gambit meant to inoculate claims of trauma and victimhood from denial, debate, and stigmatization.

When depoliticized, claims of victimhood suspend normative politics by redefining the parameters of what is "true" and therefore debatable. This is one reason claims of victimhood, once accepted, hold so much rhetorical power, as reflected in the contemporary use of "isms" to outflank political opponents.[2] By claiming to be "beyond and before politics," depoliticized victimhood can neutralize competing claims and accusations of self-interest and strategic behavior. Depoliticized claims therefore become ostensibly unassailable: the suffering represented in them, once accepted, is no longer disputable.

2. These include ableism, racism, sexism, classism, cisgenderism, heterosexism, ethnocentrism, colorism, anti-Semitism, and sectarianism.

Despite attempts to frame suffering as beyond politics, claims of victimhood are clearly not apolitical. The claim to prepolitical status instead endeavors to control political exchange by providing an unquestionable starting point to identify the harms done to an individual or group (Jeffery and Candea 2006:289). Claims of victimhood continue to pivot on a Western cultural conception of a victim and what the process of victimization represents. Achieving these is no easy feat. Again, claims of victimhood can generate sympathy, but just as likely pity (Dunn 2004). And what happens when sympathy slides toward pity? According to Goffman (1963), pity is an emotion that lowers someone's social status because it is associated with weakness. This can then lead to discrediting the victim's experience and their claim, which typically involves victim blaming and further stigma. This highlights the paradoxical nature of victimhood as a cultural construct and political category. It risks pity and stigmatization but, once acknowledged and depoliticized, can earn increased political efficacy for a victim's claims.

The Role of Celebrity in Gaining Notoriety

Because victims are often compelled to gain sympathy and recognition while forestalling pity and victim blaming, gaining widespread public support requires that suffering reflect something more than private misery. In the context of public tragedy, the harm (or harms) suffered must involve a cause (or causes) that transcends them as individual victims. Their suffering must be appreciated as something more, a risk that resonates with a general sense of precarity among a broader moral community. As I argued earlier, current news and entertainment programming and social media communication have cultivated a general sense of vulnerability—indeed, a fear of victimization (Altheide 2013; Bauman 2013a; Bude 2017)—that has nurtured greater sympathy and moral community around stories of personal suffering that helps collectivize them as causes.

The heightened sympathy and identification with the plight of victims has in turn promoted a kind of notoriety that contemporary media logics amplify: what I call *tragic celebrity*. Tragic celebrity emerges when the victim or victims come to symbolize something that reflects more broadly distressing societal factors or forces. Specifically, tragic celebrities are victims who gain supporters who self-identify with their suffering, who advocate on their behalf and the cause(s) they come to represent. Their victimization becomes a proxy, a referendum, on suffering and its immorality. Therefore, a tragic celebrity becomes the face, symbol, or icon of a publicly tragic event.

The emergence of tragic celebrity echoes many of the same mechanisms by which celebrity, in general, is achieved and gained. Scholarship on celebrity suggests that the "ascendancy of celebrity" is another one of the distinctive features of the early twenty-first century (Barry 2008; Furedi 2010:493; Gabler 2001). In the aftermath of public tragedies, tragic celebrities can emerge as victims whose harms are elevated and become icons for what is wrong and unjust, who (or what) is to blame, and what needs changing. They are the most galvanizing stories of our time.

But what specifically is celebrity? And how does it figure in public tragedies? According to Daniel Boorstin's (1992) classic treatment of the concept, celebrity is simply a function of "well-knownness." Gabler (2001) further refines the idea of celebrity by distinguishing it from fame, noting that many famous persons do not have the public followings associated with celebrities. The essence of celebrity is high visibility; the essence of fame is being well known. These are somewhat different things, even if they often converge in today's media environment. One can be famous, for example, but rarely in the public's eye, while celebrity is ipso facto being at the center of public attention. Indeed, one might even argue that fame and infamy have largely collapsed in the contemporary media environment and celebrity has subsumed both. It has not always been this way, though, as in the past public figures often stood aloof from the crush of media attention and therefore celebrity. Some still do. In today's environment, however, it is often difficult to distinguish the two since the value of fame is often associated with the celebrity it can attract.

The notion of celebrity has a long history. The word was first used in the sixteenth century to signify when ceremonies were carried out with the proper amount of respect and devotion (OED 1984:363). But by the early nineteenth century, celebrity had moved closer to its current usage, referring to writers and entertainers of that day who had achieved a vocal and devoted following. This more contemporary usage of celebrity gained further momentum with the mass circulation of texts and images and through the proliferation of live entertainment in urban contexts. Today, celebrity has come to signify someone who has attracted a large public following, which can be achieved in many ways, including, as I suggest, through tragic circumstances and publicly acknowledged suffering. Contemporary social media platforms and accelerated forms of commercialization play a key role in the shape and proliferation of celebrity. These new platforms have further fetishized celebrity by promoting different types of "influencers" and, as I have suggested, an increasingly blurry line between "fame" and "infamy."

Regardless of what has thrown them into the limelight, those who become the focus of public attention—the celebrities of our day—are objects of mass consumption, being both adulated and ridiculed. Celebrities gain fame in movies; reality television series; tweets; YouTube and Tik Tok videos; and the images, memes, merchandising, talk shows, political commentaries, and the like disseminated through them. Currently, the celebrity market takes shape as both exceptionalism—reflected in fame and notoriety—and the quotidian—as reflected in the dreams of everyday people who achieve it, seemingly against the odds (Barry 2008; Furedi 2010; Gabler 2001). What makes today's celebrity captivating is both an exceptional status that "exceeds the people" and the commonplace aspirations and fears of "the people" (Barry 2008).

If celebrities are persons who achieve public acclaim and an avid following, then tragic celebrities are victims who gain renown through their misfortunes. Their supporters identify with their suffering and advocate on their behalf (and on behalf of the causes they come to represent). Their victimization stands as a lesson about all of the risks posed by the present. Tragic celebrity therefore comports with the zeitgeist of our day—the conditions and vulnerabilities associated with risk society. Examples of tragic celebrities who have emerged from the crucible of public tragedy include Rodney King, who was brutally beaten during a traffic stop by Los Angeles police and sheriff's deputies in 1991. As King was being beaten, an amateur videographer clandestinely taped the scene just off a Los Angeles freeway exit ramp. The video was subsequently watched on the news by millions. (This was one of the first instances of new media technologies exposing previously "hidden" trauma and loss. As handheld video technology has spread, so too has the imagery now associated with public horror and public tragedy.) The 1997 death of Princess Diana of England also became an instance of trauma, loss, and public outrage, when she died in an auto accident while seeking to escape news journalists and paparazzi who were pursuing her and her new boyfriend in Paris. Then, in 1999, high school seniors Eric Harris and Dylan Klebold engaged in what was then the deadliest school shooting in U.S. history at Columbine High School in Colorado. Those killed and injured became emblematic of the trauma and loss represented in school shootings. And while tragic celebrity might be a status reserved only for those who suffer at the hands of perpetrators, the Columbine case provides a more complicated outcome in terms of the perpetrators, their infamy, and the tragic celebrity that grew from it. Indeed, the shooting inspired copycat killings by those sympathetic to Harris and Klebold's suggested "alienation." The influence of the event now even has a label, indicative of its cultural and political legacy: "the Columbine effect" (Muschert and Peguero 2010).

Media coverage of the events on September 11, 2001, provided a legion of tragic celebrities and their stories, including all those who died in the Twin Towers as well as the first responders who sought to save them and were sickened in the aftermath. September 11 also represented a turning point in public discourse regarding crises, trauma, and loss. As I argued in chapter 1, the conditions and structure of feeling that manifested in its aftermath have fueled the proliferation of public tragedies. In 2005 Hurricane Katrina further exposed just how unequal our society is, as most of the storm's victims were poor African Americans literally left behind by federal, state, and private emergency responders as the storm approached and then left. Their suffering—for the first time covered in real time and around the clock by cable news—came to embody, for some, the institutional expression of racism in America. Each of these events, and many other public tragedies and the tragic celebrities that have arisen as a consequence, have with increased frequency populated both news and entertainment programming, social media feeds, and with them the politics of our time.

PUBLIC TRAGEDY AND TRAGIC CELEBRITY: THE KILLING OF GEORGE FLOYD

To illustrate the origins of tragic celebrity in the context of public tragedy, I engaged in a frame analysis of news stories about George Floyd's arrest and murder at the hands of the Minneapolis police on May 25, 2020. George Floyd emerged as a tragic celebrity from the crucible of a public tragedy that followed his murder. His killing provoked nationwide outrage and protest as video footage of his asphyxiation circulated first on social media and then through sustained news media coverage. Soon after, the public's sympathy and outrage elevated Mr. Floyd's death to iconic status; he has become a global symbol of police brutality, racial violence, and racism in America and beyond. In a phrase, George Floyd became a tragic celebrity.

George Floyd was arrested in Minneapolis, Minnesota, for allegedly passing a counterfeit $20 bill in a nearby convenience store. He was then murdered by Derek Chauvin, a white police officer. Chauvin knelt on Floyd's neck while he was handcuffed, face down on the street next to a patrol car. Chauvin held him in that position for nearly nine minutes. Two other officers, one white and the other Asian American, assisted in immobilizing Floyd by kneeling on his back. A fourth officer, an African American, prevented onlookers from intervening on Floyd's behalf. Floyd complained that he couldn't breathe for the first four or more minutes of his arrest. He then lost consciousness. For the last three minutes of his arrest, he lay motionless and had no pulse, yet the arresting officer continued to keep his knee on Floyd's neck. While their banter, captured on video, confirmed that the arresting officers knew he had lost consciousness, none of the officers attempted to revive him. His murder was captured on two smartphones and shared widely over social media, setting off weeks of public self-examination, moral outrage, and social and political conflict. The official autopsy determined that Mr. Floyd's death was a homicide attributable to cardiopulmonary arrest caused by subdual and restraint. A secondary autopsy commissioned by Mr. Floyd's family determined that the cause of death was pressure applied to his neck (or mechanical asphyxia).

Notably, the trauma script almost immediately framed Mr. Floyd's death: a storyline that he had suffered an unnecessary death at the behest of a trustee institution—the police—that had unjustly killed him for being Black. Important also was the backdrop and setting of Mr. Floyd's death and its reporting. He was killed at a time when the Trump presidency was stoking racial animus; when COVID-19 pandemic reporting highlighted the impact of the virus on people of color; and within months of two other high-profile deaths of African Americans, Breonna Taylor and Ahmaud Arbery, who were also killed at the hands of law enforcement (or ex-law enforcement). In both cases, the media featured "white perpetrators" as responsible. In each of these cases, the news and social media also explicitly connected police brutality to a larger discourse on race relations in the United States.

The urgency of the current narrative of white/Black/law enforcement figuratively took off with the killing of Trayvon Martin in 2012 in Sanford, Florida; gained speed with the exoneration of his killer, George Zimmerman, in 2013; and further accelerated with the killing of Michael Brown and the subsequent Ferguson, Missouri, uprising of 2014. From these events and the race relations that preceded and accompanied them, the Black Lives Matter movement was founded (Ransby 2018). In the months prior to George Floyd's murder, Ahmaud Arbery was also killed by an ex-detective, his son, and a neighbor while he was jogging through a white neighborhood in Georgia. They accused him of burglarizing a house that was under construction, chased him down in their automobiles, and shot him while trying to take him into custody.

Soon after that, Breonna Taylor was mistakenly shot in bed in Louisville, Kentucky, by police officers who performed a no-knock search warrant on the wrong home in a botched drug raid. News and social media paid considerable attention to Arbery and Taylor's stories, but neither case managed to break through and "trigger" the general public to act until after George Floyd's murder and the public tragedy that subsequently emerged (in summer 2020). They had yet to become public tragedies but would soon afterward. Nonetheless, the context of related events and extensive news media coverage sensitized many Americans to police violence and racism. From this crucible, George Floyd's killing became a "culminating event" and public tragedy (cf. Sigelman et al. 1997).

An Analysis of Tragic Celebrity

To further explore these issues, I conducted a content analysis of news stories covering George Floyd's murder. To capture the coverage through which Mr. Floyd's murder became a publicly tragic event and he became a tragic celebrity, I collected news stories in the immediate aftermath of his killing and during Chauvin's trial (and conviction) for his murder. Mass media frames typically coalesce around a dominant narrative or "storyline" during the initial period of news coverage, as do public views (Best 1991; Entman 1993; Stoycheff et al. 2018). Through frame analysis, I captured the context and tone of news coverage drawing on what have variously been termed qualitative, linguistic, literary-critical, ethnographic, and stylistic methods of content analysis (Altheide 1996, 2004; Gamson and Modigliani 1989; Hall 1975).

I specifically collected and analyzed news stories from the *New York Times* (*NYT*), the *Wall Street Journal* (*WSJ*), and the *Los Angeles Times* (*LAT*) in the two months following George Floyd's murder—May 25 to July 25, 2020—and the 40 days of his murderer's trial—March 8 to April 20, 2021. Using the ProQuest news database, my initial "open search" of stories relating to Floyd's murder—a search for any mention of "George Floyd" in a news article across the three news services—resulted in 1,161 *NYT* stories, 1,036 *WSJ* stories, and 430 *LAT* stories over the two months following his killing, for a total of 2,627 stories. Using the same open-search strategy for the month of Derek Chauvin's trial—March 8 to April 20, 2021—netted 268 *NYT*, 182 *WSJ*, and 108 *LAT* articles, for a total of 558 articles. The totals across both events and time periods netted 3,185 stories, a significant number of stories by any measure, especially considering the short timeframe I searched. This provides one relatively raw measure of just how pronounced and even iconic George Floyd's murder and tragic celebrity had become.

My initial assessment of those 3,185 stories suggested that many did not expressly focus on Mr. Floyd and the circumstances of his life and death at the hands of the Minneapolis police and public reactions to it. An initial analysis of these stories showed this was the case. Therefore, I narrowed the search to news stories with "George Floyd" in the headline to focus on those stories highly likely to involve in-depth journalistic accounts of his life and death. Searching for stories in the three news services that headlined "George Floyd" during the two months following his murder netted a sample of 46 George Floyd–headlined stories (18 *LAT*, 20 *NYT*, 8 *WSJ*). Using a slightly modified search strategy for the 40 days of Derek Chauvin's murder trial, I searched for instances of "George Floyd" or "Derek Chauvin" in story headline titles, which further netted 116 more stories

(23 *LAT*, 37 *NYT*, 56 *WSJ*). That made for a sample of 162 focused and in-depth news stories about George Floyd and his murder.

I then used frame analysis to look for patterns in the journalistic and public recounting of Floyd's killing (Entman 1993; Goffman 1974; Linstrom and Marais 2012). I explored the story elements (i.e., narratives) that helped shape public perceptions of George Floyd's tragic end and his emergence from it as a tragic celebrity. The vast majority of the public would experience his death through the media, primarily the news media. The coded stories overridingly conveyed that Floyd's death exemplified the larger issue of racial victimization, both by police and, as the story progressed, by American governance institutions, culture, and society generally.

In frame analysis, one pays particular attention to story construction. How and why are news stories chosen and framed? Why do journalists and editors *select* certain events that they *emphasize* and therefore *communicate* as important? How do they *structure* their stories and relate them to other events and issues of the day (Gamson and Modigliani 1989; Gitlin 1980; Goffman 1974)? Analyzing *story selection* indicates why a story was selected and what lies at the center of its retelling. This often reflects simple news making as a journalistic enterprise in which sensationalism, drama, and shock value are part of crafting a newsworthy narrative. Investigating *story emphasis* suggests why certain aspects of a story are highlighted and why other qualities are either de-emphasized or omitted from the story's narrative. In George Floyd's case, for example, his innocence and obedience in the face of the arresting officer's brutality provided a stark contrast, emphasizing the callousness and immorality of his killing and his innocence.[3] Finally, looking at *story structure* reveals how journalists and editors temporally and symbolically configure the narrative and how they connect it, or not, to other issues and events of the day.

For example, story structure can be "episodic" or "thematic" (Iyengar and Simon 1993). *Episodic stories* emphasize concrete descriptions that depict events as unique and singular episodes in time and space and are not related to other events in other places. By contrast, *thematic stories* emphasize abstract and generalizable aspects of an event or issue, inferring that they may reflect a larger trend related to other events, in other

---

3. This was coded as "victim, blameless." See table A.6.

places, at other times. Thematic stories therefore center on generalizations with wider application, often taking shape as lessons to the broader public about worrisome trends or upsetting developments (Fishman 1978).

Overall, the coded news stories showed that news of George Floyd and his murder was *selected*, *emphasized*, and *structured* in ways that encouraged public sympathy, moral outrage, and political conflict. The predominant news frames also promoted Floyd as a tragic celebrity. This contrasts with common journalistic renderings of police killings that tend to downplay police wrongdoing (Dukes and Gaither 2017; Hirschfield and Simon 2010; Mawby 2013). For example, while the story of Floyd's arrest and horrific death was clearly *selected* for its spectacle, the collection of stories did not *emphasize* his resistance to arrest or his prior indiscretions or criminal record. The news stories I coded did not minimize the brutality reflected in Floyd's murder by suggesting it was necessary to fight crime. Nor did they *structure the story* of his killing as an *episodic* event (rather than a thematic one and therefore a localized issue). Casting his death simply as a function of either a rogue cop or a corrupt Minneapolis police department would likely have dampened the issue's broader public appeal. This, however, was not to be the case.

THE TRAUMATIC STORY OF GEORGE FLOYD'S MURDER

News stories are a product of the news and entertainment business. Therefore, they are typically *selected* both for their significance—who or what is involved—and for the spectacle, drama, and emotion they can deliver. There is no doubt that George Floyd's brutal killing was selected and received widespread and sustained news coverage because of the spectacle and the raw emotion associated with the horrific nine-minute video that circulated on social media first and gained momentum among the public (Arango et al. 2021). Reflecting this, three-quarters of the news stories that headlined "George Floyd" opened with one of three sensational references: the manner of his horrific killing; racial conflict and social protest, rioting, looting, and violence; and police responses and police violence.

The predominant storyline in the news used to explain and describe Floyd's killing also relied on core aspects of the trauma script: George Floyd was the victim of a police officer (the perpetrator) who represented societal forces (the police as a trustee institution) and social relations (race, racial animus, and racism) that were beyond Mr. Floyd's foresight or control. The confluence of these elements marked him as innocent and the harm committed as unnecessary, unjust, and therefore immoral. The video footage (and reference to it in news stories) reinforced this narrative by focusing on Mr. Floyd's passivity: he neither visibly struggled nor resisted the arresting officers and appeared unthreatening to them. Adding to the emotional spectacle and moral outrage, Mr. Floyd also audibly pleaded for his life, saying he could not breathe while praying to his mother for help.

Notably, very few of the stories documenting Floyd's arrest and death included strong claims that countered the trauma-script-focused narrative of his killing (I coded these as "counterclaims," which appeared in less than a fifth of the news stories), as is often the case with police violence. Such counterclaims take shape through comments about how perpetrators resisted arrest, threatened the police, had a "rap sheet" of prior felonies, were high on drugs, or were experiencing an episode of mental illness, all of which imply that police violence was in some manner warranted or at least excusable (Dukes and Gaither 2017; Hirschfield and Simon 2010; Mawby 2013). This was the case even though Floyd's life and disposition on the day he was killed by a police officer involved many of these commonly used counterclaims. In this case, most news stories included thematic references rather than limiting the story to a local or episodic affair, and they connected policing as an institution (coded as "institutional victimization") to Floyd's death. For instance, over three-quarters of the stories I analyzed *thematically* connected Floyd's killing to other recent and historical cases of police violence against African Americans. And in over half of the stories I coded, the arresting police officer, Derek Chauvin, was characterized as the "perpetrator" who intended to harm Mr. Floyd. Finally, one-quarter of the coded news articles emphasized Mr. Floyd's obedience and powerlessness as a victim of unwarranted police violence. (See table A.6.)

The overriding message conveyed by the news discourse was therefore that Floyd's murder was racially motivated and that it transcended Derek Chauvin as an individual person or police officer. Chauvin symbolized policing as an institution of American culture and its racism. Put another way, the bulk of news stories about Floyd's murder did not convey his killing as an *episodic*, local, or limited affair. Instead, news stories thematically connected Floyd's murder to other contemporary and historical cases, making it a controversial national political issue that reflected race relations, the animus of white cops, and policing as a racist institution in the United States. In short, news reports deployed a broader set of societal issues and events to frame and make sense of the horrific and utterly tragic aspects of Floyd's arrest and death.

THE TRIAL OF GEORGE FLOYD'S MURDERER

Nearly a year later, the same story elements and news frames predominated during Derek Chauvin's trial for Mr. Floyd's murder (March 8 through April 20, 2021). Indeed, the court case's notoriety is a testament to George Floyd's ascendant tragic celebrity. Using the same coding scheme used to analyze news coverage the month after his murder, well over half (74 of 116) of the stories written during Chauvin's trial mentioned aspects of Floyd's acclaim through reference to the monuments, memorials, and commemorations held or erected in his name. These stories also highlighted the connections between his victimization and other historical and contemporary instances of racial injustice. (See table A.6.)

The emphasis and structure of news stories during Chauvin's trial were much the same as those that emerged just after George Floyd's killing. Stories during the trial emphasized Floyd's obedience and Chauvin's brutality (coded as "victim, perpetrator" in tables A.6 and A.7). News accounts identified Chauvin as a "perpetrator" in nearly all of the trial stories. Stories restated the murder and assault charges against Chauvin, repeated trial dialogue accusing Chauvin, and quoted trial observers who commented on Chauvin's unnecessary brutality. In related news stories covering Chauvin's trial, nearly half the stories described his actions as "immoral": unjust, depraved, and unwarranted. Moral claims appeared in half of the stories both immediately following Floyd's death and during Chauvin's trial for murder.[4] "Moral claims" of this kind were also an essential aspect of Floyd's tragic celebrity because they elevated Floyd's death beyond the day to day and equated them with generalized moral principles presumably shared by the public.

During Chauvin's trial, "policing" (coded as "victim, institutional" in tables A.6 and A.7) was blamed for Floyd's death in half of the stories. In this regard, trial coverage deviated from summer 2020 coverage, in which

4. See tables A.6 and A.7.

more than three-quarters of news stories had references to blaming "the police" and "policing" in the United States for Floyd's death and for victimizing African Americans in general. This difference was likely, at least in part, an artifact of the structure of arguments in the court case itself, which did not prosecute the "institution of policing" per se, but rather a single police officer for committing murder. However, news stories blamed policing as an institution by directly and indirectly associating Floyd's killing with police violence in general. Specifically, police violence was associated with the killings of Breonna Taylor, Ahmaud Arbery, and Daunte Wright (who was killed not far away in Brooklyn Center, Minnesota, during the trial). In news stories, Chauvin's case was also compared and associated with other historically significant and high-profile instances of police brutality and misconduct involving African Americans, including the cases of Rodney King and O. J. Simpson (Campo-Flores and Jamerson 2021; Cowan 2021; Lacey 2021).

News framing of the two periods differed the most with respect to how often George Floyd was blamed for his own death (coded as "victim, blaming" in tables A.6 and A.7). During Chauvin's trial, whether it was drug addiction, personal health, or initial resistance to arrest (i.e., refusing to get into the police cruiser), references of this kind were much more numerous than in stories immediately following Floyd's death. Again, this was likely a function of the trial, where adversarial courtroom dynamics meant that trial coverage included references to counterarguments made by the defense on behalf of their client, Chauvin. For example, in the initial coverage of Floyd's killing, less than a sixth of the news stories carried victim-blaming references, such as suggesting he died due to drug use, hypertension, or struggling with officers (coded as "counterclaims"). In contrast, during Chauvin's trial, half of the coded news stories included such counterclaims and forms of victim blaming in which Floyd was either directly blamed or indirectly inferred to have caused his own death.

Trial coverage also differed in that a larger proportion of the stories were episodically structured (23 of 116 stories during Chauvin's trial versus 3 stories of the 46 just after Floyd's murder) and almost exclusively focused on Chauvin's conduct as a police officer. (See tables A.6 and A.7.) This was also an artifact of trial coverage, as a sizable share of news stories related only what happened in the case that day, that week, or to date. These stories were coded as episodic stories because they did not mention anything other than the day's specific trial details and, therefore, expressed a very restricted view of George Floyd's murder. If anything, these relatively peripheral stories skew my accounting because they provide a sense that counterclaims were more common in press accounts than they were. The vast majority of the stories that recount Floyd's life and killing in any detail did not include counterclaims of this kind.

GEORGE FLOYD'S TRAGIC CELEBRITY

George Floyd quickly emerged as a tragic celebrity following the wide circulation of the horrific video of his asphyxiation and extensive news coverage of his murder by police officer Derek Chauvin. In news media coverage I analyzed, the predominant framing highlighted elements of the trauma script to explain the event. Again, the trauma script is a cultural framework that highlights the innocence of the victim or victims who have suffered unwarranted harms. Such outcomes are socially blamed on the actions or omissions of society or, in this case, societal proxies: a police officer, the institution of policing, and a culture of racism. In Floyd's case, news stories immediately following his death and those that covered the trial of police officer Derek Chauvin largely blamed Chauvin as the perpetrator ("perpetrator blame" was represented in over three-quarters of the analyzed news stories) and policing as the U.S. institution ("institutional blame" in over half of the analyzed news stories) responsible for Floyd's death. In half of all coded news stories, the death of George Floyd was also moralized as wrong, unjust, and racist (coded as "moralized harm"). This effectively blamed Floyd's death not just on Derek Chauvin or the police, but on society, since racism transcends Chauvin and the Minneapolis police and is thematically generalizable beyond the case of Floyd's murder. Indeed, more than three-quarters of all coded news stories were structured thematically (rather than episodically), associating Floyd's death and Chauvin's trial with similar cases and with police brutality, poverty, and race relations in the United States and beyond.

On this point, it is important to emphasize that reliance on the trauma script to frame and thematically structure news stories relating to Mr. Floyd's death was not a foregone conclusion. It was by no means inevitable that his death would be eulogized in a manner that emphasized his innocence, the malevolence of a white police officer, the racial bias of policing, and racism in the United States. By all accounts, George Floyd lived a troubled life. Some political pundits and right-wing activists actively attacked the framing of his death as a public tragedy and his emergence as a tragic celebrity (Watts 2020). Across the coded news stories, many described Mr. Floyd's problems with addiction, his run-ins with the law, and his decade of incarceration. Yet they did so in ways that tended to diminish those indiscretions while emphasizing the traumatic circumstances of his death. This is very unusual news coverage of a police killing.

Rather than undermining his tragic celebrity, then, retrospective accounts of George Floyd's past were much like those common to entertainment and sports celebrities. They focused on his early troubles and his efforts to overcome them, such as his move to Minneapolis from Houston, framed as his attempt at "redemption" by starting over. For instance, an *NYT* biopic story titled "George Floyd, from 'I Want to Touch the World' to 'I Can't Breathe'" developed a narrative arc of his life, telling of his poverty-stricken youth in a tough Houston neighborhood called the Bricks. There, he excelled in sports but ran into trouble with drugs and spent time in prison for robbery. The story recounted those travails but emphasized his move to Minnesota as an effort to better himself. The news article quoted a friend: "His move would be a fresh start . . . his story one of redemption" (Fernandez and Burch 2020). An article in the *LAT*, also featuring Mr. Floyd's attempts to surmount his past troubles, quoted another friend, who said Mr. Floyd "was going to get himself straight" by moving to Minneapolis (Hennessy-Fisk 2020). These and other newspaper accounts that examined Mr. Floyd's life emphasized his recent attempts at atonement cut short by murder-by-police, not his past troubles, continued drug addiction, or illicit behavior.

Stories about Mr. Floyd's life also highlighted the comments of sympathetic informants, who amplified his symbolic connection to other notorious killings of African Americans by police and to the tragedy of racism in the United States generally. For example, a front-page story in the *NYT*, "Man of Outsized Dreams Stirred a Movement with Final Breaths," opened with memories of the aspirations of Floyd's youth and how they were snuffed out by a police officer's knee:

It was the last day of 11th grade at Jack Yates High School in Houston, nearly three decades ago. A group of close friends, on their way home, were contemplating what senior year and beyond would bring. They were black teenagers on the precipice of manhood. What, they asked one another, did they want to do with their lives? "George turned to me and said, 'I want to touch the world,'" said Jonathan Veal, 45, recalling the aspiration of one of the young men—a tall, gregarious star athlete named George Floyd whom he had met in the school cafeteria on the first day of sixth grade. To their 17-year-old minds, touching the world maybe meant the N.B.A. or the N.F.L. "It was one of the first moments I remembered after learning what happened to him," Mr. Veal said. "He could not have imagined that this is the tragic way people would know his name." The world now knows George Perry Floyd Jr. through his final harrowing moments, as he begged for air, his face wedged for nearly nine minutes between a city street and a police officer's knee. Mr. Floyd's gasping death, immortalized on a bystander's cellphone video during the twilight hours of Memorial Day, has powered two weeks of sprawling protests across America against police brutality. He has been memorialized in Minneapolis, where he died; in North Carolina, where he was born; and in Houston, where thousands stood in the unrelenting heat on Monday afternoon to file past his gold coffin and bid him farewell in the city where he spent most of his life. (Fernandez and Burch 2020)

In the months following Floyd's killing (May 25–July 25), fully three-quarters of the news articles I collected touched on his notoriety by describing his childhood memories, commentaries, and commemorations, as relayed by his family, friends, and well-wishers in street protests, multicity memorial(s), and an open funeral in Houston. These stories and their references embody George Floyd's status as a tragic celebrity. The narrative content of stories like these repeatedly referenced his name and linked it to protest events and expressions of defiance; public memorials; commemorations; other instances of police brutality; and symbolic tributes in art, including murals and theater. The stories linked public mourning and racial protest to George Floyd, making him a tragic celebrity.

The significant number of stories covering the 40 days of Chauvin's murder trial also provides de facto evidence of just how consequential George Floyd's tragic celebrity had become in the aftermath of his murder. Floyd's death and Chauvin's trial were frequently compared to the Rodney King trial (1992) and the O. J. Simpson trial (circa 1994–95), both of which galvanized the nation on issues of race, policing, and the law

(Campo-Flores and Jamerson 2021; Cowan 2021; Lacey 2021). In cities across the country, government officials justified mobilizing the police and national guard by evoking the need to avert rioting if Mr. Chauvin was found not guilty (Hennessy-Fiske 2021; Tabrizy et al. 2021). Indeed, the notoriety of Chauvin's trial, as reflected in the mobilization of security forces, the extensive coverage it received, and the political theater that took advantage of it, reflected and amplified George Floyd's tragic celebrity. By March 2021 he had become an icon, and the trial of Derek Chauvin for his murder had come to represent a referendum on race relations in the United States.

In keeping with Floyd's tragic celebrity, the vast majority of stories about his life and murder relied on a *thematic* rather than *episodic* structure to interpret the meaning of his death and the role that policing, the law, race, and societal inequality had played in it. As I've argued, thematic attention to George Floyd's horrific killing involved connecting it to other cases: other failures of policing as an institution and other race-related issues and events, all of which were noted for promoting societal-wide distress. Floyd's murder was frequently linked with other notorious police killings and even lynchings, both contemporaneously and historically. For example, in the following *LAT* story, Floyd's killing was suggested to have worsened the tragedy for families who had recently lost loved ones to police violence:

> For families who have lost a loved one to police violence, there are two truths most agree on: The pain never goes away, and every new fatal encounter with law enforcement makes it raw again. As the nation and world mourn the death of George Floyd, these five Californians continue to grieve over law enforcement killings closer to home. Their tragedies are made worse, they say, by the systemic racism that remains in the American criminal justice system and continued use of fatal force that seldom results in repercussions for the officers involved. For some, speaking out is a balm and a necessary part of an ongoing fight. For others, it is trauma endured so that the person gone is not forgotten. Here, they share their stories. (Chabria and Bermudez 2020)

And a *WSJ* story relating Chauvin's trial and conviction, "Black Americans Greet Derek Chauvin Conviction with Relief, Caution," opened by linking the trial and its verdict to other notorious racially incendiary events, including the beating of Rodney King, the trial of O. J. Simpson, and the murder of Emmet Till:

> For many Black Americans, the conviction of Derek Chauvin in the death of George Floyd inspired feelings of relief and a sense that the verdict might have been an anomaly. "I hope it will change some things. I'm praying it's a stepping stone," said Christin Hickman, a 35-year-old from Minneapolis. "But it didn't change with Emmett Till. It didn't change with Rodney King. So, you know, I'm not holding my breath." Mr. Chauvin, a former Minneapolis police officer, was convicted of all counts in the death of Mr. Floyd, which inspired nationwide protests and debate after it was captured by bystanders on video. Like the 1995 O.J. Simpson murder trial and the Rodney King police brutality case in 1992, the three-week Chauvin trial was closely watched and viewed by many Americans as a watershed moment in U.S. race relations, even hearkening to Emmett Till, a Black teenager who was murdered in Mississippi for purportedly offending a white woman in the 1950s. That episode, and the lack of accountability for the killers, helped galvanize the civil-rights movement. (Campo-Flores and Jamerson 2021)

The message delivered in stories like these, and their focus on policing and accountability, was that the police had failed African Americans and that the law and the courts had failed them too. By proxy, society had failed. These are the hallmarks of public tragedies and the conditions from which tragic celebrities are made.

Finally, for the sake of perspective, it is important to again emphasize that news stories do not generally cover police violence in the way they covered George Floyd's killing or Derek Chauvin's trial. News stories of George Floyd's murder sharply contrast with frequently used explanations of police violence in standard news accounts. Scholars have shown that police violence is more commonly explained in terms of a victim who is an immediate threat to police officers (or another person) and therefore a "perpetrator of violence" rather than a "victim of police violence" (Dukes and Gaither 2017; Hirschfield and Simon 2010). Another narrative that often explains police killings portrays them as the unfortunate consequence of police officers fulfilling their duty to protect the public (Mawby 2013). Both explanations are ultimately victim-blaming accounts that justify the deaths and clear individual officer(s) and policing as an institution to blame.

Yet in the case of Mr. Floyd's killing, the graphic nine-minute recording cohered with elements of the trauma script, which forestalled counterclaims by the Minneapolis police: that Floyd had strongly resisted arrest, that he was a threat to police, and that his death was therefore "justifiable." Rather, in the prevailing counternarrative, an obedient Mr. Floyd suffered a needless death, one for which he was largely blameless. He was the victim. Therefore, instead of individual blame being directed at the victim—George Floyd—social blame was directed at the actions of a perpetrator—Derek Chauvin as a police officer—and policing in general—a societal institution—for a racially motivated murder. The cause of the harm was blameworthy, and society was ultimately at fault (i.e., social blame). Based largely on this narrative and understanding, Mr. Floyd's death gained notoriety and, with notoriety, public outrage, which quickly elevated his killing into a public tragedy, his life as a tragic celebrity.

CONCLUSION

Recent transformations in cultural constructions of victimhood have been essential to the emergence and increased importance of public tragedies as political events. Public tragedies turn on public acknowledgment, sympathy, and moral outrage over the harms a victim or victims have endured. The cultural shift in both the power and appreciation afforded victimhood is exemplified in the tragic celebrity that now, with great frequency, arises from the crucible of public tragedy. As the political tumult associated with such events has grown, it has encouraged a new kind of celebrity, as accusations and social blame vault a victim (or victims) into the role of celebrated protagonist. Tragic celebrity exemplifies the conditions of risk society and the general public's heightened sense of vulnerability, the trauma script as a conventionalized explanation for trauma and loss, and the rise of political victimhood and its valorization of blameless suffering (cf. Kleinman, Das, and Lock 1997). Tragic celebrity reflects the renown a victim (or victims) can achieve when they become the symbol of a publicly tragic issue or event and the cause (or causes) that animates it.

As suggested, the emergence of tragic celebrity echoes many of the same mechanisms by which celebrity, in general, is achieved. If celebrities are persons who achieve public acclaim and an avid following, then tragic celebrities are victims who gain renown through the misfortune that befalls them and for which their supporters hold them to be blameless. Their victimization stands as a warning to all of the risks posed by the present. Tragic celebrities therefore emerge from public tragedies when the story of their trauma and loss becomes the center point for social and political conflict, exposing a systemic basis for suffering with which others self-identify.

George Floyd was just such a tragic celebrity. His murder was captured on smartphones and distributed over social media and, soon afterward, on broadcast and internet news. It set off months of public self-examination, moral outrage, and social and political protest against police brutality and racism in Minneapolis, across the United States, and even internationally. Floyd's death—and others that were associated with it—quickly emerged as a symbol of institutional racism, making his singular death a collective event and public tragedy. His death and persona became an iconic image of what went wrong in Minneapolis and what is wrong in a world at risk.

Floyd's murder and his media construction as a tragic celebrity are mirrored in other notable examples. In 2013, for instance, the victims of the Boston Marathon bombing gained widespread attention, sympathy, and funds via the "Boston Strong" victims' advocacy movement that sought to help fund recuperative surgery and therapy for the scores of runners and bystanders disfigured by the blasts. In 2016 the mass shooting of mainly gay patrons at the Pulse nightclub in Orlando, Florida, came to symbolize the homophobia and discrimination experienced by the LGBTQ+ community in the United States. And in another complex case of tragic celebrity, in 2018 Supreme Court nominee Brett Kavanaugh was accused of having sexually assaulted Christine Blasey Ford when they were high school teenagers. As part of the #MeToo movement, Ms. Ford's supporters saw their own experiences in her case. A media storm followed as the public inveighed about its concern, sympathy, and position on her horrific experiences.

In response, however, those who supported Mr. Kavanaugh also applied the trauma script to his experience. They lionized him as an example of someone victimized by a politically motivated smear campaign, causing him undeserved and unnecessary trauma and infamy for simple political gain (i.e., self-interest). Significant cases of tragic celebrity on the political right also include that of Kyle Rittenhouse, a 17-year-old who shot three men (two fatally) in August 2020 during civil unrest in Kenosha, Wisconsin. Rittenhouse answered an online call to arms to protect Kenosha's downtown from "leftwing rioters." The political unrest followed the shooting of a Black man, Jacob Blake, by a police officer and reflected the hostilities unleashed by George Floyd's murder. Rittenhouse was subsequently charged with murder, and prosecutors argued (at his trial in November 2021) that he had provoked protestors in the attack, while his defense lawyers argued that he had acted in self-defense. A jury found Rittenhouse not guilty of murder and other charges, judging that he had acted in self-defense. Rittenhouse became a tragic celebrity on the right, who, after his trial, traveled widely to political events where he was honored for his persecution and standing his ground against it.

Ashley Babbitt's death represents another case of tragic celebrity on the right. Babbitt was killed by a capital security officer on January 6, 2020, while storming the capital with others who sought to overturn the defeat of then president Donald Trump. Her death and its coverage in the right-wing media provoked supportive commentary comparing her treatment to George Floyd's, suggesting that she was being "smeared" by the liberal press (Prestigiacomo 2022). A swell of support online in conservative social media outlets—such as at hashtag #SayHerName and via sympathetic political elites—categorized her death as "an execution." She was eulogized as a victim and martyr (Swoyer 2021).

In yet another case, Robert LaVoy Finicum was killed in 2016 by the Oregon State Patrol on a highway north of Burns, Oregon, for failing to surrender himself for arrest. He was part of a group of property-rights and anti-tax activists who had occupied a remote federal wildlife sanctuary in rural southeastern Oregon, the Malheur National Wildlife Refuge. The armed activists and militiamen held off federal and state authorities and occupied the refuge for over a month to protest the arrest of two ranchers and what the activists viewed as federal government "overreach." Finicum, like the others, was lionized as a victim by social media commentary and the right-wing media. Protests were organized, memorials were erected, and outrage at his "execution" was expressed by those who saw their beliefs, values, and causes in him (Stack 2016).

And while not involving disaster or death per se, in 2019 the #Free-Britney movement represented another variation on politicized cases of victimization and tragic celebrity, which in this case involved fans rallying around Britany Spears over concern about the long-running, court-ordered conservatorship that denied her control over her financial assets and therefore her life. All these cases reflect the elements of public tragedy by associating the victim's trauma and loss with the trauma script. Yet these individuals and collectives also achieved "tragic celebrity" because their trauma and loss attained symbolic status for either the suffering the victims experienced or the suffering they caused. Their images and narratives continue to exert influence via the causes they and others have come to represent.[5]

This is both a partial listing and one that lacks the depth and development I gave to George Floyd's case. I've hardly scraped the surface of the many victims who suffer horribly at the hands of perpetrators, accidents, and misfortunes. Some, like the cases I have just mentioned, including Floyd's, gained sustained public attention in one way or another, but many others do not. In truth, very few victims become tragic celebrities. How, then, does one victim's trauma vault them into celebrity status while another's does not? Making a tragic celebrity involves a consistent process that parallels the more conventional celebrity associated with entertainment and fame. The typical celebrity is a performer with a compelling story, who gains sustained media attention, and a like-minded public following or "fans" (Gabler 2001). Like the public tragedies from which they often emerge, tragic celebrities are also associated with a compelling story that eulogizes them as blameless victims who have endured suffering that is blamed on society. The storyline, framed and conveyed via media coverage, social media attention, advocacy, and political manipulation, can become emblematic of "a condition" or "cause," resulting in further and more intense public recognition, sympathy, and with these, a rapidly expanding moral community. For victims of public tragedy who become tragic

5. Elsewhere in the book I take up other cases of public tragedy that also illustrate the link between politicized crisis and the emergence of tragic celebrity. These include the residents of Flint, Michigan, who suffered a municipal water crisis; the victims of the botched federal response to Hurricane Maria in Puerto Rico; and the students who mobilized to stop gun violence in the aftermath of the Marjory Stoneman Douglas High School mass shooting.

celebrities, then, the trope involves a victim (or victims), a compelling story of victimization, sustained media exposure, and a public following that coalesces around the victim (or victims) and agitates and advocates for the righting of a wrong done to them (and those associated with them). Again, the key to the narrative is the story of unnecessary and therefore traumatic loss at the hands of society or some aspect of it. It is therefore the story of trauma and loss that ultimately translates the traumatic experience of an individual victim (or victims) into collective harm, promoting a public following and, with it, the emergence of both public tragedy and tragic celebrity.

Conclusion

WHY CLAIMS OF TRAUMA AND LOSS PROMOTE PUBLIC OUTRAGE AND ENCOURAGE POLITICAL POLARIZATION

"They're shooting in my class, I'm hiding in a corner I love you," Jessica Luckman frantically texted her mother as gunman Nikolas Cruz prowled the halls.

—victim, Stoneman Douglas High School mass shooting, Parkland, Florida (Geggis, Huriash, and Pesantes 2018)

The wind came and took everything. It took the house with all my belongings. All that was inside (. . . the house is gone).

—victim, Hurricane Maria, Villa Hugo, Puerto Rico (King and Botti 2017)

The water was brown, and it had a disgusting smell. . . . It was like dirt was coming out (of the faucet).

—victim, toxic water crisis, Flint, Michigan (Goodnough, Davey, and Smith 2016)

Mr. Floyd uttered "I can't breathe" not a handful of times, as previous videotapes showed, but more than 20 times in all. He cried out not just for his dead mother but for his children too. Before his final breaths, Mr. Floyd gasped: "They'll kill me. They'll kill me."

—victim, police brutality, Minneapolis, Minnesota (Oppel and Barker 2020)

In these epigraphs, the victims of public tragedies relate their harrowing, even life-ending experiences. Every year, horrific events like these induce great suffering. Some are actively caused by individuals, such as the nearly 40,000 gun-related deaths that happen each year or acts of sexual harassment and assault, recently exposed by the #MeToo movement (Jaffe 2018). Others are not caused by mistaken or malevolent individuals but are the outcome of institutional failures that are frequently magnified by strategic denial and the victim-blaming rhetoric deployed by administrators, political elites, and their surrogates to avoid responsibility (Bovens and 't Hart 2016). As taken up in chapter 3, Flint, Michigan, is illustrative of the latter. In 2014, city officials changed its water source and purification system to save money. Although residents repeatedly complained about poor water quality, officials denied it was unsafe. Only when independent researchers tested the water and found it dangerous would officials acknowledge the problem (Clark 2018; Sze 2020). By this time, thousands of Flint residents, many of them children, had been exposed.

Still, other public tragedies like natural disasters and industrial accidents often have complex origins that are not easily tied directly to acts of individual persons or even single institutions. In 2018, the Camp Fire in Northern California, which was the deadliest (86 dead) and one of the costliest ($16.5 billion in damages) in U.S. history, had multiple causes. The proximate cause was a Pacific Gas & Electric (PG&E)–owned utility transmission tower and line that were not well maintained. But poor zoning that allowed residential development to sprawl into a mature forest compounded that problem, as did a city plan with few alternative exits. Additionally, the fire reflected years of successful political opposition by residents and developers to forest management. Decades of fire suppression efforts led to the buildup of highly combustible material. Finally, climate change and unusual snow and rain patterns helped create conditions that amplified the risk and intensity of the fire, which in the Camp Fire's case quickly became a "firestorm."

Nevertheless, because the spark that started the blaze was traced back to poorly maintained equipment, PG&E was found liable and blamed for the fire in an investigation by Cal-Fire. PG&E subsequently agreed to pay $1 billion in compensation (Smith and Bizjak 2019). Whether Paradise will ever completely recover from the fire remains to be seen.

These and the resulting forms of crisis, misfortune, and heartbreak are, unfortunately, a universal part of the human experience. In the opening chapter, I asked what sentiments and conditions have transformed responses to many events that in the past were most often understood to reflect personal misfortune, fateful disaster, or individual responsibility into today's public tragedies that seize the public's attention and galvanize the emotions of millions? I also asked what, in the present day, leads so many Americans to sympathize, even personally identify, with victims of trauma and loss in ways that can transform a limited crisis into a widely reviled public tragedy, triggering political conflict and controversy and perhaps even social transformation? As I have argued, how society responds to crises is not intrinsic to the material circumstances or the level of suffering they induce. Instead, it reflects how we perceive, understand, and remember events and those who have suffered them. This is also to say, then, that public tragedies, like the fated disasters of the past, are inherently products of our time.

In contemporary times, when the trauma script is used to frame crises and those who suffer them, the event is more likely to gain sympathy and come to represent an existential threat to the social and moral order. As such, while the material qualities of a disaster or social crisis certainly matter—that is, who (or what) was harmed, how they were harmed, how many were harmed, and why they were harmed—alone, they are insufficient to produce a public tragedy. Events that become publicly tragic are social and political accomplishments.

A GENEALOGY OF PUBLIC TRAGEDY

While public tragedies are not new to the twenty-first century, I've argued that their contemporary regularity reflects a qualitative shift in how trauma and loss are perceived and collectively responded to in the United States and elsewhere. As social proxies, public tragedies expose heightened levels of angst, dependence, distrust, and vulnerability that have emerged alongside state efforts to modernize society, and as I have made the case, as reflected in the U.S. federalization of risk. This is one of my core arguments. Unpacking public tragedies has exposed the public's relationship with authority and risk. The abiding sense of vulnerability many Americans feel is increasingly on display in the aftermath of traumatic events, which is what makes exploring them so revealing. Given the state's paradoxical role and often partisan response to crises, it should not surprise us that one or more segments of the public routinely blame the state and its surrogates for collective misfortune. Accusations of this kind have, with time, gained in power and political influence. What began early in the twentieth century with class-based movements focused on the state and its surrogates had included movements engaged in a robust social and cultural critique of society by the century's end. The "new social movements" did not focus on class-based and economic concerns (as they had in the nineteenth and early twentieth centuries). Instead, new movements sought "freedom" from oppressive and increasingly globalized, technocratic, and economic structures and traditional cultural institutions that they accused of causing significant social and psychological trauma (Melucci 1996; Touraine 1995).

However, countermovements were formed to challenge "identity movements" as they emerged, pushed for social and cultural recognition, and legally established rights and freedoms across the developed world. Social and religious conservatives, nativists, nationalists, and the "illiberal"—animated by somewhat different concerns—have also relied on a similar protest trope founded on a sense of betrayal and blameless victimization (Wieviorka 2005). They, too, have come to rely on the trauma script. They, too, see themselves as victims of societies that have forsaken them as they face global economic and cultural trends that threaten to diminish their social and material standing (Ehrenreich 2020; Gidron and Hall 2020; Hochschild 2018; Kurer 2020).

As I have argued in *After Tragedy Strikes*, the trauma script is a function of and comports with the contemporary "structure of feeling" cultivated by risk society (Williams 1961). The transition away from modernity reflects both "real" and "ideational" changes, *real* insofar as the material changes induced by human technoscientific, economic, and bureaucratic systems do indeed threaten our civilization. Yet the material risks such modern systems pose are not the whole of it. They connect to changes in social structural, cultural, and political relations that have accelerated inequality and are exacerbated by capital's newfound mobility and its timeless pursuit of new opportunities for capital accumulation. This has pushed the state toward fiscal crisis while destabilizing the post–World War II "social contract" between government, industry, and unions. It has undermined wage work and deepened the risk of poverty for an (ever) expanding share of the U.S. public (Fantasia 1988, 1995; Reinarman 1987). These conditions have expanded hardship and grievance because capital has restructured and relocated production and banking functions overseas to avoid labor costs, costly regulations, and taxation (Bluestone and Harrison 1982; Castells 1996; Castells and Tyson 1989; Dicken 2003). The deployment of computerized operations, artificial intelligence, and robotics to lower overhead costs, enhance productivity, exert greater control, and increase profit has only exacerbated these issues. It will continue to hasten these social trends and associated resentments, including clashes between liberal progressivism and populist illiberalism (Eatwell and Goodwin 2018; Goodhart 2017; Mouffe 2018; Norris and Inglehart 2019).

Again, in the context of U.S. politics, political elites routinely argue that these conditions reflect a zero-sum competition among demographic groups and identities, thereby fanning partisanship that has increasingly become more sectarian (Finkel et al. 2020). By contrast, in the early twentieth century, social and political elites tended to hew to a rhetoric of progress, claiming—whether sincere or not—that everyone in society would benefit from their efforts through an aggregate increase in prosperity. Such was the case in 1963 when President John F. Kennedy defended his use of public money to pursue state development, suggesting in a famous quote that "a rising tide lifts all the boats" (Safire 1993:627). As an idea underlying modern political and economic justifications for the welfare state, society would benefit from state building: infrastructure plans, social programs, and industrial subsidies. Over time, the power of such beliefs and their aphorisms to persuade the public ebbed as neoliberalism became the prevailing "inequality regime" in Western societies (Acker 2006; Mudge 2011; Piketty 2020).[1]

A strong belief in progress no longer ties citizens to the state or one another. In conjunction with the rise of identity politics and an abiding sense

---

1. An "inequality regime" is an ideological rationale for hierarchy (and therefore inequality) that becomes institutionalized in convention and law (Acker 2006; Piketty 2020).

of vulnerability, neoliberalism has effectively fragmented civil society and the political domain into competing interest groups (Mudge 2008, 2018). No longer unified by the promise of progress and, with it, the chimera of a shared future, public skepticism takes shape in a context of state and industry retrenchment and the championing of public-private partnerships, fiscal restraint, and deregulation. The naked promotion of zero-sum trade-offs has compelled individuals, groups, and entire classes of persons to compete, within the state structure, to gain benefits and avoid risks.

These and related changes have left a mark on the public's psyche, provoking feelings of betrayal, distrust, and vulnerability that have further cultivated an increasingly accusatory politics in which the public regularly sees their precarity and lack of control in public tragedy. Risk society, therefore, also reflects *ideational* changes that take shape in contemporary beliefs, commitments, and identities that are further mirrored in the trauma script and reliance on it to explain trauma and loss. As I have argued, risk society is characterized by a general loss of faith in progress because the social compact that animates it has not only faltered but has actively been effaced by political and economic elites. Most people view the state not as a neutral arbiter but as a partisan interest. Across the political spectrum, people believe that the government and corporate America are reneging on their commitment to American workers and to America generally (Gallup 2022; Nadeem 2022; Pew Research Center 2022). Once a unifying conviction, the idea of progress has faded with increased wage and employment precarity, the dissolution of the post–World War II liberal political consensus, and the rise of neoliberal, zero-sum politics.

Nevertheless, while many Americans seem to embrace a neoliberal conception of the state, they also hold the state responsible for not fulfilling its duty to the general public. In this regard, public tragedies involve and reflect a competitive and grievance-based, neoliberalized, and increasingly sectarian "politics of risk" that is paradoxically embedded in welfarist state expectations: one might even say a sense of entitlement (Platt 1999). Deeper yet, humanity is ultimately the underlying threat responsible for suffering. Fate, God's hands, bad luck, unintended accidents, or simple mistakes no longer hold power as believable explanations for trauma, loss, and suffering. I have also made the case through an analysis of public tragedies, human cause and, with it, social blame infuses all matters of consequence in the Anthropocene. Given the trauma script's role in motivating public tragedy and the associated movements and causes, does its frequent use portend more political dysfunction or, eventually, a move toward political rehabilitation? To answer this question, we must address what public tragedies represent as collective events and political accomplishments.

THE POLITICS OF PUBLIC TRAGEDY AND WHY THEY MATTER

Knowing that the trauma script can politically charge crisis events, transforming some of them into public tragedies that are distinct from the disasters that populate everyday life, does not explain why we might want to know and better understand their origins, increased frequency, and contemporary manifestation. Why do public tragedies matter? As I have argued throughout, there are several reasons to explore the influence that public tragedies currently exert on public sentiments and, with them, the nation's politics. The first is that unpacking public tragedies exposes sociological facets of society and with them the zeitgeist of our time. As suggested in previous chapters, there is ample evidence that collective response to trauma and loss is qualitatively and quantitatively different today than in the past. This shift has set the stage for public tragedy. We see it in increasingly common public outpourings of grief, spontaneous memorialization, protest, and collective action, and in claims that society, or some segment of it, is partly or wholly responsible for the harm(s) done. And routine blame avoidance on the part of the accused—often political elites or governance authorities or their surrogates—can and does often further polarize and politicize cases of trauma and loss, making them that much more contentious. By contrast, until the late twentieth century, God's plans, fate, bad luck, and blameless accidents or individual responsibility typically sufficed as explanations of tragic events, even when harms were known to have been caused or worsened by human actions or omissions. These explanations, often couched in liberal individualistic terms, also tended to mute social and political conflict in the aftermath of tragic events.

Public tragedies also matter for what they represent politically. As I have also argued, public tragedies are sui generis: emergent social and political phenomena that are an increasingly frequent source of public tumult and sectarian conflict. When trauma and loss are framed by the trauma script and public tragedy results, the ensuing uproar can exert tremendous influence over the "body politic" with unpredictable results: they have the power to transform social and political relations and have done so. As I have striven to show, reliance on the trauma script to frame social crises of various kinds has resulted in the proliferation of public tragedies with significant political ramifications. Not least is the conventionalization of the script and its diffusion as a new and powerful type of rhetoric used in virtually all contemporary political contests.

Because claims to the script posit a collective wrong, they fundamentally differ from claims founded in the liberal individualism long associated with U.S. political culture. Therefore, they hold the potential to shape U.S. political engagement and demands differently, too. What are the implications of this difference? The script and its public resonance and their realization in public tragedy have played an important role in exposing trauma and loss of many kinds and mobilizing large portions of the public to react collectively. By contrast, in the past, when harm such as that reflected in sexual harassment or institutional racism, among other sorts, was understood through ideas of liberal individualism and individual responsibility and as reflecting one's personal life, the response was most often muted by comparison. By moralizing historically significant injustice and naming who or what is judged responsible for it, the trauma script has indeed pushed American politics toward a reckoning of sorts and past the liberal individualism that stymied recognition of this kind in the past.

The now-frequent use of the trauma script even suggests that the United States is moving toward a more collectivist and less individualistic political discourse with potential ramifications for American political imagination, governance, and policy manifestations. Indeed, there is some evidence of this in the political attitudes of younger Americans, such as the millennial generation, who are more likely to support more collectivist outlooks and political visions. For example, millennials are much more likely than older cohorts (i.e., X, Boomer, or Silent generations) to blame societal conditions for racial minorities' inability to "get ahead these days." At the same time, they are more supportive of bigger government and government programs (Pew Research Center 2018, 2020). As I have sought to show in previous chapters, this, along with other trends, has resulted in a transformed political imagination and political rhetoric and led to a good deal of political tumult.

Yet the political use and manifestation of the trauma script has not necessarily aligned with past claims and forms of collectivism—for example, those based on social class affiliations and critiques of capitalism and poverty. On the one hand, the trauma script politically empowers through collective association. It incentivizes those who allege harm and those who advocate on their behalf to frame their injuries as a function of their membership in a collective because it yields more legitimacy and power to their claims. The harms done to them are not simply "personal troubles" but represent "public issues." The script is indeed collectivist in this regard.

On the other hand, as victims' advocates and social movement entrepreneurs have successfully used the script to gain public attention, sympathy, and outrage, they have been joined by pundits, political elites, and even journalists, news, and the entertainment media in exploiting the script's current ability to draw public attention and fuel emotional response. Accordingly, the trauma script has become a relatively common idiom to explain nearly any kind of risk, injury, or crisis (cf. Bennett 2022; Pandell 2022; Sehgal 2021). Overusing the script might have the effect of overplaying the collective aspect of personal crises because it downplays, indeed actively denies, that a given case of trauma and loss might reflect unique circumstances, accidental harm, or even individual responsibility. Here, the "authentic" use of the trauma script to address collective issues gives way to a conventionalized discourse of trauma and loss that anyone can apply regardless of the authenticity of their claim. Because of this dynamic, the trauma script will likely, with time, begin to lose some of its power to provoke and, with it, the political strength to mobilize across partisan divides and crosscutting identity constructs.

Indeed, we have already seen some of this in the increasingly polarized and sectarian politics of the first quarter of the twenty-first century. This can take shape as a backlash, in which claims of victimization often split the public rather than unify it. Political partisans interpret a claim's authenticity by who is making it. And they often reflect partisan interests once they take the shape of public tragedies. Indeed, as I have made the case across the preceding chapters, their politicization is the primary reason they become publicly tragic.

An illustrative example of these political dynamics in 2023 is the heavily reported train derailment in East Palestine, Ohio. On February 3, a train transporting toxic chemicals derailed in this small rural community. There are nearly 1,000 train derailments a year in the United States. This derailment received great national attention, public outrage, and political posturing that continued for more than two weeks after the initial derailment. This clearly set it apart from other derailments, which at best typically receive short-term, local attention (Fortin 2023).

In the initial derailment, roughly 20 of the 149 railcars carrying hazardous materials caught fire. Within hours of the crash and despite the images of mangled railcars on fire, the EPA began testing air and water and detected no concerning contamination levels. Two days after the derailment, because temperatures in the remaining unbreeched railcars carrying toxic chemicals began to rise dangerously, the authorities called for residents to evacuate for fear of a catastrophic explosion. Subsequently, Norfolk Southern Railroad, in conjunction with the federal authorities, decided to begin a controlled burn of the remaining toxic chemicals in the unbreeched railcars in lieu of their possible spontaneous ignition. Such an explosion would have expelled shrapnel and toxic materials miles from the derailment site.

The subsequent giant plume of black smoke from the controlled burn of the chemicals, framed by the small town underneath it, became a news and social media spectacle and sensation (Fortin 2023; Olorunnipa, McDaniel, and Duncan 2023; Ulloa 2023). The EPA's continued monitoring for toxic air and water returned negative results. Residents were allowed to return. Yet when they did on February 8, they soon began to report unexplained symptoms and signs of local distress: dizziness, headaches, skin rashes, nausea, odd smells, dead fish in a local creek, and local animals that had mysteriously died. As news of these issues began circulating on social media and the nightly news, a broadcast-internet media feedback loop supercharged the derailment generating still more coverage and concern nearly two weeks after the initial derailment. This was unusual for an event in which no one had died or been injured.

Public outrage, however, was very partisan. Former president Trump, Republican senator J. D. Vance, Republican senator Marco Rubio, and influential right-wing pundit Tucker Carlson either visited East Palestine or inveighed about the neglect and malfeasance of the U.S. federal response, citing its lack of urgency for a "rural, blue-collar community with few people of color" (Olorunnipa, McDaniel, and Duncan 2023; Ulloa 2023). Those who lived in East Palestine were the blameless victims of unforeseeable and unnecessary harm, which was socially blamed on the omissions of the U.S. federal government. This included the federal government, represented by partisan interests—progressives, the Democratic Party, and "liberals"—and an uncaring corporation, Norfolk Southern Railroad.

Paradoxically, while founded on social blame meant to summon public support, the trauma script, used as it was in the East Palestine case and the others I have related in prior chapters, can clearly and simultaneously promote divisions instead of unity. Indeed, it is frequently used to do so, as the East Palestine experience illustrates. Because the script relies on social responsibility to mobilize sympathy and outrage, in which one (or more) group(s) blames another group (or groups) for the harm done to them, it can generate conflict too. Such was the situation in the exemplary cases I have used to explore public tragedy. In this regard, the trauma script coheres with the zero-sum politics I have associated with risk societal relations (as developed in chapter 1). When applied to a case of trauma and loss, the discursive structure of the script, therefore, identifies victims that have been wrongly harmed and the perpetrators responsible for the harm.

Consequently, the impact of the trauma script on political relations has been less "collectivist" and more "populist" in its manifestation since the core logic of the trauma script moralizes the harms being problematized and blames them on an institution, culture, or group or all three at once. The zero-sum and accusation-based qualities of the script also coincide with the character of contemporary identity constructs and the associated affinity groups and social causes. Many current identity constructs are hyperpoliticized and "standpoint" based (Hartsock 1998) and, therefore, noninclusive insofar as they are founded on the experiences, outlooks, and grievances claimed by an affinity group. When the script's focal points and grievance-based identity politics coincide, the dynamic can even complicate coalition building and collaboration among allied interests (Beamish and Luebbers 2009).

The trauma script's influence on contemporary political discourse and relations is also a function of its use as a political gambit. As I argued in chapter 4, by invoking the trauma script to claim victimization, claimants implicitly strive to "depoliticize" those claims by marking them as outside the scope of political challenge (Jeffery and Candea 2006). They seek to inoculate themselves from denial, debate, and stigmatization by framing themselves as victims and their harms as a priori to the current political moment and crisis. Put another way, in claiming that the harms done to them reflect historically situated patterns of collective abuse, those making such claims suggest they are beyond and before current "politics." This neutralizes the accusation that they are claiming victimization for strategic reasons and are motivated by simple self-interest. Depoliticized claims, once accepted as true, become indisputable. They suspend normative politics by redefining the parameters of what is factual and debatable (Jeffery and Candea 2006:289). This is one reason why, once acknowledged, claims of victimhood currently hold so much political legitimacy and rhetorical power.

Accusations reliant on the trauma script that claim victimization are clearly not apolitical, even when those claims are authentic. Instead, allegations of this kind attempt to control political exchange by providing an incontestable starting point for claims making. The power of the depoliticization strategy is illustrated by its current use, which, as I have argued, is extensive. It is viewable, for example, in the proliferation of contemporary "isms"—ableism, racism, sexism, classism, cisgenderism, heterosexism, ethnocentrism, colorism, and anti-Semitism, among others—and the oratorical command they currently hold in political exchange. For those who have accepted them, they define unassailable and indisputable truths.

Finally, as I have suggested throughout, the discursive conventionalization of the trauma script exposes our current political moment and what is shaping it. The United States currently confronts a significant degree of political dysfunction, much of which is rooted in a contemporary structure of feeling that has promoted a deep sense of grievance about both past and present injustices and a sense of increased vulnerability to risks of a range and type (Norris and Inglehart 2019). Whether or not one is sympathetic to a specific set of claims, insulation from dialogue and dispute is not in keeping with democratic values, the principles of free exchange, or the ideal of an open political system. If one believes that democracy, as a system, requires open political dialogue, shutting down the discussion of issues and ideas because they might antagonize victims—real or imagined—is not an entirely healthy political development in the long term, where open exchange ensures that voices on the margins are included in political discussion and debate.

THE TRANSFORMATIONAL POWER OF PUBLIC TRAGEDY

Clearly, public tragedies have emerged from these epochal conditions as our time's most galvanizing social and political events. They can shape public opinion, spawn social movements, influence elections, result in policy and legal changes, and even take down governments. They can catalyze larger waves of social, cultural, and political transformation. This is another reason I have sought to better understand public tragedies—for their transformative power. We see this in U.S. public tragedies as varied and consequential as the Columbine High School Shootings (1998), the September 11 terror attacks (2001), the Great Recession (2008/2009), Hurricane Katrina (2010), the Boston Marathon Bombing (2013), the #MeToo movement (2017), the police killing of George Floyd (summer 2020), and the COVID-19 pandemic. Although each of these was a substantially different kind of event, each became publicly tragic because the trauma and loss associated with them was explained, framed, understood, and remembered through the trauma script.

To understand their power to transform, I have sought to answer a further question: Why do we understand and respond to such a diverse array of crisis events in such a singular manner? Analyzing what distinguishes public tragedies from the sad but inevitable disasters of the world exposes why public tragedies are transformative. I found public tragedies to be sui generis; they are a distinctive and now increasingly common type of social and political event that reflects and involves several co-occurring developments characteristic of risk societies. I analyzed these developments in chapters 2 through 4, to expose and better explain the contemporary emergence and proliferation of public tragedies as crisis events that are humanized as blamable moral-political failures, a process that transformed them into hyperpolitical moments.

In chapter 2, I focused on a current political reality: elites and officials have come to rely on blame-avoidance strategies. Blame avoidance has become a conspicuous feature of governance and governing processes. This strategic and political response to risk management reflects several issues native to representative government in the United States (Weaver 1986). Because any given policy or program cannot satisfy all of one's constituents, any political action will make some constituents happier than others. Structural dynamics like this support limited policy agendas and blame-avoidance tactics over credit-claiming strategies that might be associated with new policy and program cultivation.

The ascendance of blame avoidance also reflects current political environments in which the public is prone to accuse the government of mistakes, misconduct, and accidents regardless of what has transpired. Because Americans commonly assume the government should prevent or significantly diminish most if not all risk, the former often wholly or partly blame public officials and the trustee institutions they manage for any trauma and loss that occurs. Responding to accusations of blame—indeed, in proactively seeking to get out in front of it—administrative and political elites try to evade allegations and responsibility by defending themselves and their administrative efforts. Predictably, this tends to amplify suspicion and distrust among stakeholders, especially the victims, resulting in yet more political controversy and notoriety as the elements for public tragedy quickly accrue.

Once having become notorious, public tragedies further demonstrate "what is at risk" by dramatizing vulnerabilities while exposing societal authorities to criticism. Exposure and criticism almost inevitably lead to some amount of blame. Blame can reflect whatever trauma has befallen those victimized or the perception that those in charge have failed to fulfill their obligation to protect and serve. Indeed, the sense of betrayal that can come with perceptions of disloyalty can emotionally supersede whatever presumably caused the crisis to begin with: hurricanes, acts of terror, sexual assaults, and other events. This leaves public officials, political elites, and their surrogates effectively "to blame" for the suffering that people experience.

A new media logic and communication ecology has also encouraged these conditions and public sentiments. As I suggested in chapter 3, a new media logic and communication ecosystem features spectacle and fearmongering in its programming. By presenting shocking stories meant to capture and hold audience attention, news and entertainment media emphasizes fear, cultivating insecurity through stories focused on crime, terrorism, political extremism, racism, sexual assault, and environmental decline (Altheide 2013, 2017). In the second half of the twentieth century a new generation of professional journalists also adopted an exposé ethic. Exposé journalism, in turn, led to an emphasis on political officials', industry elites', and trustee institutions' mistakes, misconduct, negligence, and intentional harm. These conjoined developments have promoted both public cynicism and distrust, on the one hand, and outrage over moral and political indiscretions, on the other. This sort of news reporting and programming corresponds to the conditions, beliefs, and feelings that promote public tragedy and are reflected in the trauma script.

The emergent communication ecology has further intensified the impact of exposé news reporting because it can quickly supercharge an issue or event. Facts, but also rumor, conspiracy, and hearsay, ricochet across broadcast media, internet news, and social media platforms. A local tragedy that might otherwise fly under the public's radar can now quickly become a full-blown national crisis: powerful media feedback loops amplify both the spectacle and the emotional and political aspects of the event, while hyperaccelerated responses push it into primetime. The news media's reliance on regular displays of shock, spectacle, and fear to grab and hold audience attention reinforces the dynamics that define public tragedies as social and political events.

These media logics and communication ecology, alongside contemporary exposé journalism and its professional code, are key ingredients in producing and proliferating public tragedies. Using journalistic tropes that define what is (and is not) newsworthy, journalists expose wrongdoing and its victims and have held many wrongdoers to account. Yet over time journalism has also sowed fear, cynicism, and paradoxically, desensitization. For example, in chapter 3 I showed how consistently journalists relied on elements of the trauma script to explain stories of trauma and loss and in so doing cultivated public sympathy and outrage. Through case comparisons, I also showed that issues and events that became publicly tragic often involved news frames that highlighted innocent victims and their suffering. In addition, journalists often used news frames and implicit references that blamed trauma, loss, and victimization on the moral-political failures of trustee institutions and, therefore, on the actions or omissions of administrative officials and political and cultural elites. This encouraged politicization as sympathetic political interests sought to capitalize on the outrage and pressed to hold the organizations and institutions "at fault" accountable.

As a conventionalized discourse, the trauma script is also reflected in how the media encodes issues and events so that they resonate with social and cultural sentiments—the contemporary "structure of feeling"—regarding trauma, loss, and victimization. The script encourages moral considerations and social blame to explain the suffering of innocent victims. It culturally "calls out" a certain kind of collective response when invoked. As an explanatory discourse, the trauma script elevates an issue or event from a local and isolated case into a generalizable class of abuse. A case in point is the above mentioned East Palestine train derailment. It warns that this event could happen to anyone, anywhere, anytime—that we should be concerned because if we are the kind of people harmed by it, we too are in danger.

Along with blame-avoidance tactics deployed by political elites, a new media logic and communication ecology, and journalism's embrace of exposé, the victim industry has also played an important role in cultivating the conditions and beliefs that stand behind public tragedy. As I explored in chapter 4, the victim industry has sought to expose the systemic cultural and structural basis of victimhood. It blames "society" for the hardship of victims by blaming government and governance institutions, cultural beliefs and ideologies, and social hierarchies, privileges, and associated inequalities. Yet even with the increased cultural resonance and political power that is afforded claims to victimization today, victim blaming and marginalization are still possible. In fact, as noted previously, the centrality of social blame in the trauma script predictably results in resistance and, with that, counternarratives. Competing political narratives, therefore, compel those who suffer trauma, along with their advocates, to recount their experiences to maximize public sympathy, political recognition, and support for their injuries and suffering. This too has had its own unintended consequences as viewed in political resistance and adoption of the same trauma narrative by competing political interests.

As I have suggested, the trauma script is that narrative, a now-conventionalized explanation of harm that individuals and institutions use to frame trauma and loss to gain public support. This is important because which political framing prevails and how the public views victims and who (or what) is held responsible plays a pivotal role in public response. Notably, shifting cultural constructions of victimhood have played a central role in the emergence of public tragedies as transformative social and political events.

In *After Tragedy Strikes*, while I have sought to map public tragedies' origins, meaning, and contemporary social and political anatomy, more research is still required on the trauma script and public tragedy since they have significant implications for U.S. political culture and politics. Scholars should further investigate how the trauma script compares with established U.S. political discourses and what this portends for politics generally. Another fruitful line of research would explore whether the now frequent claims to victimhood—an identity construct strongly associated with the trauma script—foreclose productive political exchange. Conversely, might the proliferation of claims to victimhood foster an opening to a new sort of politics? Researchers should examine, over time, whether the conventionalization of the trauma script represents a distinctive but passing political moment, one that reflects and is now simultaneously shaping contemporary politics, or something that is becoming permanently baked into politics.

I have striven to show the contemporary cultural construction of shocking events and how and why the traumas they induce now frequently convey outsized notoriety, concern, and outrage. They become publicly tragic, while other objectively similar traumas do not. I have argued that while the material qualities of any given disaster, crisis, or traumatic event matter, on their own they are not enough to generate a notorious and politically consequential public tragedy. Rather, public tragedies are social and political accomplishments. Their realization occurs through outpourings of anguish and grief, spontaneous memorialization, accusation, denunciation, social blame, political demand, and social protest. By contrast, in the past, issues of injury and death were often treated as private affairs; people grieved with their immediate relations, and fate, bad luck, chance, and personal responsibility often explained harmful outcomes or were used to diffuse responsibility for them (Jorgensen-Earp and Lanzi-lotti 1998). Not long ago, trauma and loss—even death—could also be rationalized as a necessary sacrifice—the price paid for progress. One might even say that the nineteenth and early twentieth-century public reaction to the suffering of others was callous by today's standards.

No longer. Explanations such as these are not as culturally believable as they once were. They must compete with contemporary human-centric causal stories centered on societal forces, factors, and conditions in which social blame for moral and political failure and claims of victimization are now pivotal. As I have shown, this change in viewpoint reflects societal-level change toward a risk society that has set the stage for the ascendance of the trauma script and a cultural understanding of trauma and loss that pivots on claims of victimization and victimhood as an identity. Taken together, risk-societal relations, when coupled with contemporary sectarian political rhetoric in the United States, a newfound communication ecology, and a victim industry committed to exposing victimization in all its guises, go a long way toward explaining the contemporary structure of feeling and therefore the resonance that the trauma script currently has with the public. It also suggests why trauma and loss, when experienced in this way, can trigger such strong collective moral and political reactions. In a phrase, it is why these conditions and convictions so frequently trigger public tragedy.

APPENDIX   Notes on Data Collection
and Media Analysis

For chapter 2, I paired two hurricane disasters to assess and better understand how the political communications and rhetoric regarding crises can promote (or, on the contrary, suppress) public tragedy. Hurricane Maria was characterized by intense political conflict, controversy, and national notoriety, while Hurricane Harvey, an objectively catastrophic and therefore similar hurricane crisis, was not. I compared the two to show how crisis events take shape differentially through political communications among stakeholders. Political stakeholders in situations of this kind can include political elites and their political rivals; public officials and government administrators; journalists, pundits, and experts; victims, victims' advocates, and watchdog groups; and others involved in assessing or experiencing a given crisis and the trauma and loss associated with it. I expressly focused on political communications, and more specifically on the use of credit-claiming and blame-avoidance rhetorics and the role these play in fomenting or forestalling public tragedies.

    To collect news stories regarding each hurricane event, I searched using the ProQuest news database, using keywords. I collected all the stories available in the year following each hurricane event. This resulted in 245 Hurricane Harvey stories and 192 Hurricane Maria stories. To ensure my sample of stories was comparable, I relied on parallel search parameters, using similar search words and phrases, such as a search for "Hurricane Maria" or "Hurricane Harvey"; specified geographic references, including "Puerto Rico" or "Houston"; and roughly parallel date ranges given landfall dates, such as August 2017–September 2018. In a similar search, I also collected feature stories from national news magazines (i.e., *Newsweek*, *Politico*, *Salon*, etc.), official reports regarding FEMA's humanitarian relief efforts (e.g., FEMA 2017, 2018; National Hurricane Center 2018), and academic research on each hurricane event (e.g., Amadeo 2018; Joseph et al. 2020; Mooney and Dennis 2018; Santos-Burgoa et al. 2018).

Regarding the sample of news stories, I sorted them for those articles that featured "political communications" among the stakeholders (as defined earlier) involved in each event's aftermath. Such stakeholders provided observations, commentary, explanation, criticism, and the like. I then narrowed my search to news stories that featured political communications because I wanted to isolate and compare explicit political messaging, such as the political rhetoric used and the rival claims making expressed about each hurricane crisis. I coded a story as involving "political communication" if it featured claims making by stakeholders in which they politicized the hurricane crisis by either praising or criticizing the actions or omissions of relief efforts or those impacted by the storms.

For example, then president Trump and his surrogates were in several cases openly hostile to the claims made by the leaders of Puerto Rico in the aftermath of Hurricane Maria. They were also dismissive of victim claims regarding their suffering after Maria, while being boastful of the administration's alleged accomplishments in addressing hardship on the island. Over the year of coverage, my coding resulted in 38 of Hurricane Maria's 192 news stories (20%) involving such *explicit* political communications. By contrast, only 13 of Harvey's 245 news stories (5%) featured explicitly political communications over roughly the same period. Harvey was mainly cast as a success even though it was also a devastating storm.

Having collected and narrowed down the news stories featuring political communication, I then analyzed and further coded these stories along several dimensions to capture the shape of political messaging. While not coding the other materials, such as magazine articles, government reports, or academic research, I did assess them for reference to political communications, controversy, and conflict in each storm scenario. What I found in these materials assisted in code creation and therefore in my coding of news stories. Again, I wanted to capture the rhetorical strategies used by elected officials, administrative leaders, their surrogates, and spokespersons (hereafter "political elites") when they claimed credit and tried to avoid blame in the aftermath of each hurricane crisis. I asked whether these efforts and the shape they took were associated (or not) with heightened levels of political conflict and controversy.

The first dimension of political communication I sought to assess regarded how political elites cast the *severity* and *manageability* of each hurricane event. Those in charge of managing a crisis are incentivized to characterize it as severe so that they escape blame for any damage it does. To gain attention and resources, political rivals and victims' advocates, by contrast, are incentivized to characterize a crisis as severe and a response as problematic. They can accuse those in charge of mismanaging a crisis at the expense of those harmed and, in so doing, stoke outrage and political controversy.

Along with severity, I was sensitive to and coded for how public officials and their political rivals addressed the manageability of the crisis (manageable/unmanageable) or whether those responsible were held to have mismanaged hurricane response. This also involved noting the claims makers' relationship to the crisis and their response to it. Were they in some respect tasked with hurricane response, were they political rivals of those who were, or did they represent the concerns of the victims of the storms?

I also tracked what was implicitly conveyed in the news through descriptive statements and allusions to fault, failure, and wrongdoing attributed to no one in particular. I coded those as "journalistic slant." I therefore organized news stories of political communications according to whether they were made by those representing official government authorities, their political rivals, or as an example of journalistic slant.

As the coding scheme in table A.1 shows, I noted when public officials denied, affirmed, or maximized the severity of each hurricane. Public officials who directed government response tended to maximize the storm's severity. By casting the storm as "unmanageable," public officials charged with operational response suggested that they did their best in an impossible situation. By comparison, their rivals focused on and accused them of mismanagement. Those who suffered the consequences of such a storm, by casting it as severe and the government response as mismanaged, stand to gain public support given their framing of suffering as avoidable and unnecessary (had the operational response to the crisis been managed appropriately).

In the third set of codes, I tried to capture the political communications used by political elites to deflect blame, claim credit, and manage impressions in the aftermath of each hurricane event. Therefore, I coded stories in which political elites engaged in a rhetoric of *credit claiming* through which they sought to portray their efforts as commendable and effective or sought to *avoid blame* for the trauma and loss associated with each storm. Credit claiming often reflects elites' grandiose claims of success, wherein they downplay the suffering reflected in a crisis by reframing failure as success (Stone 1997). Blame avoidance can take shape in statements of denial and evasion, disqualification of critics, disassociation, reinterpretation, and scapegoating.

Finally, a word on the modest sample of political communication stories I used to analyze and explore political elite rhetorical strategies in the aftermath of both hurricane events. While the news media comparisons I was able to make regarding political communications involved a relatively modest sample of news stories,

Table A.1 Hurricane Maria, Political Communication Stories, September 1, 2017–July 1, 2018

Analytic codes	All claims, no. and % of articles with each type of political communication	Official claims, no. and % of articles with each type of political communication	Rival claims, no. and % of articles with each type of political communication	Journalistic slant, no. and % of articles with each type of political communication
Political communications	38			
Manageable crisis	6 (16%)	6 (16%)	0	0
Unmanageable crisis	8 (21%)	7 (18%)	0	1 (3%)
Mismanaged crisis	35 (92%)	0%	(17) 45%	18 (47%)
Affirm severity	8 (21%)	7 (18%)	0	1 (3%)
Deny severity	2 (5%)	2 (5%)	0	0
Maximize severity	15 (40%)	10 (26%)	2 (5%)	3 (8%)
Blame avoidance	19 (50%)	19 (50%)	0	0
Credit claiming	16 (42%)	16 (42%)	0	0

NOTE: Of the 192 news stories collected for Hurricane Maria, 38 featured "political communications." The coding, numbers, and percentages in the table are based on the 38 political communication news stories sorted by their differing rhetorical claim types: manageable crisis, unmanageable crisis, mismanaged crisis, affirm severity, deny severity, maximize severity, blame avoidance, and credit claiming.

Table A.2 Hurricane Harvey, Political Communication Stories, August 1, 2017–June 1, 2018

Analytic codes	All claims, no. and % of articles with each type of political communication	Official claims, no. and % of articles with each type of political communication	Rival claims, no. and % of articles with each type of political communication	Journalistic slant, no. and % of articles with each type of political communication
Political communications	13			
Manageable crisis	1 (8%)	1 (8%)	0	0
Unmanageable crisis	6 (46%)	4 (31%)	0	2 (15%)
Mismanaged crisis	6 (46%)	0	2 (15%)	4 (31%)
Affirm severity	7 (54%)	7 (54%)	0	0
Deny severity	0	0	0	0
Maximize severity	4 (31%)	1 (8%)	2 (15%)	1 (8%)
Blame avoidance	1 (8%)	1 (8%)	0	0
Credit claiming	5 (39%)	5 (39%)	0	0

NOTE: Of the 245 news stories collected for Hurricane Harvey, 13 featured "political communications." The coding, numbers, and percentages in the table are based on the 13 political communication news stories sorted by their differing rhetorical claim types: manageable crisis, unmanageable crisis, mismanaged crisis, affirm severity, deny severity, maximize severity, blame avoidance, and credit claiming.

the patterns exposed in my analysis were echoed in other sources I used in my investigation of each hurricane event, including news magazines (i.e., *Newsweek*, *Politico*, the *New Yorker*, the *Atlantic*), official reports regarding FEMA's humanitarian relief efforts after each storm (FEMA 2017, 2018), and academic attention to each hurricane (Duhart 2019; Einbinder 2018; Garcia-Lopez 2018; Kishore et al. 2018; Santos-Burgoa et al. 2018; Santos-Lozada and Howard 2018; Shultz and Galea 2017). As such, the modest data used to illustrate political communication in the aftermath of two hurricane events provides a reliable proxy for assessing and illustrating the prevailing national discourse framing each event. Tables A.1 and A.2 show coded story totals separately for each hurricane event.

COMPARING NEWS MEDIA CRISIS NARRATIVES (CHAPTER 3)

For chapter 3, I explored the mass media's role in preconfiguring the conditions for public tragedy through an analysis and comparison of the news regarding six paired cases of trauma and loss. My analysis suggests that news-maker emphasis on spectacle, exposé, and fear, in conjunction with a heavy reliance on the trauma script, plays a significant part in the proliferation of public tragedies. Through heavy reliance on the trauma script to explain trauma and loss, currently the news and entertainment media encourages a view that is more likely to galvanize the public, or subgroups of it, by moralizing trauma and loss while also emphasizing political conflict. My interest in chapter 3 was therefore to ascertain the role of the news media in framing crises in ways that comport with, even encourage, public tragedy. To do this, I assessed general news-making logics. I compared the narratives associated with traumatic events that had achieved widespread public notoriety and political controversy—de facto public tragedies—with similar crisis events that had not. As for chapter 2, I used the ProQuest news search database to collect news stories for analysis and comparison.

I examined online and print news coverage of six paired crisis cases: two catastrophic hurricane events, two mass high school shootings, and two community-based toxic events. Using these as exemplary cases, I sought to identify patterns in news coverage associated with public notoriety as reflected in claims of perpetration, victimization, social blame, moral failure, and political conflict and controversy. For the catastrophic hurricane events, I used the same sample of news stories for Hurricanes Maria and Harvey used in chapter 2 but subjected them to a different coding scheme guided by the distinctive theoretical frame developed in chapter 3. As detailed earlier, I collected a year's worth of news reportage for the hurricane events.

For the news coverage of the school shootings, I collected coverage of the Marshall County High School shooting in Benton, Kentucky (January 2018), and the

Stoneman Douglas High School shooting in Parkland, Florida (February 2018). I began story collection for each event six months after each had transpired and collected news stories from their origination dates to July 1, 2018. They occurred within three weeks of one another. For the Flint, Michigan, and Newark, New Jersey, toxic water events, I collected news stories for an entire year following the first news reportage of each case. Both had occurred two years before my collection efforts and involved longer histories of contamination and cover-up (Clark 2018).

I selected the six cases of trauma and loss, paired by crisis type, for the following reasons. First, I chose them for the way they depicted the causes and the types of trauma and loss they represented. Natural disasters have conventionally been deemed acts of God, school shootings provide instances that highlight individual perpetration, and the municipal water crises were clear examples of government failure. Reflecting on this, I wanted to compare how each case was conveyed (encoded) and understood (decoded) (Hall 1980), as broadly reflected in the national public discourse about them (i.e., the news), as reflected in public comments, commemorations, tributes, demonstrations, and official responses. Part of this involved determining how coverage of one kind of traumatic event, such as a hurricane, might differ from that of another type, such as a school shooting, and how these might differ from coverage of Flint, Michigan's toxic water catastrophe (Clark 2018).

I also selected the paired cases for their timing: they reflected a shared moment and hence mentalité, having taken place at very similar points in time and entailing the same or similar sociocultural elements. This reduced the number of intervening issues that might explain differences in the public discourse(s) about either case. I essentially sought to create the conditions for a naturally occurring experiment, a scenario in which the cause of trauma and loss was virtually the same, while public responses varied considerably by case. Comparing cases of this kind and in this manner offered a means of assessing how similar events achieved vastly different public profiles. One case had become controversial, widely known, infamous, and publicly tragic, while the other had not. Moreover, comparing these cases would also reveal how similar social and political rhetoric was across very different crisis types. These cases, therefore, were illustrative of the conditions I wished to understand better and explain.

I searched within ProQuest using (roughly) parallel search parameters involving keywords/phrases, geographic locations, and date ranges. My search yielded an initial sample of 1,141 news articles for the six paired cases. After sorting and examining the sample of stories for duplication and topical relevance, I found that a small number of print and electronic versions of the same story were differently titled. Where two or more stories were the same, varying only by title, I dropped the redundant stories from the database of codable stories. I also dropped stories if they did not focus on the case of interest, even though the search term was present. Such stories were also neither coded nor tallied in story totals. This left

830 stories for analysis and coding, of which 480 were *primary stories* and 350 were *secondary stories* (see table A.3).

Having gained a general sense of the news narratives for each case, I then coded for how articles explained the "cause" of harm and the suffering associated with each event. A small number of news stories referred to *fate* (God's hand, destiny, or simple bad luck, among other such mechanisms), suggesting that harm reflected either chance or powers beyond human agency. Most stories, however, explained trauma and loss by *blaming* humans, government, and society for accidents, negligence, and intentional harm, what I labeled "social blame" (Oorschot and Halman 2000). Blame also infrequently included victim blaming, where those harmed were held responsible for their injuries. Blame was also expressed, although infrequently, as "individual perpetrator blame," wherein a person was individually held accountable for trauma and loss. When articles attribute trauma and loss to other humans, they could also include moralizations and accusations of "social responsibility."

I therefore coded for accidental, negligent, intentional, and victim-centered blaming. By doing so, I sought to determine whether "individual perpetrators" were blamed for the trauma and loss or whether cause, and therefore blame, was more diffuse, falling on institutions like "the government," "society," or even American "culture" in general. This latter aspect corresponded with "social blaming." Social blame, as developed in the chapters, reflects a collective form of responsibility in which an individual's actions are held to represent a group, organization, or society in general. None of the stories I assessed and coded in my final tallies involved individuals held solely responsible. This was even the case in the school shootings. Therefore, I collapsed the three forms of blame—accident, negligence, and intentional harm—into one meta-category, social blame, to reflect how, in each of these types, it was ultimately "social blame" that was used to explained trauma and loss (see table A.4).

The use of social blame to explain cases of trauma and loss was also associated with moralizing, in which the harms done were cast as deliberate wrongdoing or at the very least, callousness and insensitivity. In the contemporary context, social outrage and political conflict are virtually inevitable when harm is moralized in this way. Therefore, to understand the role moralized harm and political conflict might have played in the narrative related to each crisis event, I coded for instances when the harm was *moralized* and when harm was associated with *political conflict*. News stories with the moralized harm/political conflict code often were expressed in relatively straightforward ways: the harm was intentional or reflected neglect on the part of a perpetrator, responsible party, or trustee. In either case, it was "wrong": those harmed had been victimized by "immoral conduct." As shown in table A.5, the crisis events that were more notorious were also more often moralized. They were also more likely to feature political conflict.

Table A.3 News Media Story Totals by Case (*LAT, NYT, WSJ*)

	Marshall County High School Shooting (1/1/18–7/1/19)	*Stoneman High School Shooting (1/1/18–7/1/19)*	*Hurricane Harvey (8/1/17–6/1/18)*	*Hurricane Maria (9/1/17–7/1/18)*	*Newark, NJ, Toxic Water (1/1/16– 12/30/17)*	*Flint, MI, Toxic Water (1/1/15– 12/30/16)*	*Total*
Primary stories	5	86	137	144	12	96	480
Secondary stories	5	165	108	48	0	24	350
Total stories	10	251	245	192	12	120	830

Table A.4 News Media Story Totals, Types of Blame by Case

	Marshall County High School (1/1/18–7/1/19)	Stoneman High School (1/1/18–7/1/19)	Hurricane Harvey (8/1/17–6/1/18)	Hurricane Maria (9/1/17–7/1/18)	Newark, NJ, Toxic Water (1/1/16–12/30/17)	Flint, MI, Toxic Water (1/1/15–12/30/16)	Total
Fate based	1	2	10	1	0	0	14
Victim blame	0	0	0	6	0	0	6
Social blame	6	227	18	105	7	130	493
Accidental harm	0	0	3	2	0	2	7
Intentional harm	5	128	1	15	0	25	174
Negligent harm	1	99	14	88	7	103	312
Total	13	456	46	217	14	260	1,006

Table A.5 News Media Story Totals, Moralized Harm and Political Failure by Case

	Marshall County High School (1/1/18–7/1/19)	Stoneman High School (1/1/18–7/1/19)	Hurricane Harvey (8/1/17–6/1/18)	Hurricane Maria (9/1/17–7/1/18)	Newark, NJ, Toxic Water (1/1/16–12/30/17)	Flint, MI, Toxic Water (1/1/15–12/30/16)	Total
Moralizing harm	4	33	2	39	1	56	135
Political conflict	1	102	14	43	1	30	191
Total and percent of total stories	5 of 10 (50%)	135 of 251 (54%)	16 of 245 (7%)	82 of 192 (43%)	2 of 12 (17%)	86 of 120 (72%)	326

ADVOCACY, PUBLIC TRAGEDY, AND TRAGIC
CELEBRITY (CHAPTER 4)

In chapter 4 I explored the construction of victimhood by victims' advocates and
its role in preconfiguring the conditions that predict public tragedy. To capture
the transition from George Floyd's killing as a public tragedy to Mr. Floyd becoming a tragic celebrity, I analyzed news stories about his murder as well as stories
that covered the trial of his murderer, Derek Chauvin. I collected news stories
in the two months following Floyd's murder—May 25 to July 25, 2020—and the
40 days over which Derek Chauvin's trial took place, March 8 to April 20, 2021.
Using the ProQuest news database, my initial "open search" of stories was for
the two months following the murder. I searched for any mention of "George
Floyd" in news articles across the three news services: *NYT*, *WSJ*, and *LAT*. This
resulted in 1,161 *NYT*, 1,036 *WSJ*, and 430 *LAT* stories, for a total of 2,627. I
used the same open-search strategy for the 40 days of Derek Chauvin's trial and
netted 268 *NYT*, 182 *WSJ*, and 108 *LAT* stories, for a total of 558. The total across
both periods and events netted 3,185 stories that mentioned Georgie Floyd's
murder, a significant number of news stories by any measure or type of event,
especially considering the short timeframe over which I searched. Initial analysis
of the 3,185 stories showed that there were simply too many stories that did not
expressly focus on Mr. Floyd's life and death and public reaction(s) to it. Therefore, I narrowed the search to news stories with "George Floyd" in the headline
to focus on those that were likely to involve in-depth journalistic accounts and
frames of reference. Searching for news stories in the three news services that
headlined "George Floyd" during the two months following his murder netted a
sample of 46 George Floyd-focused headlined stories (18 *LAT*, 20 *NYT*, 8 *WSJ*).[1]
Using a slightly modified search strategy for the 40 days of Derek Chauvin's trial,
I searched for "George Floyd" or "Derek Chauvin" in story titles, netting a sample
of 116 stories (23 *LAT*, 37 *NYT*, 56 *WSJ*). As such, I had a sample of 162 headline
stories that exemplified news coverage and with them the national public discourse regarding George Floyd's murder and societal response to it (see tables A.6
and A.7).

1. In my preliminary analysis, I found that 6 of the 52 stories were either duplicate stories
(5 stories) or not relevant (1 story).

Table A.6 Headline Stories Referencing George Floyd's Murder, May 25–July 25, 2020

Codes	Code description	LAT no.	NYT no.	WSJ no.	Total no.	Total %
Story totals	Floyd headline stories.	18	20	8	46	100
Primary story totals	Floyd is primary focus.	16	20	6	42	91
Secondary story totals	Floyd is mentioned but is subordinate to article focus.	2	0	2	4	9
Sensationalism (vs. prosaic)	Story opens with Floyd's murder, police violence, racial animus, protests, and riots.	14	15	5	34	74
Tragic celebrity	Reference Floyd's celebrity—protests inspired by his death, memorials, tributes, art and symbolism, iconic/symbolic status.	13	15	5	33	72
Victim, accidental	No fault harm: Floyd's death was unintended.	0	0	0	0	0
Victim, blameless	Floyd was an innocent victim.	1	9	2	12	26
Victim, institutional	Floyd's death involved societal forces/factors/institutions.	13	17	7	37	80
Victim, perpetrator	Floyd's death by officer was intentional (murder).	8	12	4	24	52
Counterclaims: victim blaming, situation blaming, partisan blaming	Source of Floyd's death was disputed, suggesting it was situational, blamed on Floyd, or reflects political claims.	5	2	1	8	17
Moral claims	Floyd's death was unethical, unjust, immoral, wrong, offensive, unfair, hateful.	12	8	2	22	48
Episodic stories	Localized/limited.	2	1	0	3	7
Thematic stories	Widespread/general.	16	16	7	39	85

NOTE: Results are from a frame analysis conducted on the 46 stories that headlined "George Floyd" in the three news services during the two months following his murder (18 LAT, 20 NYT, 8 WSJ). The story elements are listed and totaled by row (not column).

Table A.7 Headline Stories, Derek Chauvin's Murder Trial, March 8–April 20, 2021

Codes	Code description	LAT no.	NYT no.	WSJ no.	Total no.	Total %
Story totals	Chauvin/Floyd headline stories.	23	37	56	116	100
Primary story	Chauvin/Floyd is primary focus.	16	27	42	85	73
Secondary story	Chauvin/Floyd is mentioned, but is subordinate to article focus.	7	10	14	31	27
Sensationalism (vs. prosaic)	Story opens with Floyd's murder, police violence, racial animus, protests, and riots.	20	20	35	75	65
Tragic celebrity	Reference Floyd's celebrity—protests inspired by his death, memorials, tributes, art and symbolism, iconic/symbolic status	17	23	34	74	64
Victim, accidental	No fault harm: Floyd's death was unintended.	0	0	0	0	0
Victim, blameless	Floyd was an innocent victim.	2	4	3	9	8
Victim, institutional	Floyd's death involved societal forces/factors/ institutions.	16	21	22	59	51
Victim, perpetrator	Floyd's death by officer was intentional (murder).	20	32	51	103	89
Counterclaims: victim-blaming, situation-blaming, partisan-blaming	Source of Floyd's death was disputed, suggesting it was situational, blamed on Floyd, or reflects political claims.	2	19	36	57	49
Moral claims	Floyd's death was unethical, unjust, immoral, wrong, offensive, unfair, hateful.	15	18	20	53	46
Episodic stories	Localized/limited.	1	9	17	27	23
Thematic stories	Widespread/general.	20	27	38	85	73

NOTE: Results are from a frame analysis conducted on the 116 stories that headlined "George Floyd" or "Derek Chauvin" in the three news services during the 40 days of Derek Chauvin's murder trial (23 *LAT*, 37 *NYT*, 56 *WSJ*). The story elements are listed and totaled by row (not column).

References

Acker, Joan. 2006. "Inequality Regimes: Gender, Class, and Race in Organizations." *Gender & Society* 20(4):441–64.

Adut, Ari. 2008. *On Scandal: Moral Disturbances in Society, Politics, and Art.* Cambridge, UK: Cambridge University Press.

Alexander, Jeffrey C. 2002. "On the Social Construction of Moral Universals: The 'Holocaust' from War Crime to Trauma Drama." *European Journal of Social Theory* 5(1):5–85.

Alexander, Jeffrey C. 2004. "Toward a Theory of Cultural Trauma." *Cultural Trauma and Collective Identity* 76(4):620–39.

Alexander, Jeffrey C., Ron Eyerman, Bernard Giesen, Neil J. Smelser, and Piotr Sztompka. 2004. *Cultural Trauma and Collective Identity.* Berkeley: University of California Press.

Allcott, Hunt, and Matthew Gentzkow. 2017. "Social Media and Fake News in the 2016 Election." *Journal of Economic Perspectives* 31(2):211–36.

Altheide, David L. 1987. "Ethnographic Content Analysis." *Qualitative Sociology* 10(1):65–77.

Altheide, David L. 1994. "An Ecology of Communication: Toward a Mapping of the Effective Environment." *Sociological Quarterly* 35(4):665–83.

Altheide, David L. 1996. *Qualitative Media Analysis.* Thousand Oaks, CA: Sage Publications.

Altheide, David L. 2002. *Creating Fear: News and the Construction of Crisis.* New York: Aldine de Gruyter.

215

Altheide, David L. 2004. "Ethnographic Content Analysis." Pp. 325–26 in *The Sage Encyclopedia of Social Science Research Methods*, vol. 1. Thousand Oaks, CA: Sage.

Altheide, David L. 2006. "Terrorism and the Politics of Fear." *Cultural Studies ↔ Critical Methodologies* 6(4):415–39.

Altheide, David L. 2009. *Terror Post 9/11 and the Media*. Vol. 4. New York: Peter Lang.

Altheide, David L. 2013. "Media Logic, Social Control, and Fear." *Communication Theory* 23(3):223–38.

Altheide, David L. 2017. *Terrorism and the Politics of Fear*. 2nd ed. Lanham, MD: Rowman & Littlefield.

Amadeo, Kimberly. 2018. *Hurricane Harvey Facts, Damage and Costs: What Made Harvey So Devastating*. Beaumont, TX: Lamar University.

Anker, Elisabeth. 2005. "Villains, Victims and Heroes: Melodrama, Media, and September 11." *Journal of Communication* 55(1):22–37.

Anker, Elisabeth. 2015. "The Melodramatic Style of American Politics." Pp. 219–45 in *Melodrama after the Tears: New Perspectives on the Politics of Victimhood*, edited by J. Metelmann and S. Loren. Amsterdam, Netherlands: Amsterdam University Press.

Anker, Elisabeth Robin. 2014. *Orgies of Feeling: Melodrama and the Politics of Freedom*. Durham, NC: Duke University Press.

Apter, David E. 1965. *The Politics of Modernization*. Chicago: University of Chicago Press.

Arango, Tim, Nicholas Bogel-Burroughs, Audra D. S. Burch, Maria Cramer, John Eligon, Manny Fernandez, Christine Hauser, et al. 2021. "How George Floyd Died, and What Happened Next." *New York Times*, May 25, https://www.nytimes.com/article/george-floyd.html.

Aronowitz, Stanley. 1996. "The Politics of the Science Wars." Pp. 202–25 in *Science Wars*, edited by Andreew Ross. Durham, NC: Duke University Press.

Associated Press. 2016. "Elevated Levels of Lead Found in Newark Schools' Drinking Water." *New York Times*, March 10. https://www.nytimes.com/2016/03/10/nyregion/elevated-lead-levels-found-in-newark-schools-drinking-water.html.

Baker, Peter. 2017. "Trump Lashes Out at Puerto Rico Mayor Who Criticizes Storm Response." *New York Times*, September 30. https://www.nytimes.com/2017/09/30/us/politics/trump-puerto-rico-mayor.html.

Baker, Peter, and Caitlin Dickerson. 2017. "Trump Warns Storm-Ravaged Puerto Rico That Aid Won't Last 'Forever.'" *New York Times*, October 12. https://www.nytimes.com/2017/10/12/us/politics/trump-warns-puerto-rico-weeks-after-storms-federal-help-cannot-stay-forever.html.

Barker, Vanessa. 2007. "The Politics of Pain: A Political Institutionalist Analysis of Crime Victims' Moral Protests." *Law & Society Review* 41(3):619–64.

Barry, Elizabeth. 2008. "Celebrity, Cultural Production, and Public Life." *International Journal of Cultural Studies* 11(3):251–58.

Barry, John M. 2007. *Rising Tide: The Great Mississippi Flood of 1927 and How It Changed America.* New York: Simon and Schuster.

Baum, Andrew, Raymond Fleming, and Jerome E. Singer. 1983. "Coping with Victimization by Technological Disaster." *Journal of Social Issues* 39(2):117–38.

Bauman, Zygmunt. 1992. "The Solution Is the Problem." *Times Higher Education Supplement* 13(November):25.

Bauman, Zygmunt. 2007. *Liquid Times: Living in an Age of Uncertainty.* Cambridge, UK: Polity Press.

Bauman, Zygmunt. 2013a. *Liquid Fear.* New York: John Wiley & Sons.

Bauman, Zygmunt. 2013b. *Liquid Modernity.* New York: John Wiley & Sons.

Bea, Keith. 2012. "The Formative Years: 1950–1978." Pp. 83–114 in *Emergency Management: The American Experience 1900–2010*, edited by C. B. Rubin. New York: Routledge.

Beamish, Thomas D. 2001. "Environmental Threat and Institutional Betrayal: Lay Public Perceptions of Risk in the San Luis Obispo County Oil Spill." *Organization and Environment* 14(1):5–33.

Beamish, Thomas D. 2002. *Silent Spill: The Organization of an Industrial Crisis.* Cambridge, MA: MIT Press.

Beamish, Thomas D. 2010. "The BP Disaster and Hobson Choice of Oil Production." Think Progress. May 6. https://archive.thinkprogress.org/the-bp -disaster-and-hobsons-choice-of-oil-production-a1b88a67ab80/.

Beamish, Thomas D. 2015. *Community at Risk: Biodefense and the Collective Search for Security.* Palo Alto, CA: Stanford University Press.

Beamish, Thomas D., and Nicole Woolsey Biggart. 2009. "Markets as Regimes: Explaining Change and Stability, Competition and Consensus in Economic Contexts." Unpublished manuscript, University of California Davis.

Beamish, Thomas D., and Nicole Woolsey Biggart. 2011. "The Role of Social Heuristics in Project Centered Production Networks: Insights from the Commercial Construction Industry." *Engineering Project Organization Journal* 1(4):57–70.

Beamish, Thomas D., and Nicole Woolsey Biggart. 2015. "Social Heuristics: The Pragmatics of Convention in Decision-Making." Pp. 235–82 in *Institutions and Ideals: Philip Selznick's Legacy for Organizational Studies*, edited by Matthew S. Kraatz. Bingley, UK: Emerald Group Publishing Limited.

Beamish, Thomas D., Ryken Grattet, and Debbie Niemeier. 2017. "Climate Change and Legitimate Governance: Land Use and Transportation Law and Policy in California." *Brooklyn Law Review* 82(2):725–60.

Beamish, Thomas D., and Amy J. Luebbers. 2009. "Alliance-Building across Social Movements: Bridging Difference in a Peace and Justice Coalition." *Journal of Social Problems* 56(4):647–76.

Beamish, Thomas D., Harvey Molotch, and Richard Flacks. 1995. "Who Supports the Troops: Vietnam, the Gulf War, and the Making of Collective Memory." *Social Problems* 42(3):344–60.

Beamish, Thomas D., Harvey Molotch, Perry Shapiro, and Randolph Bergstrom. 1998. *Petroleum Extraction in San Luis Obispo County, California: An Industrial History*. Camarillo, CA: US Department of the Interior Minerals Management Service, Pacific OCS Region.

Beck, Ulrich. 1992. *Risk Society: Towards a New Modernity*. London: Sage.

Beck, Ulrich. 1999. *World Risk Society*. Cambridge, UK, and Malden, MA: Polity & Blackwell Press.

Beck, Ulrich. 2002. "The Terrorist Threat: World Risk Society Revisited." *Theory, Culture, Society* 19(4):39–55.

Beck, Ulrich. 2009. *World at Risk*. Cambridge, UK: Polity.

Beck, Ulrich, Anthony Giddens, and Scott Lash. 1994. *Reflexive Modernization: Politics, Tradition, and Aesthetics in the Modern Social Order*. Cambridge, UK: Polity.

Beck, Ulrich, and Daniel Levy. 2013. "Cosmopolitanized Nations: Re-Imagining Collectivity in World Risk Society." *Theory, Culture & Society* 30(2):3–31.

Beckett, Katherine. 1996. "Culture and the Politics of Signification: The Case of Child Sexual Abuse." *Social Problems* 43(1):57–76.

Bellah, Robert Neelly, Richard Madsen, William M. Sullivan, Ann Swidler, and Steven M. Tipton. 1996. *Habits of the Heart: Individualism and Commitment in American Life*. Berkeley: University of California Press.

Benford, Robert D., and David A. Snow. 2000. "Framing Processes and Social Movements: An Overview and Assessment." *Annual Review of Sociology* 26:611–39.

Bennett, Jessica. 2022. "If Everything Is 'Trauma,' Is Anything?" *New York Times*, February 4. https://www.nytimes.com/2022/02/04/opinion/caleb-love -bombing-gaslighting-trauma.html.

Benson, Rodney. 2004. "Bringing the Sociology of Media Back In." *Political Communication* 21(3):275–92.

Berstein, Peter. 1996. *Against the Gods: The Remarkable Story of Risk*. New York: John Wiley & Sons.

Best, Joel. 1991. "Road Warriors on Hair Trigger Highways: Cultural Resources and the Media's Construction of the 1987 Freeway Shooting Problem." *Sociological Inquiry* 61:327–45.

Best, Joel. 1997. "Victimization and the Victim Industry." *Society* 34(4):9–17.

Best, Joel. 1999. *Random Violence : How We Talk about New Crimes and New Victims*. Berkeley: University of California Press.

Biggart, Nicole Woolsey, and Thomas Beamish. 2003. "The Economic Sociology of Conventions: Habit, Custom, Practice and Routine in Market Order." *Annual Review of Sociology* 29:443–64.

Birkland, Thomas A. 1997. *After Disaster: Agenda Setting, Public Policy, and Focusing Events.* Washington, DC: Georgetown University Press.

Birkland, Thomas, and Sarah Waterman. 2008. "Is Federalism the Reason for Policy Failure in Hurricane Katrina?" *Publius: The Journal of Federalism* 38(4):692–714.

Black, Donald. 2011. *Moral Time.* Oxford, UK: Oxford University Press.

Black, Donald. 2014. *The Social Structure of Right and Wrong.* Cambridge, MA: Academic Press.

Bluestone, Barry, and Bennett Harrison. 1982. *The Deindustrialization of America: Plant Closings, Community Abandonment, and the Dismantling of Basic Industry.* New York: Basic Books.

Boin, Arjen, and Sanneke Kuipers. 2018. "The Crisis Approach." Pp. 23–38 in *Handbook of Disaster Research,* edited by H. Rodriguez, D. William, and J. E. Trainor. New York: Springer.

Boin, Arjen, and Paul 't Hart. 2007. "The Crisis Approach." Pp. 42–54 in *Handbook of Disaster Research, Handbooks of Sociology and Social Research,* edited by H. Rodriguez, E. L. Quarantelli, and R. R. Dynes. New York: Springer.

Boin, Arjen, Paul 't Hart, and Allan McConnell. 2009. "Crisis Exploitation: Political and Policy Impacts of Framing Contests." *Journal of European Public Policy* 16(1):81–106.

Bolin, Bob. 2007. "Race, Class, Ethnicity, and Disaster Vulnerability." Pp. 113–29 in *Handbook of Disaster Research, Handbooks of Sociology and Social Research,* edited by Havidán Rodríguez, William Donner, Joseph E. Trainor. New York: Springer.

Boltanski, Luc. 1999. *Distant Suffering: Morality, Media and Politics.* Cambridge, UK: Cambridge University Press.

Boltanski, Luc, and Laurent Thévenot. 2006. *On Justification: Economies of Worth.* Princeton, NJ: Princeton University Press.

Boorstin, Daniel. 1992. *The Image: A Guide to Pseudo-Events in America.* 1st ed. New York: Vintage Books.

Bosman, Julie. 2016. "Few Answers on When Flint Will Have Clean Water Again." *New York Times,* January 27, A13. https://www.nytimes.com/2016/01/28/us/few-answers-on-when-flint-will-have-clean-water-again.html.

Bourdieu, Pierre. 1999. *Acts of Resistance: Against the Tyranny of the Market.* New York and London: New Press.

Bovens, Mark and Paul 't Hart. 1996. *Understanding Policy Fiascos.* New Brunswick, NJ: Transaction Books.

Bovens, Mark, and Paul 't Hart. 2016. "Revisiting the Study of Policy Failures." *Journal of European Public Policy* 23(5):653–66.

Bovens, Mark, Paul 't Hart, Sander Dekker, and Gerdien Verheuvel. 1999. "The Politics of Blame Avoidance: Defensive Tactics in a Dutch Crime-Fighting

Scenario." Pp. 123–47 in *When Things Go Wrong*, edited by H. Anheier. Thousand Oaks, CA: Sage Publications.

Bovens, Mark, Paul 't Hart, and Sanneke Kuipers. 2006. "The Politics of Policy Evaluation." Pp. 319–35 in *The Oxford Handbook of Public Policy*, edited by R. E. Goodin, M. Moran, and M. Rein. Oxford, UK: Oxford University Press.

Bovens, Mark, Paul 't Hart, and B. Guy Peters. 2002. *Success and Failure in Public Governance: A Comparative Analysis*. Cheltenham, UK: Edward Elgar Publishing.

Bowles, Samuel, David Gordon, and Thomas Weisskopf. 1984. "Beyond the Wasteland: A Democratic Alternative to Economic Decline." *Science and Society* 48(2):224–29.

Brecher, Jeremy. 1997. *Strike!* Cambridge, MA: South End.

Brenan, Megan. 2019a. "Americans Equally Worried about Mass Shooting and Terrorism." *Politics: Gallup Poll Social Series*, October 11, https://news .gallup.com/poll/267383/americans-equally-worried-mass-shooting -terrorism.aspx.

Brenan, Megan. 2019b. "Americans' Trust in Government to Handle Problems at New Low." *Politics: Gallup Poll Social Series*, January 31. https://news .gallup.com/poll/246371/americans-trust-government-handle-problems-new -low.aspx.

Brenan, Megan. 2021. "Crime Fears Rebound in U.S. after Lull during 2020 Lockdowns." *Politics: Gallup Poll Social Series*, November 10. https://news .gallup.com/poll/357116/crime-fears-rebound-lull-during-2020-lockdowns .aspx?thank-you-subscription-form=1.

Brenan, Megan. 2022. "Parent, Student School Safety Concerns Elevated." *Education*, September 1. https://news.gallup.com/poll/399680/parent -student-school-safety-concerns-elevated.aspx.

Brenner, Robert. 2003. *The Boom and the Bubble: The US in the World Economy*. New York,: Verso.

Brenner, Robert. 2020. "Escalating Plunder." *New Left Review* 123(May/June): 5–22.

Brown, Phil, and Edwin J. Mikkelsen. 1990. *No Safe Place: Toxic Waste, Leukemia, and Community Action*. Berkeley: University of California Press.

Brown, Phil, Carmen M. Vélez Vega, Colleen B. Murphy, Michael Welton, Hector Torres, Zaira Rosario, Akram Alshawabkeh, José F. Cordero, Ingrid Y. Padilla, and John D. Meeker. 2018. "Hurricanes and the Environmental Justice Island: Irma and Maria in Puerto Rico." *Environmental Justice* 11(4):148–53.

Bude, Heinz. 2017. *Society of Fear*. New York: John Wiley & Sons.

Bullard, Robert. 1994. *Dumping on Dixie: Race, Class, and Environmental Quality*. 2nd ed. Boulder, CO: Westview Press.

Bullard, Robert D., and Beverly Wright. 2009. *Race, Place, and Environmental Justice after Hurricane Katrina: Struggles to Reclaim, Rebuild, and Revitalize New Orleans and the Gulf Coast.* Boulder, CO: Westview Press.

Burke, Kenneth. 1973. *The Philosophy of Literary Form.* Berkeley: University of California Press.

Burke, Kenneth. 1984. *Attitudes toward History: With a New Afterword.* Berkeley: University of California Press.

Burns, Alexander, and Julie Turkewitz. 2018. "They've Tuned In, on Guns: Will They Turn Out?" *New York Times*, March 23, A1. https://www.nytimes.com/series/tune-in-turn-out.

Butler, David. 2012a. "Focusing Events in the Early Twentieth Century: A Hurricane, Two Earthquakes, and a Pandemic." Pp. 13–50 in *Emergency Management: The American Experience 1900–2010*, edited by C. B. Rubin. New York: Routledge.

Butler, David. 2012b. "The Expanding Role of the Federal Government: 1927–1950." Pp. 51–82 in *Emergency Management: The American Experience 1900–2010*, edited by C. B. Rubin. New York: Routledge.

Button, Gregory. 2016. *Disaster Culture: Knowledge and Uncertainty in the Wake of Human and Environmental Catastrophe.* London: Routledge.

Calhoun, Craig. 1998. "The Public Good as a Social and Cultural Product." Pp. 20–35 in *Private Action and the Public Good*, edited by E. S. Clemens and W. W. Powell. New Haven, CT: Yale University Press.

Calhoun, Craig. 2004. "A World of Emergencies: Fear, Intervention, and the Limits of Cosmopolitan Order." *Canadian Review of Sociology and Anthropology* 41(4):373–95.

Campbell, Bradley, and Jason Manning. 2014. "Microaggression and Moral Cultures." *Comparative Sociology* 13(6):692–726.

Campbell, Bradley, and Jason Manning. 2018. *The Rise of Victimhood Culture: Microaggressions, Safe Spaces, and the New Culture Wars.* London: Palgrave Macmillan/Springer Nature.

Campo-Flores, Arian, and Joshua Jamerson. 2021. "Black Americans Greet Derek Chauvin Conviction with Relief, Caution." *Wall Street Journal*, April 21. https://www.wsj.com/articles/black-americans-greet-derek-chauvin-conviction-with-relief-caution-11618963514?reflink=desktopwebshare_permalink.

Cappella, Joseph A., and Kathleen H. Jamieson. 1996. "News Frames, Political Cynicism, and Media Cynicism." *Annals of the American Academy of Political and Social Science* 546(1):71–84.

Carlton, Jim, and Loren Elliott. 2018. "As Texas Recovers from Harvey, Port Arthur Struggles; Blue-Collar Gulf Coast City Still Digging Out from Hurricane." *Wall Street Journal*, August 13. https://www.wsj.com/articles/as-texas-recovers-from-harvey-port-arthur-struggles-1534152600.

Carson, Rachel. 1962. *Silent Spring*. Boston, MA: Houghton-Mifflin.

Cartwright, Gary. 1991. *Galveston: A History of the Island*. New York and Toronto: Atheneum and Maxwell Macmillan Canada/Maxwell Macmillan International.

Case, Anne, and Angus Deaton. 2021. *Deaths of Despair and the Future of Capitalism*. Princeton, NJ: Princeton University Press.

Castells, Manuel. 1996. *The Information Age: Economy, Society, Culture*. Vol. 1, *The Rise of the Network Society*. Oxford, UK: Blackwell.

Castells, Manuel, and Laura d'Andrea Tyson. 1989. "High Technology and the Changing International Division of Production: Implications for the US Economy." Pp. 13–50 in *The Newly Industrializing Countries in the World Economy*, edited by Randall Purcell. Boulder, CO: Lynne Rienner.

Castillo, Carlos, Mohammed El-Haddad, Jürgen Pfeffer, and Matt Stempeck. 2014. "Characterizing the Life Cycle of Online News Stories Using Social Media Reactions." Pp. 211–23 in *Proceedings of the 17th ACM Conference on Computer Supported Cooperative Work & Social Computing*. https://dl.acm.org/doi/10.1145/2531602.2531623.

Chabria, Anita, and Esmeralda Bermudez. 2020. "The Enduring Pain of Police Violence; Families Who Lost Loved Ones Revisit Their Unhealed Trauma after George Floyd's Death." *Los Angeles Times*, June 14, A1. https://www.latimes.com/california/story/2020-06-14/police-violence-victims-california-george-floyd-protests.

Chadwick, Andrew. 2017. *The Hybrid Media System: Politics and Power*. Oxford, UK: Oxford University Press.

Chadwick, Andrew, and Philip N. Howard, eds. 2009. *Routledge Handbook of Internet Politics*. London: Routledge.

Chevigny, Paul. 2003. "The Populism of Fear: Politics of Crime in the Americas." *Punishment & Society* 5(1):77–96.

Christie, Nils. 1986. "The Ideal Victim." Pp. 17–30 in *From Crime Policy to Victim Policy: Reorienting the Justice System*, edited by E. A. Fattah. New York: St. Martin's Press.

Clark, Anna. 2018. *The Poisoned City: Flint's Water and the American Urban Tragedy*. New York: Metropolitan Books.

Cohen, Stanley. 2011. *Folk Devils and Moral Panics: The Creation of the Mods and Rockers*. New York: Routledge.

Coleman, James S. 1965. "Modernization: Political Aspects." Pp. 172–85 in *The International Encyclopedia of the Social Sciences*. Vol. 10, edited by D. L. Sills. New York: Macmillan.

Cooney, Mark. 1998. *Warriors and Peacemakers: How Third Parties Shape Violence*. New York: NYU Press.

Cooney, Mark. 2014. "Death by Family: Honor Violence as Punishment." *Punishment & Society* 16(4):406–27.

Cowan, Jill. 2021. "Derek Chauvin Verdict Reverberates Across California." *New York Times*, April 21. https://www.nytimes.com/2021/04/21/us/california-derek-chauvin-verdict.html.

Crutzen, Paul J. 2006. "The 'Anthropocene.'" Pp. 13–18 in *Earth System Science in the Anthropocene*, edited by E. Ehlers and T. Krafft. Berlin: Springer.

Crutzen, Paul J., and Christian Schwägerl. 2011. "Living in the Anthropocene: Toward a New Global Ethos." *Yale Environment 360* 1(January 24). http://hdl.handle.net/11858/00-001M-0000-0014-7F13-F.

Dauber, Michele Landis. 2013. *The Sympathetic State: Disaster Relief and the Origins of the American Welfare State*. Chicago: University of Chicago Press.

Davies, James Chowning. 1974. "The J-Curve and Power Struggle Theories of Collective Violence." *American Sociological Review* 39(4):607–10.

Davis, Joseph E. 2005a. *Accounts of Innocence: Sexual Abuse, Trauma, and the Self*. Chicago: University of Chicago Press.

Davis, Joseph E. 2005b. "Victim Narratives and Victim Selves: False Memory Syndrome and the Power of Accounts." *Social Problems* 52(4):529–48.

Destler, Chester McArthur. 1946. "Entrepreneurial Leadership among the 'Robber Barons': A Trial Balance." *Journal of Economic History* 6(S1):28–49.

Dicken, Peter. 2003. *Global Shift: Reshaping the Global Economic Map in the 21st Century*. 4th ed. New York: Guilford Press.

Dimock, Michael. 2020. "How Americans View Trust, Facts, and Democracy Today." The Pew Research Center, February 19, https://pew.org/38gSYyx.

Dodier, Nicolas. 1993. "Review Article: Action as Combination of 'Common Worlds.'" *Sociological Review* 41(3):556–71.

Dodier, Nicolas. 1995. "The Conventional Foundations of Action: Elements of a Sociological Pragmatics." *Reseaux* 3(2):145–66.

Doka, Kenneth J. 2003a. "Memorialization, Ritual and Public Tragedy." Pp. 179–90 in *Living with Grief: Coping with Public Tragedy*, edited by M. Lattanzi-Licht and K. J. Doka. New York: Hospice Foundation of America/Brunner/Routledge.

Doka, Kenneth J. 2003b. "What Makes a Tragedy Public?" Pp. 3–14 in *Living with Grief: Coping with Public Tragedy*, edited by M. Lattanzi-Licht and K. J. Doka. New York: Hospice Foundation of America/Brunner/Routledge.

Douglas, Mary. 1966. *Purity and Danger*. London: Routledge and Kegan Paul.

Douglas, Mary. 1990. "Risk as Forensic Resource." *Daedalus* 119(4):1–16.

Downs, Anthony. 1972. "Up and down with Ecology—the Issue-Attention Cycle." *Public Interest* 28:38–50.

Downton, James, and Wehr Paul. 1998. "Persistent Pacifism: How Activist Commitment Is Developed and Sustained." *Journal of Peace Research* 35(5):531–50.

Dreier, Peter. 2006. "Katrina and Power in America." *Urban Affairs Review* 41(4):28–549.

Duhart, Olympia. 2019. "Emotional Appraisals in the Wake of Hurricanes Harvey and Maria." *Wake Forest Law Review* 54(4): 973–1000.

Dukes, Kristin Nicole, and Sarah E. Gaither. 2017. "Black Racial Stereotypes and Victim Blaming: Implications for Media Coverage and Criminal Proceedings in Cases of Police Violence against Racial and Ethnic Minorities." *Journal of Social Issues* 73(4):789–807.

Dunn, Amina. 2020. *Most Voters Are "Fearful" and "Angry" about the State of the U.S., but a Majority Now Are "Hopeful," Too.* Washington, DC: Pew Research Center.

Dunn, Jennifer L. 2004. "The Politics of Empathy: Social Movements and Victim Repertoires." *Sociological Focus* 37(3):235–50.

Dunn, Jennifer L., and Melissa Powell-Williams. 2007. "'Everybody Makes Choices': Victim Advocates and the Social Construction of Battered Women's Victimization and Agency." *Violence against Women* 13(10):977–1001.

Durkheim, Emile. 1951. *Suicide: A Study in Sociology.* New York: The Free Press.

Earl Bennett, Stephen, Staci L. Rhine, Richard S. Flickinger, and Linda L. M. Bennett. 1999. "'Video Malaise' Revisited: Public Trust in the Media and Government." *Harvard International Journal of Press/Politics* 4(4):8–23.

Eatwell, Roger, and Matthew Goodwin. 2018. *National Populism: The Revolt against Liberal Democracy.* New York: Penguin.

Edelman, Murray. 1988. *Constructing the Political Spectacle.* Chicago: University of Chicago Press.

Editorial Board, The. 2017. "Texas, Thou Hast Sinned: Progressives Blame Houston's Success for the Hurricane Disaster." *Wall Street Journal*, August 31. https://www.wsj.com/articles/texas-thou-hast-sinned-1504221194?reflink=desktopwebshare_permalink

Ehrenreich, Barbara. 2020. *Fear of Falling: The Inner Life of the Middle Class.* New York: Hachette Book Group.

Eikenberry, Angela M., Verónica Arroyave, and Tracy Cooper. 2007. "Administrative Failure and the International NGO Response to Hurricane Katrina." *Public Administration Review* 67(1):160–70.

Einbinder, Nicole. 2018. "How the Response to Hurricane Maria Compared to Harvey and Irma." *FRONTLINE & WGBH Educational Foundation*, May 1. https://www.pbs.org/wgbh/frontline/article/how-the-response-to-hurricane-maria-compared-to-harvey-and-irma/.

Eliot, T. S. 1991. *T. S. Eliot: Collected Poems, 1909–1962.* New York: HarperCollins.

Entman, Robert M. 1989. *Democracy without Citizens: Media and the Decay of American Politics.* Oxford, UK: Oxford University Press.

Entman, Robert M. 1993. "Framing: Toward Clarification of a Fractured Paradigm." *Journal of Communication* 43(4):51–58.

Entman, Robert M. 2010. "Media Framing Biases and Political Power: Explaining Slant in News of Campaign 2008." *Journalism* 11(4):389–408.

Erikson, Kai T. 1976. *Everything in Its Path: Destruction of Community in the Buffalo Creek Flood*. New York: Simon and Schuster.

Erikson, Kai T. 1990. "Toxic Reckoning: Business Faces a New Kind of Fear." *Harvard Business Review* (January/February):118–26.

Erikson, Kai T. 1994. *A New Species of Trouble: Explorations in Disaster, Trauma, and Community*. 1st ed. New York: W. W. Norton.

Ewick, Patricia, and Susan Sibley. 1995. "Subversive Stories and Hegemonic Tales: Towards a Sociology of Narrative." *Law and Society Review* 29(2): 197–226.

Eyerman, Ron. 2001. *Cultural Trauma: Slavery and the Formation of African American Identity*. Cambridge and Malden, MA: Cambridge University Press.

Eyerman, Ron. 2015. *Is This America? Katrina as Cultural Trauma*. Austin: University of Texas Press.

Eyerman, Ronald, Jeffrey C. Alexander, and Elizabeth Butler Breese, eds. 2015. *Narrating Trauma: On the Impact of Collective Suffering*. London: Routledge.

Fantasia, Rick. 1988. *Cultures of Solidarity: Consciousness, Action, and Contemporary American Workers*. Berkeley: University of California Press.

Fantasia, Rick. 1995. "From Class Consciousness to Culture, Action, and Social Organization." *Annual Review of Sociology* 21:269–87.

Fantasia, Rick, and Kim Voss. 2004. *Hard Work Remaking the American Labor Movement*. Berkeley: University of California Press.

Fassin, Didier, and Richard Rechtman. 2009. *The Empire of Trauma: An Inquiry into the Condition of Victimhood*. Princeton, NJ: Princeton University Press.

Fattah, Essat A. 2000. "Victimology: Past, Present, Future." *Criminologie* 33(1):17–46.

FEMA. 2017. *Historic Disaster Response to Hurricane Harvey in Texas*. News Release. HQ-17-133. Austin, TX: Federal Emergency Management Agency. https://www.fema.gov/press-release/20210318/historic-disaster-response -hurricane-harvey-texas.

FEMA. 2018. *Hurricane Season FEMA After-Action Report*. Washington, DC: Federal Emergency Management Agency. https://www.fema.gov/sites/default /files/2020-08/fema_hurricane-season-after-action-report_2017.pdf.

Fernandez, Manny, and Audra D. S. Burch. 2020. "Man of Outsize Dreams Stirred a Movement With Final Breaths." *New York Times*, June 9, A1. https://www.nytimes.com/article/george-floyd-who-is.html?smid=url-share.

Finkel, Eli J., Christopher A. Bail, Mina Cikara, Peter H. Ditto, Shanto Iyengar, Samara Klar, Lilliana Mason, Mary C. McGrath, Brendan Nyhan, and David G. Rand. 2020. "Political Sectarianism in America." *Science* 370(6516): 533–36.

Fishman, Robert. 1978. "Crime Waves as Ideology." *Social Problems* 25(5):531–43.

Fominaya, Cristina Flesher, and Rosemary Barberet. 2013. "Defining the Victims of Terrorism." Pp. 129–46 in *Violence and War in Culture and the Media: Five Disciplinary Lenses*, edited by A. Karatzogianni. Londo: Routledge.

Fortin, Jacey. 2017. "America's Tap Water: Too Much Contamination, Not Enough Reporting, Study Finds." *New York Times*, May 4, https://www.ny times.com/2017/05/04/us/tapwater-drinking-water-study.html.

Fortin, Jacey. 2023. "Ohio Train Derailment: Separating Fact From Fiction." *New York Times*, February 28. https://www.nytimes.com/2023/02/28/us /ohio-train-derailment-east-palestine.html?smid=url-share.

Foucault, Michel. 1984. "Nietzche, Genealogy, and History." Pp. 76–100 in *The Foucault Reader*, edited by P. Rabinow. New York: Pantheon Book.

Fraser, Nancy. 1990. "Rethinking the Public Sphere: A Contribution to the Critique of Actually Existing Democracy." *Social Text* 25(26):56–80.

Freeman, Joshua B. 2018. *Behemoth: A History of the Factory and the Making of the Modern World*. New York: W. W. Norton.

Freudenburg, William R. 1993. "Risk and Recreancy: Weber, the Division of Labor, and the Rationality of Risk Perceptions." *Social Forces* 71(4):909–32.

Freudenburg, William R. 2000. "The Risk Society Reconsidered: Recreancy, the Division of Labor, and Risks to the Social Fabric." Pp. 107–22 in *Risk in the Modern Age: Social Theory, Science, and Environmental Decision Making*, edited by M. J. Cohen. New York: St. Martins Press.

Freudenburg, William R. 2001. "Risk, Responsibility and Recreancy." Pp. 87–108 in *Environmental Risks: Perception, Evaluation and Management*, vol. 9, edited by J. N. Gisela Böm, Timothy McDaniels, and Hans Spada. Bingley, UK: Emerald Group Publishing.

Freudenburg, William R., and Robert Gramling. 2011. *Blowout in the Gulf: The BP Oil Spill Disaster and the Future of Energy in America*. Cambridge, MA: MIT Press.

Freudenburg, William R., and Susan K. Pastor. 1992. "Technological Risks: Toward a Sociological Perspective." *Sociological Quarterly* 33(3):389–412.

Friedman, Jeffrey A. 2019. "Priorities for Preventive Action: Explaining Americans' Divergent Reactions to 100 Public Risks." *American Journal of Political Science* 63(1):181–96.

Fukuyama, Francis. 2022. *Liberalism and Its Discontents*. New York: Farrar, Straus and Giroux.

Furedi, Frank. 2004. *Therapy Culture: Cultivating Vulnerability in an Uncertain Age*. London: Routledge.

Furedi, Frank. 2006. *Culture of Fear Revisited: Risk-Taking and the Morality of Low Expectation*. 4th ed. London: Continuum.

Furedi, Frank. 2007. *Politics of Fear*. London: Bloomsbury Publishing.

Furedi, Frank. 2010. "Celebrity Culture." *Society* 47(6):493–97.

Furedi, Frank. 2018. *How Fear Works: Culture of Fear in the Twenty-First Century*. London: Bloomsbury Publishing.

Gabler, Neal. 2001. "Toward a New Definition of Celebrity." USC Annenberg: The Norman Lear Center. https://learcenter.org/publication/toward-a-new-definition-of-celebrity-2/.

Galaway, Burt, and Leonard Rutman. 1974. "Victim Compensation: An Analysis of Substantive Issues." *Social Service Review* 48(1):60–74.

Gallup. 2021. "Terrorism." Retrieved April 6, 2023. https://news.gallup.com/poll/4909/Terrorism-United-States.aspx.

Gallup. 2022. "Confidence in Institutions." Retrieved January 4, 2022. https://news.gallup.com/poll/1597/Confidence-Institutions.aspx.

Gamson, William A. 1990. *The Strategy of Social Protest*. Belmont, CA: Wadsworth.

Gamson, William A. 1992. *Talking Politics*. Cambridge, UK: Cambridge University Press.

Gamson, William A. 1995. "Constructing Social Protest." Pp. 85–106 in *Social Movement Culture*. Vol. 4, *Social Movements, Protests, Contention*, edited by H. J. and B. Klandermas. Minneapolis: University of Minnesota.

Gamson, William A., and Andre Modigliani. 1989. "Media Discourse and Public Opinion on Nuclear Power: A Constructionist Approach." *American Journal of Sociology* 95(1):1–37.

Gans, Herbert. 1980. *Deciding What's News*. New York: Vintage.

Garcia-Lopez, Gustavo A. 2018. "The Multiple Layers of Environmental Injustice in Contexts of (Un) Natural Disasters: The Case of Puerto Rico Post-Hurricane Maria." *Environmental Justice* 11(3):101–8.

Gaskins, Benjamin, and Jennifer Jerit. 2012. "Internet News: Is It a Replacement for Traditional Media Outlets?" *International Journal of Press/Politics* 17(2):190–213.

Geggis, Anne, Lisa J. Huriash, and Erika Pesantes. 2018. "Texts under 'Code Red'; Parkland Students' Words Evoke Terror and Heartbreak amid Shooting." *Los Angeles Times*, March 11, A14. https://enewspaper.latimes.com/infinity/article_share.aspx?guid=3157f3f8-0dd1-493c-a458-d4ce3f76818a.

Gencarelli, Thomas F. 2000. "The Intellectual Roots of Media Ecology in the Work and Thought of Neil Postman." *New Jersey Journal of Communication* 8(1):91–103.

Gephart, Robert P. 1993. "The Textual Approach: Risk and Blame in Disaster Sensemaking." *Academy of Management Journal* 36(6):1465–1514.

Gibbs, Lois Marie, and Murray Levine. 1982. *Love Canal: My Story*. Albany: SUNY Press.

Giddens, Anthony. 1984. *The Constitution of Society*. Berkeley: University of California Press.

Giddens, Anthony. 1990. *The Consequences of Modernity*. Palo Alto, CA: Stanford University Press.

Giddens, Anthony. 1998. *Conversations with Anthony Giddens*. Making Sense of Modernity. Palo Alto, CA: Stanford University Press.

Giddens, Anthony. 1999. "Risk and Responsibility." *Modern Law Review* 62(1):1–10.

Giddens, Anthony, and Christopher Pierson. 1998. *Conversations with Anthony Gidden: Making Sense of Modernity*. Palo Alto, CA: Stanford University Press.

Gidron, Noam, and Peter A. Hall. 2020. "Populism as a Problem of Social Integration." *Comparative Political Studies* 53(7):1027–59.

Gitlin, Todd. 1980. *The Whole World Is Watching: Mass Media in the Making and Unmaking of the New Left*. Berkeley: University of California Press.

Glassner, Barry. 2009. *The Culture of Fear: Why Americans Are Afraid of the Wrong Things*. 10th anniversary ed. New York,: Basic Books.

Godbey, Emily. 2006. "Disaster Tourism and the Melodrama of Authenticity: Revisiting the 1889 Johnstown Flood." *Pennsylvania History: A Journal of Mid-Atlantic Studies* 73(3):273–315.

Goffman, E. 1963. *Stigma: Notes on the Management of Spoiled Identity*. Englewood Cliffs, NJ: Prentice-Hall.

Goffman, Erving. 1959. *The Presentation of Self in Everyday Life*. Garden City, NY: Doubleday.

Goffman, Erving. 1974. *Frame Analysis: An Essay on the Organization of Experience*. Cambridge, MA: Harvard University Press.

Goode, Erich, and Nachman Ben-Yehuda. 2010. *Moral Panics: The Social Construction of Deviance*. New York: John Wiley & Sons.

Goodhart, David. 2017. *The Road to Somewhere: The Populist Revolt and the Future of Politics*. Oxford, UK: Oxford University Press.

Goodnough, Abby, Monica Davey, and Mitch Smith. 2016. "When the Water Turned Brown." *New York Times*, January 23, A1. https://www.nytimes.com/2016/01/24/us/when-the-water-turned-brown.html.

Goodwin, Jeff, James M. Jasper, and Francesca Polletta. 2001. *Passionate Politics: Emotions and Social Movements*. Chicago: University of Chicago Press.

Gorski, Philip S., and Samuel L. Perry. 2022. *The Flag and the Cross: White Christian Nationalism and the Threat to American Democracy*. Oxford, UK: Oxford University Press.

Gotham, Kevin Fox. 2007. "Critical Theory and Katrina: Disaster, Spectacle and Immanent Critique." *City & Community* 11(1):81–99.

Gottlieb, Julian. 2015. "Protest News Framing Cycle: How the *New York Times* Covered Occupy Wall Street." *International Journal of Communication* 9:231–53. https://ijoc.org/index.php/ijoc/article/view/2880/1297.

Graber, Doris A., and Johanna Dunaway. 2017. *Mass Media and American Politics*. Washington, DC: CQ Press.

Green, Nathan C. 2000. *Story of the 1900 Galveston Hurricane*. Gretna, LA: Pelican Publishers.

Gurr, Ted R. 1970. *Why Men Rebel*. Princeton, NJ: Princeton University Press.

Gusfield, Joseph R. 1980. *Symbolic Crusade: Status Politics and the American Temperance Movement*. Westport, CT: Greenwood Press.

Gusfield, Joseph R. 1984. *The Culture of Public Problems: Drinking-Driving and the Symbolic Order*. Chicago: University of Chicago Press.

Habermas, Jürgen. 1975. *Legitimation Crisis*. Boston, MA: Beacon Press.

Habermas, Jürgen. 1979. *Communication and the Evolution of Society*. Boston, MA: Beacon Press.

Habermas, Jürgen. 1991. *The Structural Transformation of the Public Sphere: An Inquiry into a Category of Bourgeois Society*. Cambridge, MA: MIT Press.

Hall, Peter D. 1987. "A Historical Overview of the Private Nonprofit Sector." Pp. 32–65 in *The Nonprofit Sector: A Research Handbook*, edited by Walter W. Powell. New Haven, CT: Yale University Press.

Hall, Stuart. 1975. "Introduction." Pp. 11–24 in *Paper Voices: The Popular Press and Social Change, 1935–1965*, edited by A. C. H. Smith, E. Immirzi, and T. Blackwell. London: Rowman and Littlefield.

Hall, Stuart. 1980. "Encoding/Decoding." Pp. 507–17 in *Culture, Media, Language*, edited by S. Hall, D. Hobson, A. Lowe, and P. Willis. London: Routledge.

Hallin, Daniel C. 1989. *The Uncensored War: The Media and Vietnam*. Berkeley: University of California Press.

Hammond, William M. 1998. *Reporting Vietnam: Media and Military at War*. Lawrence: University Press of Kansas.

Hanna-Attisha, Mona, Jenny LaChance, Richard Casey Sadler, and Allison Champney Schnepp. 2016. "Elevated Blood Lead Levels in Children Associated with the Flint Drinking Water Crisis: A Spatial Analysis of Risk and Public Health Response." *American Journal of Public Health* 106(2):283–90.

Hardin, Russell. 2002. *Trust and Trustworthiness*. New York: Russell Sage Foundation.

Hardin, Russell. 2004. *Distrust*. New York: Russell Sage Foundation.

Hartsock, Nancy C. M. 1998. "The Feminist Standpoint: Developing the Ground for a Specifically Feminist Historical Materialism." Pp. 565–92 in *Karl Marx*, edited by K. B. Anderson and B. Ollman. Oxfordshire, UK: Taylor & Francis Group.

Harvey, David. 1982. *The Limits to Capital*. London: Basil Blackwell.

Harvey, David. 1989. *The Condition of Postmodernity: An Enquiry into the Origins of Cultural Change*. London: Routledge.

Harvey, David. 2014. *Seventeen Contradictions and the End of Capitalism*. Oxford, UK: Oxford University Press.

Hawdon, James, and John Ryan. 2011. "Social Relations That Generate and Sustain Solidarity after a Mass Tragedy." *Social Forces* 89(4):1363–84.

Hayes, Rebecca A., Julia Crouse Waddell, and Peter M. Smudde. 2017. "Our Thoughts and Prayers Are with the Victims: Explicating the Public Tragedy as a Public Relations Challenge." *Public Relations Inquiry* 6(3):253–74.

Healy, Jack. 2018. "Gun Country Backlash When Rural Students Speak Out for Limits." *New York Times*, May 23, A13. https://www.nytimes.com/2018/05/22/us/marshall-county-kentucky-student-gun-protests.html?smid=url-share.

Hennessy-Fiske, Molly. 2020. "George Floyd's Houston Memorial Reminds Friends What They Survived." *Los Angeles Times*, June 8. https://www.latimes.com/world-nation/story/2020-06-08/george-floyds-homecoming-reminds-friends-what-they-survived.

Hennessy-Fiske, Molly. 2021. "Ex-Officer's Trial Has Minneapolis on Edge; City, Fearing a Repeat of Unrest, Has Boosted Security as Defendant in George Floyd's Death Heads to Court." *Los Angeles Times*, March 8, A4. https://www.latimes.com/world-nation/story/2021-03-07/the-first-trial-starts-next-week-for-police-in-george-floyd-death.

Hennessy-Fiske, Molly, Ruben Vives, and Melissa Etehad. 2017. "'Aid Isn't Getting to People Fast Enough'; Puerto Rico Residents Suffer as Help Comes Slowly: After so Many Storms, Can a Thinly Stretched FEMA Come Through?" *Los Angeles Times*, September 28, A1. https://www.latimes.com/nation/la-na-puerto-rico-aid-20170927-story.html.

Henry, Gary T., and Craig S. Gordon. 2001. "Tracking Issue Attention: Specifying the Dynamics of the Public Agenda." *Public Opinion Quarterly* 65(2):157–77.

Hilgartner, Stephen, and Charles L. Bosk. 1988. "The Rise and Fall of Social Problems: A Public Arenas Model." *American Journal of Sociology* 94:53–78.

Hirschfield, Paul J., and Daniella Simon. 2010. "Legitimating Police Violence: Newspaper Narratives of Deadly Force." *Theoretical Criminology* 14(2):155–82.

Hochschild, Arlie Russell. 2018. *Strangers in Their Own Land: Anger and Mourning on the American Right*. New York: The New Press.

Hoffman, Andrew J., and William Ocasio. 2001. "Not All Events Are Attended Equally: Toward a Middle-Range Theory of Industry Attention to External Events." *Organization Science* 12(4):414–34.

Insurance Information Institute. 2018. *Spotlight on Catastrophes: Insurance Issues*. Insurance Information Institute, Inc. https://www.iii.org/article/spotlight-on-catastrophes-insurance-issues.

Ivers, Dan. 2016. "Officials Say Contaminated Water at Newark Schools 'Urgent', but No Flint." NJ.com. Retrieved May 15, 2020. https://www.nj.com/essex/2016/03/elevated_lead_levels_found_in_newark_schools_drink.html.

Iyengar, Shanto, and Adam Simon. 1993. "News Coverage of the Gulf Crisis and Public Opinion: A Study of Agenda-Setting, Priming, and Framing." *Communication Research* 20(3):365–83.

Jaffe, Sarah. 2018. "The Collective Power of #MeToo." *Dissent* 65(2):80–87.

Jarvie, Jenny, Molly Hennessy-Fiske, and Matt Pearce. 2017. "New Assault Douses Coast; Houston Sees Sun, but Nearby Cities 'At God's Mercy' as Heavy Rainfall Moves East." *Los Angeles Times*, August 31, A10. https://www.latimes.com/nation/la-na-texas-tropical-storm-harvey-20170830-story.html.

Jasper, James M. 1997. *The Art of Moral Protest: Culture, Biography, and Creativity in Social Movements*. Chicago,: University of Chicago Press.

Jeffery, Laura, and Matei Candea. 2006. "The Politics of Victimhood." *History and Anthropology* 17(4):287–96.

Johnson, Cedric. 2011. *The Neoliberal Deluge: Hurricane Katrina, Late Capitalism, and the Remaking of New Orleans*. Minneapolis: University of Minnesota Press.

Jones, Jefferey. 2020. "Black, White Adults' Confidence Diverges Most on Police." Gallup. Retrieved August 15, 2020. https://news.gallup.com/poll/317114/black-white-adults-confidence-diverges-police.aspx.

Jones, Jeffrey M. 2022. "Confidence in U.S. Institutions Down; Average at New Low." Gallup. Retrieved January 4, 2023. https://news.gallup.com/poll/394283/confidence-institutions-down-average-new-low.aspx.

Jorgensen-Earp, Cheryl R., and Lori A. Lanzilotti. 1998. "Public Memory and Private Grief: The Construction of Shrines at the Sites of Public Tragedy." *Quarterly Journal of Speech* 84(2):150–70.

Joseph, Samantha Rivera, Caroline Voyles, Kimberly D. Williams, Erica Smith, and Mariana Chilton. 2020. "Colonial Neglect and the Right to Health in Puerto Rico after Hurricane Maria." *American Journal of Public Health* 110(10):1512–18.

Kahneman, Daniel, Paul Slovic, and Amos Tversky. 1982. *Judgment under Uncertainty: Heuristics and Biases*. Cambridge, UK: Cambridge University Press.

Kahneman, Daniel, and Amos Tversky, eds. 2000. *Choices, Values, and Frames*. Cambridge, UK: Cambridge University Press.

Kalleberg, Arne L. 2000. "Nonstandard Employment Relations: Part-Time, Temporary and Contract Work." *Annual Review of Sociology* 26(1):341–65.

Kalleberg, Arne L., Barbara F. Reskin, and Ken Hudson. 2000. "Bad Jobs in America: Standard and Nonstandard Employment Relations and Job Quality in the United States." *American Sociological Review* 65(2):256–78.

Karni, Annie, and Patricia Mazzei. 2019. "Trump Lashes Out Again at Puerto Rico, Bewildering the Island." *New York Times*, April 2. https://www.nytimes.com/2019/04/02/us/trump-puerto-rico.html.

Kavolis, Vytautas. 1977. "Moral Cultures and Moral Logics." *Sociological Analysis* 38(4):331–44.

Kellner, Douglas. 2003. *Media Spectacle*. London: Routledge.

Kellner, Douglas. 2004. "9/11, Spectacles of Terror, and Media Manipulation: A Critique of Jihadist and Bush Media Politics." *Critical Discourse Studies* 1(1):41–64.

Kellner, Douglas. 2007. "The Katrina Hurricane Spectacle and Crisis of the Bush Presidency." *Cultural Studies ↔ Critical Methodologies* 7(2):222–34.

Kellner, Douglas. 2014. "Media Propaganda and Spectacle in the War on Iraq: A Critique of U.S. Broadcasting Networks." *Cultural Studies ↔ Critical Methodologies* 4(3):329–38.

Kellner, Douglas. 2015a. *Guys and Guns Amok: Domestic Terrorism and School Shootings from the Oklahoma City Bombing to the Virginia Tech Massacre*. London: Routledge.

Kellner, Douglas. 2015b. *Media Spectacle and the Crisis of Democracy: Terrorism, War, and Election Battles*. London: Routledge.

Keynyn, Brysse, Naomi Oreskes, Jessica O'Reilly, and Michael Oppenheimer. 2013. "Climate Change Prediction: Erring on the Side of Least Drama?" *Global Environmental Change* 23(1):327–37.

King, Andrew, and David Botti. 2017. "In a Puerto Rican Village: 'The Wind Came and Took Everything.'" *New York Times*, September 27. https://nyti.ms/2fAMa9j.

Kinnick, Katherine N., Dean M. Krugman, and Glen T. Cameron. 1996. "Compassion Fatigue: Communication and Burnout toward Social Problems." *Journalism & Mass Communication Quarterly* 73(3):687–707.

Kinnvall, Catarina, and Jennifer Mitzen. 2020. "Anxiety, Fear, and Ontological Security in World Politics: Thinking with and beyond Giddens." *International Theory* 12(2):240–56.

Kishore, Nishant, Domingo Marqués, Ayesha Mahmud, Mathew V. Kiang, Irmary Rodriguez, Arlan Fuller, Peggy Ebner, Cecilia Sorensen, Fabio Racy, and Jay Lemery. 2018. "Mortality in Puerto Rico after Hurricane Maria." *New England Journal of Medicine* 379(2):162–70.

Kleinman, Arthur, Veena Das, and Margaret M. Lock. 1997. *Social Suffering*. Berkeley: University of California Press.

Knight, W. 2023. "Runaway AI Is an Extinction Risk, Experts Warn." *Wired*, Business News, May 30. https://www.wired.com/story/runaway-ai-extinction-statement/.

Kreps, G. A. 1990. "The Federal Emergency Management System in the United States: Past and Present." *International Journal of Mass Emergencies and Disasters* 8(3):275–300.

Kristof, Nicolas. 2017. "We Don't Deny Harvey, So Why Deny Climate Change?" *New York Times*, September 3. https://www.nytimes.com/2017/09/02/opinion/sunday/hurricane-harvey-climate-change.html?searchResultPosition=1.

Kropf, Nancy P., and Barbara L. Jones. 2014. "When Public Tragedies Happen: Community Practice Approaches in Grief, Loss, and Recovery." *Journal of Community Practice* 22(3):281–98.

Kruse, Kevin, and Julian Zelizer. 2019. "Perspective | How Policy Decisions Spawned Today's Hyperpolarized Media." *Washington Post*, January 17. https://www.washingtonpost.com/outlook/2019/01/17/how-policy-decisions-spawned-todays-hyperpolarized-media/.

Kuhn, Thomas S. 1970. *The Structure of Scientific Revolutions*. 2nd ed. Chicago: University of Chicago Press.

Kuipers, Sanneke, and Paul 't Hart. 2014. "Accounting for Crises." Pp. 589–602 in *The Oxford Handbook of Public Accountability*, edited by M. Bovens, R. E. Goodin, and T. Schillemans. Oxford, UK: Oxford University Press.

Kurer, Thomas. 2020. "The Declining Middle: Occupational Change, Social Status, and the Populist Right." *Comparative Political Studies* 53(10–11): 1798–1835.

Lacey, Marc. 2021. "A Veteran of the O. J. Simpson Legal Drama Has One Eye on the Set This Time." *New York Times*, March 29. https://www.nytimes.com/2021/03/29/us/oj-simpson-derek-chauvin-trial.html?smid=url-share.

Lamb, Sharon. 1999a. "Constructing the Victim: Popular Images and Lasting Labels." Pp. 108–38 in *New Visions of Victims: Feminists Struggle with the Concept*, edited by S. Lamb. New York, NY: New York University Press.

Lamb, Sharon, ed. 1999b. *New Versions of Victims: Feminists Struggle with The Concept*. New York, NY: New York University Press.

Lamont, Michèle, and Laurent Thévenot, eds. 2000. *Rethinking Comparative Cultural Sociology. Repertoires of Evaluation in France and the United States*. Cambridge, UK: Cambridge University Press.

Lash, Scott. 2000. "Risk Culture." Pp. 47–62 in *The Risk Society and Beyond: Critical Issues for Social Theory*, edited by U. Beck, Barbara Adam, and Jost Van Loon. London: Sage Press.

Lash, Scott, Bronislaw Szerszynski, and Brian Wynne. 1996. *Risk, Environment and Modernity: Towards a New Ecology*. Thousand Oaks, CA: Sage.

Latour, Bruno. 1987. *Science in Action*. Cambridge, MA: Harvard University Press.

Latour, Bruno. 2004. "Why Has Critique Run out of Steam? From Matters of Fact to Matters of Concern." *Critical Inquiry* 30(2):225–48.

Latour, Bruno. 2012. *We Have Never Been Modern*. Cambridge, MA: Harvard University Press.

Lattanzi-Licht, Marcia, and Kenneth J. Doka, eds. 2003. *Living with Grief: Coping with Public Tragedy*. New York: Hospice Foundation of America/ Brunner/Routledge.

Leonhardt, David, and Ian Prasad Philbrick. 2018. "Donald Trump's Racism: The Definitive List, Updated." *New York Times*, January 15. https://www.nytimes.com/interactive/2018/01/15/opinion/leonhardt-trump-racist.html.

Letters to the Editor. 2018. "Young People at the Forefront of Gun Control." *New York Times*, February 21, A22. https://www.nytimes.com/2018/02/20/opinion/students-gun-control.html.

Letukas, Lynn. 2014. *Primetime Pundits: How Cable News Covers Social Issues.* Washington, DC: Lexington Books/Rowman & Littlefield.

Leung, Angela K. Y., and Dov Cohen. 2011. "Within-and between-Culture Variation: Individual Differences and the Cultural Logics of Honor, Face, and Dignity Cultures." *Journal of Personality and Social Psychology* 100(3):507–26.

Levine, Adeline. 1982. *Love Canal: Science, Politics, and People.* Lexington, MA: Lexington Books.

Levy, Jonathan. 2012. *Freaks of Fortune: The Emerging World of Capitalism and Risk in America.* Cambridge, MA: Harvard University Press.

Levy, Marion J., Jr. 1967. "Social Patterns and Problems of Modernization." Pp. 189–208 in *Readings on Social Change*, edited by W. E. Moore and R. M. Cook. Englewood Cliffs, NJ: Prentice-Hall.

Leyden, Liz. 2018. "In Echo of Flint, Mich., Water Crisis Now Hits Newark." *New York Times*, October 30. https://www.nytimes.com/2018/10/30/nyregion/newark-lead-water-pipes.html?smid=url-share.

Lichterman, Paul. 1996. *The Search for Political Community: American Activists Reinventing Commitment.* New York: Cambridge University Press.

Lindsay, Bruce R. 2014. *FEMA's Disaster Relief Fund: Overview and Selected Issues.* Congressional Research Service. https://crsreports.congress.gov/product/pdf/R/R43537 and http://fas.org/sgp/crs/homesec/R43537.pdf.

Lindsay, Bruce R., and Francis X. McCarthy. 2015. *Stafford Act Declarations 1953-2014: Trends, Analyses, and Implications for Congress.* Congressional Report 7–5700. Washington, DC: Congressional Research Service. https://sgp.fas.org/crs/homesec/R42702.pdf.

Linstrom, Margaret, and Willemien Marais. 2012. "Qualitative News Frame Analysis: A Methodology." *Communitas* 17:21–38. https://journals.ufs.ac.za/index.php/com/article/view/991.

Lippard, Lucy R. 1999. *On the Beaten Track: Tourism, Art and Place.* New York: New Press.

Lipstadt, Deborah E. 1993. *Beyond Belief: The American Press and the Coming of the Holocaust, 1933–1945.* New York: Simon and Schuster.

Littlefield, Robert S., and Andrea M. Quenette. 2007. "Crisis Leadership and Hurricane Katrina: The Portrayal of Authority by the Media in Natural Disasters." *Journal of Applied Communication Research* 35(1):26–47.

Lloréns, Hilda. 2018. "Imaging Disaster: Puerto Rico through the Eye of Hurricane María." *Transforming Anthropology* 26(2):136–56.

Loren, Scott, and Jörg Metelmann. 2016. *Melodrama after the Tears: New Perspectives on the Politics of Victimhood.* Amsterdam, Netherlands: Amsterdam University Press.

Loseke, Donileen R. 2001. "Lived Realities and Formula Stories of 'Battered Women.'" Pp. 107–26 in *Institutional Selves: Troubled Identities in a Postmodern World*, edited by J. F. Gubrium and J. A. Holstein. Oxford, UK: Oxford University Press.

Luker, Kristin. 1984. *Abortion and the Politics of Motherhood*. Berkeley: University of California Press.

Lukianoff, Greg, and Jonathan Haidt. 2015. "The Coddling of the American Mind." *Atlantic* 316(2):42–52.

Lukianoff, Greg, and Jonathan Haidt. 2018. *The Coddling of the American Mind: How Good Intentions and Bad Ideas Are Setting up a Generation for Failure*. New York: Penguin.

Lum, Casey M. K. 2006. *Perspectives on Culture, Technology and Communication: The Media Ecology Tradition*. New York: Hampton Press.

Malle, Bertram F., Steve Guglielmo, and Andrew E. Monroe. 2014. "A Theory of Blame." *Psychological Inquiry* 25(2):147–86.

Marcuse, Herbert. 1964. *One-Dimensional Man: Studies in the Ideology of Advanced Industrial Society*. Boston, MA: Beacon Press.

Margetts, Helen, Peter John, Scott Hale, and Taha Yasseri. 2015. *Political Turbulence: How Social Media Shape Collective Action*. Princeton, NJ: Princeton University Press.

Marsh, Barnaby. 2002. "Heuristics as Social Tools." *New Ideas in Psychology* 20(1):49–57.

Mauldin, William, and Michael Bender. 2017. "Trump Slams 'Ingrates' and Media for Not Recognizing Puerto Rico Relief Progress: Trump Returns to Twitter after Criticizing San Juan's Mayor While Administration Officials Come to President's Defense." *Wall Street Journal*, October 1. https://www.wsj.com/articles/trump-slams-ingrates-and-media-for-not-recognizing-puerto-rico-relief-progress-1506881817.

Mawby, Rob. 2013. *Policing Images*. London: Willan.

Mayhew, David R. 1974. *Congress: The Electoral Connection*. Vol. 26. New Haven, CT: Yale University Press.

Mazur, Allan. 2010. *True Warning and False Alarms: Evaluating Fears about Health Risks and Technologies, 1948–1971*. New York: Routledge.

McCarthy, Justin. 2020. *Perceptions of Increased U.S. Crime at Highest since 1993*. Politics: Gallup Poll Social Series. Washington, DC: Gallup.

McComb, David G. 1986. *Galveston: A History*. 1st ed. Austin: University of Texas Press.

McCombs, Maxwell. 2014. *Setting the Agenda: Mass Media and Public Opinion*. Malden, MA: Polity Press.

McCombs, Maxwell, and Sebastián Valenzuela. 2014. "Agenda-Setting Theory: The Frontier Research Questions Edited." Pp. 633–48 in *The Oxford Handbook of Political Communication*, edited by K. Kenski and K. H. Jamieson. Oxford, UK: Oxford University Press.

McCullough, David G. 1968. *The Johnstown Flood*. New York: Simon and Schuster.

McEvoy, Arthur F. 2018. "The Triangle Shirtwaist Factory Fire of 1911: Social Change, Industrial Accidents, and the Evolution of Common-Sense Causality." *Law & Social Inquiry* 20(2):621–51.

McGraw, Kathleen M. 1991. "Managing Blame: An Experimental Test of the Effects of Political Accounts." *American Political Science Review* 85(4): 1133–57.

McWhirter, Cameron, and Valerie Bauerlein. 2018. "Shooting Victims: A 'Jokester' Coach; an Avid Soccer Player; Youth Volunteers." *Wall Street Journal*, February 15. https://www.wsj.com/articles/shooting-victims-a-jokester-coach-an-avid-soccer-player-youth-volunteers-1518719090.

Meek, Allen. 2016. "Cultural Trauma and the Media." Pp. 27–37 in *The Interdisciplinary Handbook of Trauma and Culture*, edited by Y. Ataria, D. Gurevitz, H. Pedaya, and Y. Neria. New York: Springer International.

Melucci, Alberto. 1996. *Challenging Codes: Collective Action in the Information Age*. Cambridge, UK: Cambridge University Press.

Meyer, David S. 1995. "Framing National Security: Elite Public Discourse on Nuclear Weapons during the Cold War." *Political Communication* 12(2): 173–92.

Mills, C. Wright. 2000. *The Sociological Imagination*. Oxford, UK: Oxford University Press.

Mitchell, Charles E. 1999. "Violating the Public Trust: The Ethical and Moral Obligations of Government Officials." *Public Personnel Management* 28(1):27–38.

Moeller, Susan D. 2002. *Compassion Fatigue: How the Media Sell Disease, Famine, War and Death*. New York: Routledge.

Molotch, Harvey L. 1979. "Media and Movements." Pp. 71–93 in *The Dynamics of Social Movements*, edited by M. Zald and J. McCarthy. Winthrop, MN: Winthrop Press.

Molotch, Harvey L. 2006. "Death on the Roof: Race and Bureaucratic Failure." *Space and Culture* 9(1):31–34.

Montinola, Gabriella R. 2004. "Corruption, Distrust, and the Deterioration of the Rule of Law." Pp. 298–324 in *Distrust*, edited by R. Hardin. New York: Russell Sage Foundation.

Moody, Michael, and Laurent Thévenot. 2000. "Comparing Models of Strategy, Interests, and the Public Good in French and American Environmental Disputes." Pp. 273–305 in *Rethinking Comparative Cultural Sociology. Repertoires of Evaluation in France and the United States*, edited by M. Lamont and L. Thévenot. Cambridge, UK: Cambridge University Press.

Mooney, Chris, and Brady Dennis. 2018. "Extreme Hurricanes and Wildfires Made 2017 the Most Costly U.S. Disaster Year on Record." *Washington Post*,

January 8. https://www.washingtonpost.com/news/energy-environment/wp
/2018/01/08/hurricanes-wildfires-made-2017-the-most-costly-u-s-disaster
-year-on-record/.

Morris, David B. 1996. "About Suffering: Voice, Genre, and Moral Community."
Daedalus 125(1):25–45.

Mouffe, Chantal. 2018. *For a Left Populism*. London: Verso Books.

Mudge, Stephanie L. 2008. "What Is Neo-Liberalism?" *Socio-Economic Review*
6(4):703–31.

Mudge, Stephanie Lee. 2011. "What's Left of Leftism? Neoliberal Politics in
Western Party Systems, 1945–2004." *Social Science History* 35(3):337–80.

Mudge, Stephanie L. 2018. *Leftism Reinvented: Western Parties from Socialism
to Neoliberalism*. Cambridge, MA: Harvard University Press.

Muschert, Glenn W., and Anthony A. Peguero. 2010. "The Columbine Effect and
School Antiviolence Policy." Pp. 117–48 in *New Approaches to Social Problems
Treatment*, edited by M. Peyrot and S. Lee Burns. Bingley, UK: Emerald
Group Publishing.

Nadeem, Reem. 2022. *Americans' Views of Government: Decades of Distrust,
Enduring Support for Its Role*. Washington, DC: Pew Research Center.
https://www.pewresearch.org/politics/2022/06/06/americans-views-of
-government-decades-of-distrust-enduring-support-for-its-role/.

Nader, Ralph. 1965. *Unsafe at Any Speed: The Designed-In Dangers of the
American Automobile*. New York: Grossman Publishers.

National Hurricane Center. 2018. *Costliest U.S. Tropical Cyclones Tables
Updated*. Miami, FL: National Oceanic and Atmospheric Administration.
https://www.ncdc.noaa.gov/billions/dcmi.pdf.

NCEI. 2019. *U.S. Billion-Dollar Weather and Climate Disasters*. Washington,
DC: NOAA National Centers for Environmental Information. https://www
.ncdc.noaa.gov/billions/.

Neal, Arthur G. 1998. *National Trauma and Collective Memory: Major Events
in the American Century*. Armonk, NY: M. E. Sharpe.

Neuman, W. Russell, Marion R. Just, and Ann N. Crigler. 1992. *Common
Knowledge: News and the Construction of Political Meaning*. Chicago:
University of Chicago Press.

Newburn, Tim, and Trevor Jones. 2005. "Symbolic Politics and Penal Populism:
The Long Shadow of Willie Horton." *Crime, Media, Culture* 1(1):72–87.

Newport, Frank. 2017. "Four in 10 Americans Fear Being a Victim of a Mass
Shooting." Social & Policy Issues no. 17-09-010. Gallup. https://news.gallup
.com/poll/220634/four-americans-fear-victim-mass-shooting.aspx.

Nielsen, Rasmus Kleis, and Kim Christian Schrøder. 2014. "The Relative
Importance of Social Media for Accessing, Finding, and Engaging with
News: An Eight-Country Cross-Media Comparison." *Digital Journalism*
2(4):472–89.

Niewyk, Donald L., ed. 1992. *The Holocaust: Problems and Perspectives of Interpretation*. Belmont, CA: Wadsworth.

Norris, Pippa, and Ronald Inglehart. 2019. *Cultural Backlash: Trump, Brexit, and Authoritarian Populism*. Cambridge, UK: Cambridge University Press.

Nussbaum, Martha C. 2001. *The Fragility of Goodness: Luck and Ethics in Greek Tragedy and Philosophy*. Cambridge, UK: Cambridge University Press.

Nussbaum, Matthew. 2017. "Trump Gets Do-Over, Comforts Harvey Victims." *Politico*, September 2. https://www.politico.com/story/2017/09/02/trump -hurricane-harvey-victims-do-over-242282.

Ochs, Juliana. 2006. "The Politics of Victimhood and Its Internal Exegetes: Terror Victims in Israel." *History and Anthropology* 17(4):355–68.

Olorunnipa, Toluse, Justine McDaniel, and Ian Duncan. 2023. "How a Small-Town Train Derailment Erupted into a Culture Battle." *Washington Post*, February 27. https://www.washingtonpost.com/politics/2023/02/25 /derailment-east-palestine-culture-wars/.

Oorschot, Wim van, and Loek Halman. 2000. "Blame or Fate, Individual or Social?" *European Societies* 2(1):1–28.

Oppel, Richard A., Jr., and Kim Barker. 2020. "They'll Kill Me, Floyd Pleaded, Records Reveal." *New York Times*, July 9, 1. https://www.nytimes.com/2020 /07/08/us/george-floyd-body-camera-transcripts.html.

Oreskes, Naomi, and Erik M. Conway. 2011. *Merchants of Doubt: How a Handful of Scientists Obscured the Truth on Issues from Tobacco Smoke to Global Warming*. London: Bloomsbury Publishing USA.

Organski, Abramo F. K. 1965. *The Stages of Political Development*. New York: Knopf.

Ott, Brian L., and Eric Aoki. 2002. "The Politics of Negotiating Public Tragedy: Media Framing of the Matthew Shepard Murder." *Rhetoric & Public Affairs* 5(3):483–505.

The Oxford English Dictionary (OED). 1984. 5th ed. Oxford, UK: Oxford University Press.

Painter, William L. 2019. *The Disaster Relief Fund: Overview and Issues*. CRS Report no. R45484. Washington, DC: Congressional Research Service. https://crsreports.congress.gov/product/pdf/R/R45484/19.

Pandell, Lexi. 2022. "How Trauma Became the Word of the Decade." *Vox*, January 17. https://www.vox.com/the-highlight/22876522/trauma-covid -word-origin-mental-health.

Parker, Kim, Rich Morin, and Juliana Menasce Horowitz. 2019. *Looking to the Future, Public Sees an America in Decline on Many Fronts*. Pew Research Center. https://www.pewresearch.org/social-trends/2019/03/21/public-sees -an-america-in-decline-on-many-fronts/.

Parsons, Talcott. 1951. *The Social System*. Glencoe, IL: Free Press.

Parsons, Talcott. 1985. *Talcott Parsons on Institutions and Social Evolution: Selected Writings*. Chicago: University of Chicago Press.

Pastor, Manual, Robert Bullard, James K. Boyce, Alice Fothergill, Rachel Morello-Frosch, and Beverly Wright. 2006. *In the Wake of the Storm: Environment, Disasters, and Race after Katrina*. New York: Russell Sage Foundation.

Pearce, Matt. 2018. "Parkland Shooting Survivors Not in Mood 'to Play Nice': Young Gun-Control Activists Reject Critics Who Call Them Disrespectful." *Los Angeles Times*, February 28, A2. https://enewspaper.latimes.com/infinity /article_share.aspx?guid=9a459479-2eb2-4e6f-ae80-d0cc6cfc6051.

Pearson, Andrew. 2018. "Vietnam '67: How Vietnam Changed Journalism." *New York Times*, March 29. https://www.nytimes.com/2018/03/29/opinion /vietnam-war-journalism.html.

Pew Research Center. 2018. *The Generation Gap in American Politics: Wide and Growing Divides in Views of Racial Discrimination*. Washington, DC: Pew Research Center. https://www.pewresearch.org/politics/2018/03/01/2 -views-of-scope-of-government-trust-in-government-economic-inequality/.

Pew Research Center. 2019. *Key Findings about Americans' Declining Trust in Government and Each Other*. Washington, DC: Pew Research Center. https://www.pewresearch.org/fact-tank/2019/07/22/key-findings-about -americans-declining-trust-in-government-and-each-other/.

Pew Research Center. 2020. *Most Americans Point to Circumstances, Not Work Ethic, for Why People Are Rich or Poor*. Washington, DC: Pew Research Center. https://www.people-press.org/2020/03/02/most-americans-point-to -circumstances-not-work-ethic-as-reasons-people-are-rich-or-poor/.

Pew Research Center, Peter. 2022. *Public Trust in Government: 1958–2022*. Washington, DC: Pew Research Center. https://www.pewresearch.org /politics/2022/06/06/public-trust-in-government-1958-2022/.

Piketty, Thomas. 2020. *Capital and Ideology*. Cambridge, MA: Harvard University Press.

Platt, Rutherford H. 1999. *Disasters and Democracy: The Politics of Extreme Natural Events*. Washington, DC: Island Press.

Politico Staff. 2017. "Trump Tweets Praise of Hurricane Harvey Rescuers." *Politico*, August 27. https://www.politico.com/story/2017/08/27/trump -hurricane-harvey-texas-242071.

Polletta, Francesca. 2006. *It Was Like a Fever: Storytelling in Protest and Politics*. Chicago: University of Chicago Press.

Postman, Neil. 1979. "Teaching as a Conserving Activity." *Instructor* 89(4): 38–42.

Postman, Neil. 1980. "The Reformed English Curriculum." Pp. 160–68 in *High School 1980: The Shape of the Future in American Secondary Education*, edited by A. Eurich. New York: Pittman.

Postman, Neil. 2005. *Amusing Ourselves to Death: Public Discourse in the Age of Show Business*. New York: Penguin.

Poushter, Jacob, and Moira Fagan. 2020. *Americans See Spread of Disease as Top International Threat, Along with Terrorism, Nuclear Weapons, Cyberattacks*. Washington, DC: Pew Research Center. https://www.pewresearch.org/global/2020/04/13/americans-see-spread-of-disease-as-top-international-threat-along-with-terrorism-nuclear-weapons-cyberattacks/.

Prestigiacomo, Amanda. 2022. "'Remarkable Act of Victim-Blaming': AP Slammed for Running 'Smear' Piece on Ashli Babbitt; That's Not What They Did for George Floyd." *DailyWire*, January 4. https://www.dailywire.com/news/remarkable-act-of-victim-blaming-ap-slammed-for-running-smear-piece-on-ashli-babbitt-thats-not-what-they-did-for-george-floyd.

Quarantelli, Enrico L. 1998. *What Is a Disaster? Perspectives on the Question*. East Sussex, UK: Psychology Press.

Quarantelli, Enrico L. 2006. *Catastrophes Are Different from Disasters: Some Implications for Crisis Planning and Managing Drawn from Katrina*. Social Science Research Council. Newark: University of Delaware. https://items.ssrc.org/understanding-katrina/catastrophes-are-different-from-disasters-some-implications-for-crisis-planning-and-managing-drawn-from-katrina/.

Rainie, Lee, Scott Keeter, and Andrew Perrin. 2018. *Trust and Distrust in America*. Washington, DC: Pew Research Center. https://www.pewresearch.org/politics/2019/07/22/trust-and-distrust-in-america/.

Rainie, Lee, and Andrew Perrin. 2019. *Key Findings about Americans' Declining Trust in Government and Each Other*. Washington, DC: Pew Research Center. https://www.pewresearch.org/fact-tank/2019/07/22/key-findings-about-americans-declining-trust-in-government-and-each-other/.

Randazzo, Sara. 2017. "In Harvey's Wake, a Rush to the Courthouse: Lawyers Jockey for Position in Litigation against Federal Government over Decision to Release Water from Dams." *Wall Street Journal*, October 23. https://www.wsj.com/articles/in-harveys-wake-a-rush-to-the-courthouse-1508756401.

Ransby, Barbara. 2018. *Making All Black Lives Matter*. Oakland: University of California Press.

Reeves, Andrew. 2011. "Political Disaster: Unilateral Powers, Electoral Incentives, and Presidential Disaster Declarations." *Journal of Politics* 73(4):1142–51.

Reinarman, Craig. 1987. *American States of Mind: Political Beliefs and Behavior among Private and Public Workers*. New Haven, CT: Yale University Press.

Rice, Bradley R. 1995. *The Commission Form of City Government*. Austin: Texas State Historical Association. http://www.tshaonline.org/handbook/online/articles/moco1.

Rio, Giulia McDonnell Nieto del. 2021. "For Flint, Mich., the Public Health Traumas Never Seem to Stop." *New York Times*, January 4. https://www.ny times.com/2021/01/14/us/for-flint-mich-the-public-health-traumas-never -seem-to-stop.html.

Ritzer, George. 2010. *Enchanting a Disenchanted World: Continuity and Change in the Cathedrals of Consumption*. Thousand Oaks, CA: Pine Forge Press.

Roberts, Patrick. 2006. "FEMA after Katrina." *Policy Review* 137(15):15–33.

Robles, Frances. 2018a. "FEMA Was Sorely Unprepared for Puerto Rico Hurricane, Report Says." *New York Times*, July 12. https://www.nytimes.com /2018/07/12/us/fema-puerto-rico-maria.html.

Robles, Frances. 2018b. "Trump Calls Storm Response in Puerto Rico, Where 3,000 Died, 'One of the Best.'" *New York Times*, September 11. https://www .nytimes.com/2018/09/11/us/trump-puerto-rico-maria-response.html.

Robles, Frances, Lizette Alvarez, and Nicholas Fandos. 2017. "In Battered Puerto Rico, Governor Warns of a Humanitarian Crisis." *New York Times*, September 25, A14. https://www.nytimes.com/2017/09/25/us/puerto-rico -maria-fema-disaster-.html.

Roose, Kevin. 2023. "A.I. Poses 'Risk of Extinction,' Industry Leaders Warn." *New York Times*, May 30. https://www.nytimes.com/2023/05/30/technology /ai-threat-warning.html.

Rostow, W. W. 1990. *The Stages of Economic Growth: A Non-Communist Manifesto*. 3rd ed. Cambridge, UK: Cambridge University Press.

Rothe, Anne. 2011. *Popular Trauma Culture: Selling the Pain of Others in the Mass Media*. New Brunswick, NJ: Rutgers University Press.

Rothenberg, Bess. 2002. "The Success of the Battered Woman Syndrome: An Analysis of How Cultural Arguments Succeed." *Sociological Forum* 17(1):81–103.

Rothenberg, Bess. 2003. "'We Don't Have Time for Social Change': Cultural Compromise and the Battered Woman Syndrome." *Gender & Society* 17(5): 771–87.

Roulet, Thomas J., and Rasmus Pichler. 2020. "Blame Game Theory: Scape-goating, Whistleblowing and Discursive Struggles Following Accusations of Organizational Misconduct." *Organization Theory* 1(4):2631787720975192.

Rozsa, Mathew. 2017. "Puerto Rico's Governor Begs: 'We Need Equal Treatment' from FEMA." *Salon*, October 19. https://www.salon.com/2017/10/19/puerto -ricos-governor-begs-we-need-equal-treatment-from-fema/.

Rubin, Beth A. 1995. "Flexible Accumulation: The Decline of Contract and Social Transformation." *Research in Social Stratification and Mobility* 14:297–323.

Rubin, Claire B., ed. 2012. *Emergency Management: The American Experience 1900–2010*. London: Routledge.

Ryan, William. 1971. *Blaming the Victim*. 1st ed. New York: Pantheon Books.

Safire, William. 1993. *Safire's New Political Dictionary: The Definitive Guide to the New Language of Politics*. New York: Random House Reference.

Santos-Burgoa, Carlos, John Sandberg, Erick Suárez, Ann Goldman-Hawes, Scott Zeger, Alejandra Garcia-Meza, Cynthia M. Pérez, Noel Estrada-Merly, Uriyoan Colón-Ramos, and Cruz María Nazario. 2018. "Differential and Persistent Risk of Excess Mortality from Hurricane Maria in Puerto Rico: A Time-Series Analysis." *Lancet Planetary Health* 2(11):e478–88.

Santos-Lozada, Alexis R., and Jeffrey T. Howard. 2018. "Use of Death Counts from Vital Statistics to Calculate Excess Deaths in Puerto Rico Following Hurricane Maria." *JAMA* 320(14):1491–93.

Schram, Sanford F., and Joe Soss. 2001. "Success Stories: Welfare Reform, Policy Discourse, and the Politics of Research." *Annals of the American Academy of Political and Social Science* 577(1):49–65.

Schudson, Michael. 1989. "The Sociology of News Production." *Media, Culture & Society* 11(3):263–82.

Schudson, Michael. 2018. *Why Journalism Still Matters*. Cambridge, UK: Polity Press.

Seaton, Jean. 1988. "Reporting Atrocities: The BBC and the Holocaust." Pp. 50–75 in *The Media in British Politics*, edited by J. Seaton and B. Pimlott. London: Ashgate Publishing.

Seaton, Jean. 1996. "Misery and the Media." *Contemporary Politics* 2(2):59–78.

Sehgal, Parul. 2021. "The Case against the Trauma Plot." *New Yorker*, December 27.

Self, Will. 2021. "A Posthumous Shock: How Everything Became Trauma." *Harper's Magazine*, November 11.

Semetko, Holli A., and Patti M. Valkenburg. 2000. "Framing European Politics: A Content Analysis of Press and Television News." *Journal of Communication* 50(2):93–109.

Seon-Kyoung, An, and Karla K. Gower. 2009. "How Do the News Media Frame Crises? A Content Analysis of Crisis News Coverage." *Public Relations Review* 35(2):107–12.

Shepard, Steven. 2018. "Gun Control Support Surges in Polls." *Politico*, February 28. https://www.politico.com/story/2018/02/28/gun-control-polling -parkland-430099.

Short, James F. 1984. "The Social Fabric of Risk: Toward the Social Transformation of Risk Analysis." *American Sociological Review* 49(6):711–25.

Shultz, James M., and Sandro Galea. 2017. "Mitigating the Mental and Physical Health Consequences of Hurricane Harvey." *JAMA* 318(15):1437–38.

Sibler, Ilana Friedrich. 1993. "Monasticism and the 'Protestant Ethic': Asceticism, Rationality, and Wealth in the Medieval West." *British Journal of Sociology* 44(1):103–23.

Sigelman, Lee, Susan Welch, Timothy Bledsoe, and Michael Combs. 1997. "Police Brutality and Public Perceptions of Racial Discrimination: A Tale of Two Beatings." *Political Research Quarterly* 50(4):777–91.

Simon, Jonathan. 2007. *Governing through Crime: How the War on Crime Transformed American Democracy and Created a Culture of Fear.* Oxford, UK: Oxford University Press.

Simons, Herbert W. 2007. "From Post-9/11 Melodrama to Quagmire in Iraq: A Rhetorical History." *Rhetoric and Public Affairs* 10(2):183–93.

Sinclair, Upton. 2003. *Jungle: The Uncensored Original Edition.* New York: Simon & Schuster.

Slovic, Paul. 1993. "Perceived Risk, Trust, and Democracy." *Risk Analysis* 13(6): 675–82.

Slovic, Paul. 1994. *Role of Trust in Risk Perception and Risk Management, April 1992.* Eugene, OR, and Ann Arbor, MI: Inter-university Consortium for Political and Social Research.

Slovic, Paul. 2000. "Perceived Risk, Trust, and Democracy." Pp. 500–514 in *Judgment and Decision Making: An Interdisciplinary Reader,* edited by T. Connolly, H. R. Arkes, and K. R. Hammond. Cambridge, UK: Cambridge University Press.

Smith, Brent L., and C. Ronald Huff. 1992. "From Victim to Political Activist: An Empirical Examination of a Statewide Victims' Rights Movement." *Journal of Criminal Justice* 20(3):201–15.

Smith, Darrell, and Tony Bizjak. 2019. "PG&E Agrees to $1 Billion in Settlements with California Towns, Counties Ravaged by Wildfire." *Sacramento Bee,* June 18. https://www.sacbee.com/news/california/article231701773 .html.

Smith, Heather J., and Thomas F. Pettigrew. 2015. "Advances in Relative Deprivation Theory and Research." *Social Justice Research* 28(1):1–6.

Smith, Mitch. 2016. "Flint Wants Safe Water, and Someone to Answer for Its Crisis." *New York Times,* January 9, A16. https://www.nytimes.com/2016/01 /10/us/flint-wants-safe-water-and-someone-to-answer-for-its-crisis.html.

Smith, Vicki. 1998. "The Fractured World of the Temporary Worker: Power, Participation, and Fragmentation in the Contemporary Workplace." *Social Problems* 45(4):411–30.

Smith, Vicki. 2001. *Crossing the Great Divide: Worker Risk and Opportunity in the New Economy.* Ithaca, NY: ILR Press.

Sokal, Alan, and Jean Bricmont. 1999. *Fashionable Nonsense: Postmodern Intellectuals' Abuse of Science.* New York: Macmillan.

Soskis, Benjamin. 2020. "A History of Associational Life and the Nonprofit Sector in the United States." Pp. 23–80 in *The Nonprofit Sector: A Research Handbook,* edited by Walter W Powell and Patricia Bromley. Palo Alto, CA: Stanford University Press.

Sparks, Chris. 2003. "Liberalism, Terrorism and the Politics of Fear." *Politics* 23(3):200–206.

Stack, Liam. 2016. "Orlando Shooting: What We Know and Don't Know." *New York Times*, June 12, 13. https://www.nytimes.com/2016/01/03/us/oregon-ranchers-will-return-to-prison-angering-far-right-activists.html.

Starr, Chauncy. 1969. "Social Benefit versus Technological Risk." *Science* 165(3899):1232–38.

Steffen, Will, Jacques Grinevald, Paul Crutzen, and John McNeill. 2011. "The Anthropocene: Conceptual and Historical Perspectives." *Philosophical Transactions of the Royal Society A: Mathematical, Physical and Engineering Sciences* 369(1938):842–67.

Steinberg, Ted. 2006. *Acts of God: The Unnatural History of Natural Disaster in America*. Oxford, UK: Oxford University Press.

Stone, Deborah A. 1997. *Policy Paradox: The Art of Political Decision Making*. New York: W. W. Norton.

Stoycheff, Elizabeth, Raymond J. Pingree, Jason T. Peifer, and Mingxiao Sui. 2018. "Agenda Cueing Effects of News and Social Media." *Media Psychology* 21(2):182–201.

Straub, Adam M. 2021. "'Natural Disasters Don't Kill People, Governments Kill People': Hurricane Maria, Puerto Rico–Recreancy, and 'Risk Society.'" *Natural Hazards* 105(2):1603–21.

Sue, Derald Wing. 2010. *Microaggressions and Marginality: Manifestation, Dynamics, and Impact*. Hoboken, NJ: John Wiley & Sons.

Sue, Derald Wing, Christina M. Capodilupo, Gina C. Torino, Jennifer M. Bucceri, Aisha Holder, Kevin L. Nadal, and Marta Esquilin. 2007. "Racial Microaggressions in Everyday Life: Implications for Clinical Practice." *American Psychologist* 62(4):271.

Swoyer, Alex. 2021. "Paul Gosar Defends 'Executed' Ashli Babbitt during Capitol Riot Hearing." *Washington Times*, May 12. https://www.washingtontimes.com/news/2021/may/12/paul-gosar-defends-executed-ashli-babbitt-during-c/.

Symonds, Martin. 1980. "The 'Second Injury' to Victims." *Evaluation and Change* 7(1):36–38.

Szasz, Andrew. 1994. *Ecopopulism: Toxic Waste and the Movement for Environmental Justice*. Minneapolis: University of Minnesota Press.

Sze, Julie. 2006. *Toxic Soup Redux: Why Environmental Racism and Environmental Justice Matter after Katrina*. Understanding Katrina: Insights from the Social Sciences. Social Science Research Council. https://items.ssrc.org/understanding-katrina/toxic-soup-redux-why-environmental-racism-and-environmental-justice-matter-after-katrina/.

Sze, Julie. 2020. *Environmental Justice in a Moment of Danger*. Oakland: University of California Press.

Sztompka, Piotr. 2000. "Cultural Trauma: The Other Face of Social Change." *European Journal of Social Theory* 3(4):449–66.

Tabrizy, Nilo, Ainara Tiefenthäler, Débora Souza Silva, Elie M. Khadra, and Shane O'Neill. 2021. "Video: From Rodney King to George Floyd: Reliving the Scars of Police Violence." *New York Times*, April 19. https://nyti.ms /3ncSDFT.

Tarrow, Sidney G. 2011. *Power in Movement: Social Movements and Contentious Politics.* Cambridge, UK: Cambridge University Press.

TCEQ. 2018. *Hurricane Harvey Response 2017: After Action Review.* Austin: Texas Commission on Environmental Quality. https://wayback.archive-it.org /414/20210526232856/https://www.tceq.texas.gov/response/hurricanes /hurricane-harvey.

Tewksbury, David, and Jason Rittenberg. 2009. "Online News Creation and Consumption: Implications for Modern Democracies." Pp. 186–200 in *Routledge Handbook of Internet Politics*, edited by Andrew Chadwick and Philip N. Howard. Oxfordshire, UK: Taylor & Francis Group.

't Hart, Paul. 1993. "Symbols, Rituals and Power: The Lost Dimensions of Crisis Management." *Journal of Contingencies and Crisis Management* 1(1):36–50.

Thévenot, Laurent, Michael Moody, and Claudette Lafaye. 2000. "Forms of Valuing Nature: Arguments and Modes of Justification in French and American Environmental Disputes." Pp. 222–72 in *Rethinking Comparative Cultural Sociology. Repertoires of Evaluation in France and the United States*, edited by M. Lamont and L. Thévenot. Cambridge, UK: Cambridge University Press.

Tierney, Kathleen. 2012. "Disaster Governance: Social, Political, and Economic Dimensions." *Annual Review of Environment and Resources* 37:341–63.

Touraine, Alain. 1995. "The Crisis of Progress." Pp. 45–56 in *Resistance to New Technology: Nuclear Power, Information Technology, and Biotechnology*, edited by M. Bauer. Cambridge, UK: Cambridge University Press.

Tuchman, Gaye. 1972. "Objectivity as Strategic Ritual: An Examination of Newsmen's Notions of Objectivity." *American Journal of Sociology* 77(4): 660–79.

Tuchman, Gaye. 1978. *Making News: A Study in the Construction of Reality.* New York: Free Press.

Ulloa, Jazmine. 2023. "East Palestine Crisis Tests a Trump-Backed Senator." *New York Times*, February 24. https://www.nytimes.com/2023/02/24/us /politics/east-palestine-ohio-jd-vance.html?smid=url-share.

US House of Representatives. 2006. *A Failure of Initiative: Final Report of the Select Bipartisan Committee to Investigate the Preparation for and Response to Hurricane Katrina.* Vol. 109. Washington, DC: US Government Printing Office.

Veil, Shari R., Timothy L. Sellnow, and Megan Heald. 2011. "Memorializing Crisis: The Oklahoma City National Memorial as Renewal Discourse." *Journal of Applied Communication Research* 39(2):164–83.

Victor, Daniel. 2018. "Advertisers Drop Laura Ingraham after She Taunts Parkland Survivor David Hogg." *New York Times*, March 29. https://www.ny times.com/2018/03/29/business/media/laura-ingraham-david-hogg.html.

Vinik, Danny. 2018. "How Trump Favored Texas over Puerto Rico." *Politico*, March 27. https://www.politico.com/story/2018/03/27/donald-trump-fema -hurricane-maria-response-480557.

Vliegenthart, Rens. 2019. "The Media Agenda." Pp. 271–81 in *Comparative Policy Agendas: Theory, Tools, Data*, edited by S. Walgrave, F. Baumgartner, B. Christian, and E. Grossman. Oxford, UK: Oxford University Press.

Voigt, Lydia, and William E. Thornton. 2015. "Disaster-Related Human Rights Violations and Corruption: A 10-Year Review of Post–Hurricane Katrina New Orleans." *American Behavioral Scientist* 59(10):1292–1313.

Watts, Marina. 2020. "Everything Candace Owens Has Said about George Floyd So Far." *Newsweek*, June 5. https://www.newsweek.com/everything -candace-owens-has-said-about-george-floyd-so-far-1508959.

Weaver, R. Kent. 1986. "The Politics of Blame Avoidance." *Journal of Public Policy* 6(4):371–98.

Weber, Max. 1978. *Economy and Society: An Outline of Interpretive Sociology*. Berkeley: University of California Press.

Weed, Frank J. 1990. "The Victim-Activist Role in the Anti-Drunk Driving Movement." *Sociological Quarterly* 31(3):459–73.

Weed, Frank J. 1997. "The Framing of Political Advocacy and Service Responses in the Crime Victim Rights Movement." *Journal of Sociology and Social Welfare* 24(3):43–62.

Welch, Matt. 2017. "Don't Encourage Danger." *Los Angeles Times*, September 18, A13.

Wieviorka, Michel. 2005. "After New Social Movements." *Social Movement Studies* 4(1):1–19.

Wildavsky, Aaron B. 1988. *Searching for Safety*. New Brunswick, NJ: Transaction Books.

Wilkinson, Iain, and Arthur Kleinman. 2016. *A Passion for Society*. Oakland: University of California Press.

Williams, Bruce A., and Michael X. Delli Carpini. 2011. *After Broadcast News: Media Regimes, Democracy, and the New Information Environment*. Cambridge, UK: Cambridge University Press.

Williams, Raymond. 1961. *The Long Revolution*. Cardigan, UK: Parthian Books. Reprinted in 2001.

Williams, Rhys H. 1995. "Constructing the Public Good: Social Movements and Cultural Resources." *Social Problems* 42(1):124–44.

Willison, Charley E., Phillip M. Singer, Melissa S. Creary, and Scott L. Greer. 2019. "Quantifying Inequities in US Federal Response to Hurricane Disaster in Texas and Florida Compared with Puerto Rico." *BMJ Global Health* 4(1):e001191.

Wyman, David S. 1984. *The Abandonment of the Jews: America and the Holocaust, 1941–1945*. Lexington, MA: Plunkett Lake Press.

Young, Alison. 2007. "Images in the Aftermath of Trauma: Responding to September 11th." *Crime, Media, Culture* 3(1):30–48.

Zhang, Yini, Yidong Wang, Jordan Foley, Jiyoun Suk, and Devin Conathan. 2017. "Tweeting Mass Shootings: The Dynamics of Issue Attention on Social Media." *Proceedings of the 8th International Conference on Social Media & Society* 59(July):1–5. https://dl.acm.org/doi/abs/10.1145/3097286.3097345 ?casa_token=azWgpNzjzekAAAAA:YU7cWqr8kbQkxUUVQcPG3G6WHR f8mgcV88ZVmX_Anoq8OcGfyVX3t_Av57RyzvDiccodayepXf97mA.

Zuboff, Shoshana. 2015. "Big Other: Surveillance Capitalism and the Prospects of an Information Civilization." *Journal of Information Technology* 30(1): 75–89.

Zuboff, Shoshana. 2019. "Surveillance Capitalism and the Challenge of Collective Action." *New Labor Forum* 28(1):10–29.

Index

32; as a perception, 32; as a universal concern, 32–34; vulnerability and, 34–37, 65–68. *See also* risk society
risk disputes, 16; political victimhood, and 56; as reflecting risk versus benefit 34
risk paradox, 30–31, 34, 37–39, 63–64, 65, 69
risk society, 10, 21–22; Cold War security programs and, 49–51; collective memory and cultural trauma, 63–65; compared with modern society, 32–34; crisis response as entitlement, 55; fear and social blame, 117–18; federalization of risk, 26–27, 55; government role in risk interdiction and crisis response, 28–34; laissez faire state and crises, 39–44; political victimhood, emergence of, 55–65; politicization of objectivity and science, 35; public tragedies as galvanizing political events, 36–37; public tragedies *vs.* private harms, 17–19, 182–85; risk and vulnerability, 34–37, 65–68; risk as a universal concern, 32–34; risk distribution, policies about, 32; social and institutional distrust, 19–21; tragic, contemporary meaning of, 15–17; transformational power of public tragedy, 192–97; trauma script as function of, 183–84; victim claims making and political discourse, 61; victim mentalité and, 37–39
Rittenhouse, Kyle, 177
Roosevelt, Franklin D., 47
Ryan, William, 58–59

Salvation Army, 45
Sanford, Florida, 163
scapegoating, 79, 80, 86, 201
Seaton, Jean, 110–111
second wave victimization, 155
sectarianism, media and, 31, 105; politics of risk and 185; as outcome of public tragedy,187, 197; U.S. politics and, 3, 10, 19, 65, 188; zero-sum claims-making and, 184
September 11, 2001 terror attacks, 113–16, 161
silence, as blame avoidance tactic, 80
Simpson, O.J., 169, 172
slavery, as cultural trauma, 148
social blame: conditions for public tragedies, 9–11, 26; conventionalized script of trauma and loss, 7–8; as core aspect of public tragedy, 4–5; defined, 5; fiascos, claiming credit, and avoiding blame, 76–77; generational differences in,

187–88; Hurricane Katrina and, 54; media framing of public tragedy, 123–40; mobilizing for political recognition, 155–58; new media logic, trauma reporting and public tragedy, 118; personal blamelessness and, 11–14; politics of public tragedy, importance of, 186–92; public tragedies *vs.* private harms, 17–19; social and institutional distrust, 19–21; tragic, contemporary meaning of, 14–17; victim industry and, 146–47
social heuristic, 12; media encoding and, 104
social institutions, erosion of, 31
social media, 22–23; feedback loops and, 107, 109, 116–17, 140, 145, 194; George Floyd murder and, 161–76; microaggressions and, 150; new media logic, trauma reporting and public tragedy, 28, 101–3, 116–18, 125; public tragedies *vs.* private harms, 18–19, 38; tragic celebrity and, 160, 161, 177–80; vindictive protectiveness and culture of victimhood, 149–50. *See also* media
social movement entrepreneurs: conventionalized script of trauma and loss, 8; politics of public tragedy, importance of, 188; role in shaping public reaction to tragedy, 4–5
social movements: exposé journalism and, 112; risk society and, 59, 60; role in cultivating sympathy for victims, 144–45; tactics to get media access, 107–8; transformational power of public tragedy, 192–97; trauma script and, 10, 11–12, 19, 23, 141; twenty-first century movements, change in focus, 183
social order, effect of modernity on, 31–32
social scripts: conventionalized script of trauma and loss, 7–8; defined, 7
societal proxies, 12
solution-problem dynamic, 32–34
Spears, Britney, 178
speech, freedom of on college campuses, 148–50
state government: Department of Homeland Security (DHS) partnership with, 53–54. *See also* government
Stone, Deborah, 78
Stoneman Douglas High School shooting, Florida, 120–21, 128–29; as moral-political failure, 136, 139–40; social blame and, 131–33
story emphasis, 165
story structure, 165

Founded in 1893,
UNIVERSITY OF CALIFORNIA PRESS
publishes bold, progressive books and journals
on topics in the arts, humanities, social sciences,
and natural sciences—with a focus on social
justice issues—that inspire thought and action
among readers worldwide.

The UC PRESS FOUNDATION
raises funds to uphold the press's vital role
as an independent, nonprofit publisher, and
receives philanthropic support from a wide
range of individuals and institutions—and from
committed readers like you. To learn more, visit
ucpress.edu/supportus.